Praise for *all my dead cats and other losses*

"Like death, grief and mourning are part of the lived human experience. There are no rules or timelines on grieving, despite American society dictating one 'right' way to grieve and punishing those who fail. Grief and mourning bring about BIG FEELINGS, feelings we often consider private, but they don't have to be that way. *All My Dead Cats and Other Losses* looks at the many types of grief, social responses to it, and how we can create and support collective ways of grieving. It stands out among a sea of books in this genre. Insightful, tender, and compassionate, a must-read for everyone since we are all touched by grief."

—Alice Wong, author of *Year of the Tiger*

"Beautifully grounded in personal and social experiences, offering a broad yet intimate exploration of grief tethered to the tiny creatures we share our lives with."

—Cat Dorman and Steff Boulton,
cofounders of Dead Pet Girls

"s.e. smith is a wise and unfailingly generous companion as they welcome us into a compassionate call to reframe our culture of grieving. *All My Dead Cats and Other Losses* transforms the isolating unknowns of loss and mortality into something embodied, communal, ethical, and ultimately joyful. Reading this book made me feel less alone."

—Tajja Isen, author of *Some of My Best Friends*

"*All My Dead Cats and Other Losses* is the book we desperately need—one that moves beyond platitudes and stages to face the raw, complicated, and transformative truth of grief. With clarity and compassion, smith helps us name what we're so often told to hide:

that mourning is not a problem to fix or something to get over, but a vital part of living."

—Sarah Chavez, executive director of
The Order of the Good Death

"I've been looking for a book like this for some time—something that not only explores death and dying, and grief and mourning, but also one that opens up the questions whose answers too often go assumed and unasked: Who is worth mourning? Are there other ways of grieving? smith's approach is intellectually curious and generous, and *All My Dead Cats and Other Losses* is a worthwhile read for both those actively grieving and those interested in how to think about death, dying, and—perhaps most importantly—how to live fully."

—Colin Dickey, author of *Ghostland*

"Grief is complicated, no matter who is navigating it, but in an individualist, capitalist society like the one we reside in, grief is even more layered. But as smith brilliantly explores in this must-read book, grief is a collective endeavor that requires us to understand the complexities of death, name our grief, and live alongside it rather than attempt to shun it. If you have been trying and failing to grieve, or watched others trying and failing to grieve, then *All My Dead Cats and Other Losses,* and all the wisdom it provides, is the book to have on your shelf and pass along to those who are in the throes of loving and losing."

—Evette Dionne, award-winning author of
Lifting as We Climb and *Weightless*

all my dead cats and other losses

HARPERONE
An Imprint of HarperCollins*Publishers*

all my dead cats

and other losses

practicing good grief in a culture that fears mourning

s.e. smith

 For information, address HarperCollins Publishers, 195 Broadway, New York, NY 10007. In Europe, HarperCollins Publishers, Macken House, 39/40 Mayor Street Upper, Dublin 1, D01 C9W8, Ireland.

HarperCollins books may be purchased for educational, business, or sales promotional use. For information, please email the Special Markets Department at SPsales@harpercollins.com.

hc.com

FIRST EDITION

Designed by Yvonne Chan

Library of Congress Cataloging-in-Publication Data has been applied for.

ISBN 978-0-06-344599-4

Printed in the United States of America

26 27 28 29 30 LBC 5 4 3 2 1

In memory of Jenny Rose Gealey

Contents

Prologue + Into the Charnel House viii

Chapter 1 + Sofie // Childhood 12

Chapter 2 + Mr. Shadow // Anticipation 38

Chapter 3 + Mr. Bell // Sudden 62

Chapter 4 + Leila // Guilt 88

Chapter 5 + Tab4 // Witness 114

Chapter 6 + Loki // Performance 142

Chapter 7 + Ember // Disenfranchised 170

Chapter 8 + Ash and Tricycle // Inevitability 198

Chapter 9 + Little Grey // Euthanasia 228

Chapter 10 + All My Dead Ghosts // Complicated 256

Afterword: Memento Mori 281

Acknowledgments 289

Notes 293

Prologue

Into the Charnel House

In the late 1980s as a child in Greece, one of my favorite places to go was the cemetery, a packed assortment of jagged-toothed grave markers under the glaring sun, twisted olive trees offering little shade under their delicate silver leaves. My memory of the cemetery is always fixed in a hot day, insects droning dully, heat waves shimmering, ocean sparkling, the white of the surrounding buildings and brilliant blue of their trim so intense that it was almost blinding. We would go to the cemetery when I didn't have school and my father was trying to entertain me until the evening arrived and we could fry the fish we bought directly off the boat in the harbor and sit in the backyard, wilting in the lingering warmth.

I liked wandering through the graves, loved it even more when there was a funeral and all the drama that accompanied it, but I really wanted to go to the charnel house.

Greece is one of many countries that exhume their dead and place the bones in an ossuary, a building in which bones are stored in boxes, taking up less space than graves in a nation where burial is the expected method of disposition. There is simply not enough room in the ground for all the dead people. Cremation rates remain extremely low in Greece, where the first crematorium opened in 2019[1] despite resistance from the Greek Orthodox Church, which forbids cremation, forcing some citizens to travel to Bulgaria or Germany with their dead.

In Greece, the process of exhumation and transfer was somber, but also a last opportunity to connect intimately with the decedent, to touch that which was once hidden under the skin. Outsiders may find this strange or gruesome, but is it so wrong to renew the memory of someone who has passed by celebrating the remains of their form?

In the tight quarters of the chaotically packed rows of graves, family members and the priest would gather and the bones would be ceremoniously laid out on a cloth next to the grave, with the gravedigger keeping close track in order to avoid losing one of the 206, counting them out with care and picking through them to find rings and belt buckles, buttons and rivets, rotting boots and tattered remains of shawls. Some families would be superstitious, believing that if the body had not decayed sufficiently in the years it spent in the grave, they were cursed, or a witch, and needed to be reburied or subjected to mysterious additional rites that I never had an opportunity to observe. The bones would be painstakingly packaged in a wooden box that would be added to the charnel house, and the grave prepared for the next decedent, the next round of wailing over the coffin as it was lowered into the earth. I loved watching these proceedings, peering through the stiff black dresses of widows and sisters and listening to the mumbling of the priest. Afterward, everyone would progress to the house.

The charnel house was blessedly cool, a welcome break from the blasting heat outside, and the sounds of the insects were muffled. If you imagine rows of neat, carefully labeled shelving sloping off into the darkness, you would be wrong. The ossuary was a tumble of boxes, some of which were actively breaking open or losing their plaques, decorated with moss and small plants if they were close to the entrance, green tendrils yearning for the sun. It had a dark, earthy scent, thick under your tongue, an old-bones smell that I sometimes catch on the wind thousands of miles and decades away. I liked picking my way back as far as possible, shuffling my tiny feet to avoid bones as best I could, but sometimes I failed, and they snapped under my weight in the gloom. I would point or hold them up for my father to see, finding a sense of place in their rough surfaces.

I could recognize some of the last names I saw on the boxes, trace my fingers over the death dates and try to calculate how old they were. The bones of Armenian genocide survivors lay alongside those of Greek genocide survivors, a silent testimony to struggle and suffering and forced displacement that would be mirrored nearly one hundred years later, when Lesbos took a markedly different approach to refugees, replacing a pile of bones with a heaving mound of lifejackets. I saw skulls and long bones, the tiny, graceful bones of the fingers, some still clinging to their sinew, strangely formed pelvises and blade-like scapulae.

One might assume that I was a ghoulish child who matured into a goth, but that's not really what happened, although in high school it was unusual to catch me wearing anything that wasn't black, and I sported the obligatory black box dye job. I was a curious child obsessed by this thin and friable boundary between life and death, the moment at which being alive ended and being dead began, and what followed. I became an adult equally fascinated with death and dying, but most particularly interested in how we interact with these facts of life when grief touches us. We are all future corpses, as Order of the Good Death founder Caitlin Doughty likes to note, and I am a meticulous planner for the inevitable: Leafing through a childhood notebook recently, I found detailed suggestions for my funeral, down to recommended attire for immediate family and a playlist (pre-Spotify, we're talking a painstakingly recorded cassette tape).

If we are future corpses, though, that means we are all also future mourners, waiting for the hourglass to stop. As with the census, cooperation is mandatory and death will pound on your door if you try to dodge your responsibilities. My preplanning for grief was much more haphazard, because unlike a death, it goes on indefinitely, and it cannot be summed up in the flyleaf of a notebook or staved off with some Violent Femmes.

Even as the good death movement has promoted a world in which people have a more positive relationship with death, though we have quite a way to go, society has flailed, and failed, when it comes to open conversations about grief, to find, as it were, a good grief. When these discussions do happen, they don't always feel relatable, failing to connect with people's individual experiences and understanding of loss, with loss itself not necessarily a literal death but another radical shift in the timeline of our lives. By nature, loss is an absence, something gone, something that cannot be patched up or regrown. That's a significant event for most people, in some way or another, and worth pausing for.

My approach to grief has been deeply shaped by the deaths of my animals, especially my cats. I've always had cats, from the household cats of early childhood to the one sleeping on the couch right now. Living such shorter lives as they do, pets carry a constant, steady reminder that death will come to us, whether sudden or prolonged, marked by helplessness or shock, sometimes frustrating and inconvenient—things we are not supposed to say out loud. Each unique death told me something about myself and the culture I live in, even as it felt like the world passed me by, missing the moment. I find animals' lives and deaths instructive and fascinating because they are part of us, intimately woven into our lives, sometimes the living creatures we see most, while occupying a fundamentally alien role as creatures across a species divide.

The close presence and loyalty of our pets sometimes simplifies our relationships but can also make their deaths more acute: The dog who passes away after sixteen years may have loved unconditionally and transitioned with their owner through early adulthood into forming a household and building a life, turning into the last marker of a pivotal time, which can provoke powerful emotions that transcend those surrounding the death itself.

Anyone who has lived with animals is familiar with "It was just a cat (or dog)," a casual dismissal of a deep and sometimes complicated relationship. There is a callousness there but also a fear and a sense of helplessness in the face of sorrow. If grief for humans makes people uncomfortable and uncertain in a culture where people want to fix things, and the inability to fix something stymies their responses, grief for animals is even more discomfiting. "Just get another dog," they say, confidently believing that this is the thing that will make the grief stop, not recognizing that these can be pivotal deaths in many people's lives. Stopping to mark the death of a beloved pet makes people squirm: Can we move on to the next thing now?

Most books about the things animals teach us seem to revolve around generic, saccharine "life lessons" that feel like being dumped into a swimming pool of sugar water. Or they're designed to be inspirational tearjerkers—the voyage of a dog taken on a whirlwind tour for their final year of life, or the cat who slept on the beds of the dying in nursing homes. They fail to capture the diversity and spectrum of our relationships with animals—a disservice to animals and their people alike—and are, in their own way, discomfiting, troubling, and unrelatable for some readers.

I will never know or understand what my cat is thinking.

As a journalist, whenever I report on topics related to pet death, I get an outpouring of responses. Many are simply emails telling me about beloved pets who died, from people who say, explicitly or between the lines, that they don't know who to talk to about this, and they feel isolated and alone. I find it fascinating and tragic that strangers feel so abandoned in grief that they reach out to someone they don't know, seeking reassurance, absolution, or comfort, sometimes including feelings of guilt and distress around the choices they made, such as declining care they couldn't afford or not bringing an animal to the vet sooner, sometimes years later. Most clearly write feeling they have no other choice, trapped in grief they cannot process because of society's indifference to their pain. Friends and family are tired of hearing about it, coworkers are dismissive and cruel about their mourning process, even their own vet's office is summary and brisk, taking cash or credit card before the body is even cold. Some of their stories are tragic and deeply distressing, as the creatures that played a constant role in their lives leave a ragged hole behind. No one was willing to say "I'm sorry for your loss" and sit with the meaning of what that might look like. I sometimes joke that I turned into a grief therapist by way of a society that frowns upon any discussion of pet death beyond the most superficial, but in a sense, it's not a joke at all.

People just want to be seen.

My interest in our relationship with death and how we handle the lives of our animals has become a constant thread; I find myself returning, again and again, to the ways in which our animals inform our lives. Pet death is not a "practice" death, but it is something that tends to be very personal and very common, shaping people's understanding of grief and often offering direct parallels to experiences of human death and the complexities of our relationships to each other, who is allowed to grieve, and how. Being seen through the eyes of loyal companions opens up another layer: Pet loss is a deeply private grief, a hidden undercurrent, and in exploring it, we often come to realize that there's a similar secrecy to human grief, a desire to package up a death and put it on the shelf out of reach rather than confronting it, let alone sharing that grief with others.

I am also deeply informed by my childhood in the charnel house, and how that intensely personal connection with death is viewed with such revulsion and fear in other cultures. Handling the bones of the dead wasn't harmful, and kissing the foot of a dead saint didn't traumatize me, but the very white American horror at the thought of such intimacy has been a telling element of my conversations about death. Death should be sanitized and it should happen with minimal fuss. Screaming and crying at the graveside is not what we do.

What if we did, though? What if we interacted with loss in more diverse ways?

Exploring and honoring and simply acknowledging death can look like any number of things to any number of people; wandering through a charnel house or watching an exhumation is not required, though it may be intriguing and instructive. But the world we have built for ourselves is intolerable and unsustainable. We are all going to die, we are all going to experience loss, and the time to deal with this reality is not in a frenzy at the moment of loss, but in the form of a daily gentle current that acknowledges the grief in ourselves and all around us, and the inevitability of what lies at the end of the road.

I find myself constantly returning to acceptable forms of grief, which come in a very narrow band in contemporary white American society, the society in which I live and mourn, the society I know most intimately. There are rituals to be followed and expectations to meet, and those who do not comply may be ostracized or even pathologized, their grief treated as a sickness to be corrected, a personal matter.

This comes through clearly in responses to pet loss, which often challenge the why and how of the way people grieve, such as a man baffled by his husband's gutted response to the death of a puppy who was only in their lives a short while. In conversations about pet death, people often, unprompted, also talk about the deaths of humans in their lives, connecting the dots, with similar themes emerging. I hear about feelings of guilt and anger, confusion and shame, jealousy and conflict over their human losses. They feel like they can't talk about these feelings with the people they are closest to, and sometimes they fester. And they struggle with social expectations around how they are supposed to mourn, the belief that there is a linear process of grief to follow, a checklist that will make this process easier, keep things moving along. This too shall pass.

This is unhelpful not just for grievers and the people who love them, but for death workers and others involved in the inevitable passage of life, from the veterinarian euthanizing a beloved family pet to the hospice nurse supporting a dying patient and their family. More open discussions of grief, and its myriad expressions, will benefit all of us, make room for the rich and varied forms of this natural human experience.

Avoidance of conversations about loss also means that we rarely give ourselves room to think about the fact that loss is not always about death. Loss can be about any number of huge life events: The end of a relationship. Eviction from the family home. Isolation during cancer treatment. Sometimes those losses are even positive, but still subjects of grief because they represent changes, sometimes frightening ones, in our lives: Sending a foster kitten to their new home. Switching careers. Leaving your family behind to seek opportunities in a new city. Not everyone experiences these things as losses or responds to them in the same way, but acknowledging that they *can* be experienced as losses is an important element of integrating grief into our lives.

This is not a book about pet loss—at least, it is not just about pet loss, though you will meet my dead cats and read small slices of their stories. Instead, it is about the larger climate and culture surrounding the way we grieve, because all my conversations about pet loss ultimately turn deeply human, relatable to much more than the animals we share our lives with. I find that opening scary conversations about loss and grief with the deaths of pets sometimes feels less intimidating and more approachable, acting as a gateway drug, as it were, to other conversations about how fiercely we love and how intensely we feel when we face a loss.

This is a book about grief and mourning as collective activities best undertaken in community, and the strength found in relying on each other rather than trying to do everything ourselves, alone. It is a rebuke to a culture of individualism and a call for collectivism. In grief, we can all offer support according to our ability, to others according to their needs, but this is a project that requires many of us. What a treasure, a gift, an honor it is to witness someone and lift them up, rather than turn away.

Together, we are going to explore the often deeply broken way we grieve, and what might yield a better and healthier future. We'll look at the ways in which grief is sometimes treated as a medical diagnosis and a problem in need of fixing, rather than a natural part of the human experience that we simply must live through. We will also name—and explore—common manifestations of grief, such as disenfranchised grief and anticipatory grief, because sometimes naming things and seeing that they happen to other people can bring a sense of relief or compassion. We'll also examine the ways in which grievers can feel isolated, unheard, and unsupported, and we'll think about ways in which we can be better friends to each other and kinder to the strangers in our lives.

I want this book to start conversations. If grief is uncomfortable to observe—we all naturally want to make people feel better, and we struggle in unfixable situations—and difficult to experience, we don't have to do it alone, and we shouldn't. Rather than fleeing that discomfort, we must sit with it, as a former colleague once remarked in a very different context, whether it is our grief or someone else's. We can find common ground with one another and perhaps discover something about ourselves in the process. Openly discussing grief and mourning, allowing ourselves to be a little messy—these are the things we can do to transform our lives. Suppressing grief—or feeling like you need to present yours in a particular way to be valid—just leaves it smoldering in a corner, waiting to flare up at the worst possible moment.

This is not necessarily a book for mourners or dying people; it is a book for everyone, at any time, although of course I hope that mourners who are struggling can find something that resonates in these pages. Arguably, the best time to think about loss is when you're not in the midst of it. Sometimes these conversations are easier when they are more abstract. In thinking about loss as a very normal, if complicated, part of human existence, you may help a future version of yourself, or someone you care about, or a complete stranger; be the person who hands a handkerchief to a sobbing person on the train, not someone who switches to another car.

Everyone is somebody's baby.

Emphasizing with those in grief, understanding that grief is not fixable but it can be livable, is vital and necessary, if also frightening. Death, loss, and grief are unknowns, but we can approach both together if we have the courage, and that begins with honest conversations about how we navigate grief, and how we can do better. Good grief is not beyond us—though the work to get there may be difficult.

Chapter 1

Sofie // Childhood

Moving back to the United States, to the rundown house on Chestnut Street, Redwood Elementary a short walk away, was a culture shock. No crumbling castle at the top of the hill, no nuns with rulers, no olive trees, no incense-laden air in church on Saturdays, no goats, no fireflies. My classmates ran around the playground with a familiar frenzied chaos, but I got placed in the slow readers group after a frustrating evaluation with the school psychologist who saw the stories of my daily life and my mix of Greek and English as evidence that I wouldn't be able to keep up in an American classroom.

Everything was confusing and alien, until a long-haired calico cat showed up in the yard and claimed us as her own.

Sofie the Sofa Cat, as she came to be known, traveled with my father and me to Caspar when my parents separated, becoming a constant in an inconstant life. She was patient when I dressed her up in little outfits, slept with me in my bed on the couch, waited for me by the bus stop, until the autumn day my father picked me up at school with a somber expression, idling outside as children flooded out, shrieking and laughing. My father's appearance in our battered white Volvo sedan with the holes in the rear floorboards was an unusual event, and one that usually presaged some form of exciting adventure.

My father told me that Sofie was dead—struck by a car on the road outside our house, where people often drove faster than they should have in our small hamlet. I, of course, wanted to see the body, to see her, but, my father informed me, the driver had taken her away for burial.

I'm not sure why my father thought this was a good idea. I suspect, in retrospect, that her body was probably badly damaged, bearing the ravages of an impact at high speed, and perhaps he feared traumatizing me. He might have also been in a state of shock and panic when the driver knocked on his door to confess, thinking ahead to having to break the news and navigate the reaction of a young child already in a sense of tumult and a difficult adjustment to a very different life.

Or maybe he bought into, on some level, the common idea that children—even a child who delighted in the charnel house—need to be protected from death, that it should be hidden away from them to prevent distress.

Whatever the reason, it denied me an opportunity for ritual or ceremony. Sofie was simply there in the morning and gone in the afternoon, but not gone in a definitive way that I could see and feel. It seeded a strange fixation: Was she really dead? Had she gone somewhere else? Who was the driver? Was it someone my father knew? That I knew?

I convinced myself that I knew who he was, eyed the house on the corner next to the red barn along the winding bus route, wondering if the blue truck outside was The Truck, if he had actually buried Sofie like he said he would or thrown her away like garbage. Sofie existed in a state of both living and dead, and for years, when I saw a long-haired calico in a window or stalking butterflies in a garden, I would have a thrill as my heart leaped: Had Sofie been there all along? Waiting for me?

I couldn't articulate these big feelings to my father, nor to his girlfriend at the time, who had recently lost her own beloved golden retriever, a dog I'd met and played with a handful of times and had an abstract, uncertain relationship with. Instead, those feelings festered, transmuting into a form of resentment over everything I had been denied, becoming a ferocious reminder of the social status of children in America, and the way children are denied their own status as grievers, their own ability to make decisions about how they mourn the inevitable losses in their lives.

The answer to "How do we support grieving children?" is both obvious and unsatisfactory: "It depends on the child."

Unpacking that answer in more detail doesn't just involve questions of developmental stages and lived experience, perceived and actual capacity. It requires fundamentally reconceptualizing how we think of children, because we live in a society where children's autonomy, individuality, and very personhood are called into question, with adults making all their major life decisions for them, from where they go to school to what kind of health care they receive. This is, we tell ourselves and each other, for their own good, but the end result is to reduce children's status as whole members of society, with their own emotions and experiences; parents are told to "control your brats" in much the same way we shout at an off-leash dog. Seeing children as human beings is still, regrettably, a revolutionary act that requires resisting centuries of Western thought.

"Adults tend to be very patronizing, even within my own family. That's when it hurts the most," says Jamie Minden, senior director of global organizing for Zero Hour, a youth-led organization fighting climate change. Minden has never known a world that isn't in the depths of climate calamity, and she is steeped in climate grief, which she has difficulty articulating to the adults around her—the decision-makers who created the world she now has to live in.

"People I look up to, depend on, care about—there's this narrative I hear again and again, the assumption that we don't know what we're talking about because we're young, we don't have the perspective, when we get older we'll understand."

Youth organizers like Minden are accustomed to encountering this logic, which is, in a way, rooted in the same attitudes my father drew upon when he told the driver to go ahead and take Sofie with him: Children should be insulated until they hit some magical threshold of growing up and are able to deal with the real adult world.

"I think for me grief about the climate crisis is intertwined with grief about the Anthropocene as a whole," Minden wrote when I followed up to check in a few months later. "It is not talked about enough that the sheer size and scale of life on Earth has diminished so rapidly, we are not living on the same Earth our ancestors experienced. . . . We are not only losing species but the sheer scale of life on Earth is a fraction of what it once was, and hardly anyone is reckoning with it. The perspective of frustration I shared in my interview is partly a result of this lonely grief I feel for the sheer loss of life on our planet, grief for the life our world used to host that is gone or will soon be gone while we are careening toward a future that is even less livable because of the actions of the greedy few."

It's a grinding feeling for young adults who in fact understand exactly what is going on around them; denying their grief and assuring them that they'll know better when they're older is a patronizing act of infantilization and denial of our shared humanity. Despite having lived through childhood and these experiences themselves, a surprising number of parents fall short here.

"So many people still, in 2024, their experience of parenting and their understanding of parenting is as some kind of mix of dictator and cruise director rather than that you're a partner to your kid," says Heather Corinna, founder of the long-running sex education website Scarleteen and author of *S.E.X.* and *What Fresh Hell Is This?* Corinna is a longtime advocate for youth rights and access to high-quality, factually informed sexual health, and relationships education, with work that has served children and youth all over the world for decades. They are deeply frustrated with the autocratic approach to children and parenting that dominates in the United States, viewing it as a disservice to children and youth, and they see it as a particularly sharp issue in grief. If people grow up via rites of passage where they learn about what it's like to live in the world, a loss is a rather significant inflection point and one that offers room for growth and learning, if children are allowed to do that. The adults who act as their allies in that process, advocating with them, instead of for them, with Corinna wryly noting that some parents will "hate your guts" for actively listening to their children and supporting their expressed needs, create space for kids to make mistakes and find grace through them.

Adults in the traditional Western framework are protectors and guardians, standing between children and pain and suffering, teaching them the ways of the world, and yet there is a middle ground between leaving children dangerously exposed and wrapping them in so much insulation that they never have a chance to grow into themselves. Adults must step in because humans, for a variety of evolutionary reasons, take a long time to develop. A foal can stand within minutes, a kitten can eat solid food within weeks. A human infant is frail, requiring round-the-clock attendance for months and years of nurturing care, both physical and emotional. Children are in turn laden with expectations as they grow up under the tutelage of adults who also model normative behavior around a variety of life events, including grief, in an endless feedback loop.

In some families, children may be "protected" from grief by being left out of the conversation—a common experience for many white kids, for example. In others, such as big Latine families, they may have active and expected social roles in the familial process of grief, attending funerals and other events to commemorate the passage of a loved one. In both cases, children are generally not encouraged to think for themselves and explore their own emotions around a loss. Rather, they are being trained to adhere to cultural expectations, an early lesson in the normative standards of behavior that children will face throughout their lives. These traditions and the logic that props them up are passed down from generation to generation.

Underlying attitudes about children's rights in the mainstream culture of the United States are an outgrowth of colonialism and the beliefs brought to North America by European settlers, who carried decided ideas about the role and capacity of children with them.

John Calvin, a powerful force in the Puritan thought that characterized North America under British colonists, and later heavily influenced the nascent nation of the United States, wrote that "fathers ought diligently to form their children under a system of holy discipline,"[1] describing a family structure in which children, a "gift of god," needed extensive instruction, discipline, and oversight to grow into full members of the church—and participants in society. For Puritans, being full members of the church was also a requirement for salvation. Thus, for Puritan parents, bringing their children up within the fold of the church was a moral imperative, and while Calvinists valued education, they also valued a specific *kind* of education—and one, again, in which children were instructed, not engaged as partners in a learning process, a theme seen in contemporary education as well, where teachers are authority figures to be obeyed. Calvin's work in his own city of Geneva[2] also informed Protestant thinkers and reformers who worked in education systems across Europe and, by extension, in European colonies, further shaping attitudes about children's role in societies across the world, a marked departure from many cultures where children are more actively included.

If children are to be seen and not heard, taught about the way life must be and not encouraged to explore for themselves, they must also learn about death and grief in rigid, restrictive ways that do not permit much room for freedom of expression, for asking questions, for occupying conversations in a world that can be confusing and frightening. Our failure to meet children where they are, as human beings—and, critically, as human beings who are distinct individuals with very different needs—can be an impediment in conversations about loss. In part, this is because adults may fear being honest with themselves, let alone others: How can we explain death to children when we do not fully understand it ourselves? When it also feels unfair, unfathomable, unjust, unreal, to us?

We live in a world of adult certainty: Grown-ups must be confidently definitive and binaristic in a world that in truth is lived in shades of gray. Saying "I don't know," or sitting with a child who feels bewildered and unmoored, not knowing what to say, admitting that grief cannot be fixed, is a terrifying prospect.

The slow development of humans over the course of years—and arguably a whole lifetime—makes generalizations about "children" impossible, when a matter of months can represent a huge developmental shift and the material experience of the world is so variable, and when children themselves are so incredibly diverse for a variety of reasons, developmental, cultural, and otherwise. There endures, in the United States, a common popular perception that the brain is not "fully mature" until age twenty-five,[3] implying that people under this age—especially those under eighteen—are not fully capable of engaging with the world as rational actors. *You'll understand when you're older.*

Brain development, in fact, continues throughout one's life, with this most marvelous of organs constantly growing and responding to new information, events, and inputs; we are always learning, right up until the end. While it is true that the prefrontal cortex, which oversees complex cognitive tasks such as risk assessment, is not necessarily fully developed in younger adults,[4] the trajectory of that development varies tremendously from person to person, as does the ability to apply lessons of life in general. And the plasticity of the young mind is actually a developmental advantage,[5] helping young humans develop skills to navigate the world. The kids are alright, I promise.

And while there is a tendency to identify some behaviors, especially those around impulse control, as "childish," an adult can manifest the same impulsive behaviors as a young child, just as a very confident and self-aware child can exhibit considerable emotional regulation—sometimes in particular around grief—because they are sensitive to the troubled moods of the adults in their lives.

For children, the world is filled with novelty and firsts, a phenomenon that leads many adults to frame them as "innocent" and in need of protection to retain that innocence. A better approach might involve thinking of children instead as humans who are rapidly learning about the world and need help as they explore it in order to thrive and grow into adaptive, adjusted adults. This requires supporting children's emotional, physical, and neurobiological development. This doesn't mean throwing children into the deep end with no protections, but it does mean acknowledging that the deep end exists and that children should be prepared for it with some pool floats while recognizing the neurological development that influences the life stages that shape children's behavior, such as the literalness of many young children that sometimes tangles deeply with the way they confront and process death and loss.

For example, when adults say that someone has "gone away," a young child's response may be to query when that person is coming home, where they have gone. When someone has "died," that new and abstract concept may still evade comprehension; when we say that someone's body has "stopped working" in an attempt to explain this large, very final thing that has happened, the natural follow-up question is when it will start working again or if it can be fixed. This is not necessarily a product of "innocence" but a sign of how children are processing new information and events that they haven't witnessed before, in a world where death in particular tends to be clocked in abstract, sometimes archaic and confusing euphemisms.

Passed away. Gone to a better place. Moved on to the next world. Crossing the rainbow bridge. These euphemisms can be mystifying and even frightening for children in a way that more concrete words are not, even as adults may find children "blunt" or even "careless" in the way they respond to big events such as death. Kids ask truly wild questions and make statements that seem absurd to us sometimes, because we've forgotten that these experiences are new and they're still figuring things out.

For some children, the first experience of death is that of a family pet or the pet of a friend. The death of a beloved animal who may have been a constant presence in a child's life, including in the decline that may have preceded death, is a major life event. It is also one in which young children are not necessarily heavily involved, with an adult tendency to, again, protect children from the realities of sudden death or the terminal illnesses that pets often go through, followed by decisions about euthanasia. Children may be told *about* these things, but they are not necessarily invited to be in conversation *with* them. As a friend asked me, baffled when I commented in surprise that he didn't invite his young child to ask questions about the death of a family pet, be present at the euthanasia, or even see the body or hold some sort of memorial, "Why would I want to do that? He wouldn't understand and it would only traumatize him."

His comment, rooted in kindness and his fierce love for his child, reminded me of a much earlier conversation, long before he had children, in which he talked about his existential fear of death and the prospect of simply not existing anymore, not knowing what, if anything, would happen next. When we ourselves are frightened of death and the unknown, it can be challenging to know what to say to children, and we unwittingly pass on that fear. When the first time we have these conversations is in the midst of a loss, we are processing our feelings, not just about the loss itself, but about seeing children experience major life events for the first time. It's hard to make good decisions about issues you have been avoiding in the midst of turmoil, especially under the pressure of the very valid pain parents experience when their children are also in pain, when their first instinct is to protect.

Professor Angus Johnston, a historian who focuses on student activism and youth rights at the City University of New York's Hostos Community College, tells me these conversations need to start *before* a loss, and they should happen routinely, normalizing loss as a part of family conversations and lore—something deeply woven into his own family. Death conversations happen all the time, not just between parents and children, but between children and grandparents, between disabled and nondisabled family members. It is a constant, ongoing conversation and, as such, means that when the topic comes up, it's not a somber, sit-down talk that brings everything to a screeching halt.

"We are just really afraid about talking to kids in a bunch of different ways, but specifically we have this idea that kids have this innocence which we need to protect, and we need to preserve, and we need to keep going as long as we can," he says. "And I think in a lot of ways, that's exactly wrong, that's exactly backward. Obviously, there are some things that kids need to be protected from, but in a lot of respects, one of the ways that we get into a lot of trouble is that we fail to start talking to kids about important stuff when it is early enough to have that conversation be easy."

Approaching conversations about children and loss requires adults to acknowledge their discomfort and process it on their own time—a compelling case for building a network of personal supports so they can be more present for the children in their lives. And that also requires parents to think ahead to a time when they won't be present in the lives of their children, which is also a scary thing to think about but one that ultimately, Johnson says, gives him hope for the future too.

"They'll be able to take that information with them when they go out into the world and you're not around," he says, speaking to our obligation to children and the sense of inevitable release that comes with parenting, which should be preparing children for life in the world.

You do not forget your first dead body—human or animal—

and the sense of *absence* that it projects, the spark of whatever made it alive gone, leaving something inert and somehow smaller than it was before. At any age it's a jarring event. Does that mean it is one that should be avoided, shrouded in mystique? Or is it a moment in which children should be invited to participate—if they want—to ground their understanding of death in something present, real, and concrete?

Parents and families also need to engage with the fact that death is not necessarily literal, that many kinds of losses can play roles in children's lives, and these losses may be personal or collective, broad in scope or very intimate. Exploring different kinds of losses and their roles in children's lives necessitates understanding an individual child's feelings about change. One child may experience a life event as a loss while another may not; trying to predict a child's feelings either way can be an exercise in futility. Even a seemingly positive event can feel like a loss to adults, and the same holds true for children; leaving a childhood home for a new city can represent a loss of familiar places and people. A loss can be deeply personal: the death of a family member, moving away from a best friend. It can also be much more broad: being surrounded by a dying climate and feeling helpless to create change or growing up in a community wracked by war and suffering.

Race, class, and social status can play a role in how children come to understand the role of loss in their lives. It may be a parent swallowed up in the abyss of the injustice system, a family torn apart by immigration authorities, a descent into the maw of the child welfare machine, the loss of roots and culture in a transnational adoption. These losses are poorly understood by society—indeed, sometimes children are expected to be *grateful* for them, as in the case of adoptees "saved" or "rescued" from their home nations or communities.

At the same time we patronize children, making assumptions about their relationship to the world and their ability to participate in decision-making and, at times, society in general, we are also saddling them with tremendous burdens, as Minden noted when we talked about the climate crisis.

The United States is filled, for example, with the constant drumbeat of school shootings, a phenomenon so extreme that between the first and second drafts of this chapter, the most current example was already several school shootings ago. Children in the United States are going to school in a climate of mandatory active shooter drills, surrounded by teachers who are engaged in an endless, taxing mental calculus as they survey their classrooms for things to hide behind, objects to use as weapons. Some children have always known this grief, while their teachers grieve the shift from the profession they signed up for, and may remember a time when school campuses didn't feel like they were under an eternal state of lockdown.

This is not a thing you "understand when you're older," it is simply a rank injustice to witness at any age. As the iconic Onion headline goes:[6] "'No Way to Prevent This,' Says Only Nation Where This Regularly Happens."

This is also a moment in the cultural zeitgeist characterized by extreme misinformation, with children caught in a vortex of falsities that is increasingly difficult for people of any age to untangle. Bombarded by constant conflicting, hostile, and confusing information, children attempt to pick through the threads to determine what is reality and what is not, again failed by the adults around them. This too is a form of loss, one children may not even be fully aware of: The experience of growing up in a world where nothing is definitively real is its own climate of terrifying unknowns.

The same society that hotly insists children lack capacity to engage fully with the world may wring its hands over children "being forced to grow up too soon" but seems to view this as an acceptable bycatch of being alive in American society. It is what it is.

There's another element to grieving children that is often underdiscussed: the fact that the caregivers supporting those children may be going through their own grieving processes, intensified by their own relationships with the deceased, or the missing, or the forever changed, an experience that is, for some caregivers, very isolating. This holds especially true for cis women, who are still stereotyped and relied upon as the primary caregivers for children, especially in emotional contexts, particularly women of color. Despite growing social awareness of the issue, there's a persistent gender gap in caregiving,[7] with women overall, whether employed outside the home or not, spending more time on childcare and the difficult conversations that come with it.

In a discussion with Nicole Chung, author of *A Living Remedy,* who lost her father and mother in short succession, she told me there were "many days where I was so focused on [my children, then ages seven and nine], I felt like I couldn't take care of myself, couldn't take care of or sit with my own grief." Many other caregivers expressed similar sentiments, struggling to navigate huge life events themselves while being present for their charges and worrying about meeting the needs of those children in their care.

Even as Chung felt like she "was falling off a cliff" following the abrupt loss of her father, she was navigating her children's grief, expected to intuitively figure out how best to help them. For her, anchoring some of that in traditions, such as allowing them to attend the funeral and see him in his casket, came to be an important part of that process. So was the physicality of death, an acknowledgment dear to the heart of a child who grew up alongside the charnel house.

"It was so important for my seven-year-old to see, to actually touch him, to touch his hands, to reach out and touch his beard. It was a sweet moment but really devastating; something about the physicality of that experience was really crucial for understanding" for kids who were still grappling with the idea of loss. Since physical visitation was built into family traditions, it created natural space and expectations for children to be part of that process.

"The thought of going" to a funeral initially "brought me no comfort," she said. "Being there with my kids, I saw it was important for other reasons too, accepting this reality, no matter how much I didn't want it to be. I didn't have that with my mother because she died in the spring of 2020 when I couldn't travel to be there. Experiencing both losses in very different ways, I wish I had been able to have that with my mom too; my kids didn't have that either. I came out of my father's funeral with a deeper understanding and appreciation of those rituals and how important they can be."

Concerns about the well-being of caregivers should be surfaced more frequently, says Sam Middleton, a senior clinician at Uplift, a Philadelphia-based organization that supports grieving children and caregivers. No one is born knowing how to function through grief, and few of us get instructions in it until we're going through it. Failing to talk about death is an intergenerational problem as we fail to provide people with the emotional tools in childhood that could in turn guide them in helping their own kids.

"It's okay for another adult to be your adult," Middleton said, stressing that people of all ages need help in grieving, as well as access to opportunities to explore their feelings in a safe environment. "Whoever it is, you as an adult deserve to have the support that we give to kids. Having a space to exist with your grief can make it easier to carry, and that makes it so much easier to translate it to a conversation with your kid."

Caregivers can't, and don't, have all the answers. It's okay to ask for help from people with professional and lived experience. This requires seeing grief as a collective enterprise where interdependence allows people to distribute the weight, rather than expecting everyone to travel through loss alone, adrift and unable to reach a hand out to others. This is a big part of Middleton's work, which engages with children and caregivers together and separately and provides them with opportunities to gather in community with people experiencing similar losses.

Nicole Chung and other parents also speak to the value of allowing their children to see them grieving, acknowledging that this can be an important part of their children's mourning process as well while it also feels incredibly vulnerable, and some parents may fear frightening or upsetting their children with their own grief. The same holds true for having frank conversations with kids that meet them on their level, which requires knowing and interacting with them as autonomous individuals, and, sometimes, admitting that a question is unanswerable, or that a grieving parent will do their best to find an answer, even though it might not be completely satisfactory. Grief is a project parents and children can embark upon together.

Children are individuals, and their experiences of grief can manifest very differently both from each other and from the adults around them, especially at different developmental stages, which are more of an approximation than hard, clear lines.

Katherine Streit, associate director of school services and professional trainings at Uplift, told me a story that stuck with her from her own clinical practice.

"I had a family, a little boy was playing with a friend, the little boy's baby brother had just died. The friend said, 'My brother's birthday is tomorrow,' and the little boy asked what they're doing to celebrate and said, 'My brother won't have any more birthdays because he's dead.' The starkness and bluntness can be a little overwhelming for adults to hear if they're not ready for that.

"We're kind of talking about grief bands," she continued when we discussed how children of varying ages approach loss, though grief responses can vary radically from child to child and can fluctuate deeply from day to day. At all ages, "any profound loss or trauma can lead to regression, the loss of a previously acquired skill." That can manifest in a variety of ways, from difficulty with emotional regulation to incontinence, and is a natural element of grief, not a sign of pathology or something wrong, though it can be tough to navigate. The goal shouldn't be to "get over" that grief, but to integrate a deeper acceptance of a loss in a setting where children feel comfortable talking about it and expressing their feelings—whether verbally or through art, movement, and other means, aided by adults who are willing to move through this with them.

"First and foremost, we need to create spaces for their conversations," she added. "Kids are much smarter than we give them credit for."

For Corinna, supporting children in grief starts with simply talking to them.

"What do you need? What can I do? Here's what I can offer," they say, stressing that while the specifics of this conversation may vary by age, the fundamental underlying truths remain the same. Telling children what they can expect from the days, months, and years to come can also take some of the frightening mystery out of a loss, even if it can be hard to say words like "died" or to explain that someone in a casket may look different than the person a child remembers. Children want to be heard, respected, honored, and presented with as much information as possible to make their own choices at a time of grief—even if those are not choices that parents or other adults necessarily agree with, such as wanting, or refusing, to see the body of a deceased loved one, wanting or not wanting to attend a memorial or funeral, wanting or not wanting to see a dying loved one before they pass. Centering the child as mourner creates space for a child to have some small degree of control at a time when everything may seem very much out of control, which can act as a form of grounding. It is worth observing that the same level of preparation and opportunity to opt in or out isn't age restricted and benefits adults too, Corinna says.

Children are also, Corinna notes, not assigned the same kinds of "death tasks" adults deal with, such as negotiating with the funeral home, writing obituaries, planning memorials, and other activities that can occupy grieving people, sometimes turning into a coping—or avoidance—tool. Young children in particular may not be engaged in logistical activities, or they may not find it beneficial to be assigned death busywork. This can be a terrifying prospect for adults, says Corinna: "You have to just vibe with them, you can't be in that [administrative] mode, you have to be in someone's feelings," a place where many adults do not want to be in a society that shies away from deep conversations about death and distress.

Corinna argues that adults—parents or not—can play a powerful role in the lives of grieving children as advocates, not shielding children from realities but collaborating with them, especially when those children are surrounded by adults who may be burdening them with their own expectations. Any adult can be a safe space, an anchor, in a child's mourning.

Caregivers concerned for the welfare of the young people in their charge do have a duty of care, an ethical and legal obligation. Loss can be bewildering and unmooring, especially when it is not broadly and culturally recognized as a loss. Inadequate supports at a time of mourning can leave a lasting legacy, and sensitivity to individual children is important for understanding the level of help they need.

While grief can present in a myriad of ways, there are times when the expression and experience of grief for a child becomes overwhelming to the point of dysfunction, leaving the child trapped in grief rather than healing with it, and learning to recognize that tipping point is important. The question of when grief is genuinely maladaptive, with a child having symptoms of distress that require more active intervention, is complicated by the society in which we live because it is one in which access to care is often provided through a medical model.

Even a child in a place of adaptive grief, learning and growing through the experience of loss, can benefit from structured supports such as counseling, therapy, peer groups, and other opportunities to talk about their feelings in a format that welcomes curiosity and doesn't stigmatize emotional expression. That care might continue for weeks, months, and even years as children integrate a new understanding of the world. Affirming care can be costly and hard to access, given the nationwide shortage in mental health providers, which is especially acute in rural and low-income areas. For children who do have insurance—and thanks to gains from the Affordable Care Act of 2010, close to 95 percent of children did by 2024,[8] though cuts to ACA subsidies and Medicaid, which covers nearly half of U.S. children, in 2025 under H.R. 1 (the "One Big Beautiful Bill") are likely to increase the number of uninsured children—that insurance may decline coverage unless an approved clinician has provided a diagnosis, and that treatment may be limited in term or scope. Thus a child may be trapped in a place where they need a diagnosis and an accompanying code for an insurance company to get care. "If you get that diagnosis," says

Streit, "the doctor is trying to advocate for something you need. Don't ever feel like you're doing grief wrong."

"Kids should be able to explore whenever they need to," she says, noting that the same questions may come up over and over again; this isn't necessarily a cause for concern, and neither is behavior that may seem erratic. "Kids have this profound ability that we don't really have, to hold play and joy and grief all at once." A child might be in tears one moment and playing the next, asking questions about death and then asking for permission to go run around outside. Children may have difficulty expressing their emotions and needs, she notes, and may show that through behavior, rather than words. Those behaviors may vary depending on who they are with. A child might act out at school, for example, while not behaving the same way at home. These are not unexpected grief responses.

For her, the biggest red flag for a grieving child is an indicator that the grief has become tangled in trauma, which may form a callus over loss instead of allowing it to heal. She looks for signs of "profound disruption," such as "emotional distress that goes on and on and on with no end in sight. It's the way they're grieving, it's the body and brain's way of keeping them safe from the depths of their grief," but in the long term those attempts at self-protection can backfire.

"If they don't find joy in anything anymore, if they shut down for periods of months and months," it raises concerns for Streit, as does extensive denial, because while some aspects of denial can be part of a child's grieving process, "if five years later the child is still saying 'Daddy's not dead,' that's something we really want to look at."

In cases where children are having such acute grief that they are unable to process it, that still doesn't mean that they are broken or in need of fixing, Streit stresses. But a professional may be able to help support child and caregiver alike through the process of navigating the pathway of grief, finding where the stones and stumbling blocks are, working together on moving through them. And sometimes the best help comes from someone who isn't a professional but a fellow traveler. At Uplift, clinicians such as Streit work closely with kids in groups, which can provide a safe moderated space for talking about grief with other children who are also on their own journeys, sharing wisdom and strength with each other.

Ultimately, we cannot defend against the inevitable. It's impossible to insulate or inoculate children against loss because it is part of the reality of being alive, the rough with the smooth. Our response to that loss and a child's experience of it have big stakes that can determine the trajectory of a child's life and how that child moves forward to carry that grief with them. A grief denied or minimized is a grief that will remain a raw wound.

It is vital to recognize children as individuals with their own specific needs, needs that a child can often express on their own, if adults stop to listen, communicating with kids on their own level. Adults must acknowledge that a lack of control, and assumptions about what a child can or cannot handle, can amplify grief: Giving children some authority over their own lives, no matter how small, empowers them. Letting children set their own pace and terms, making decisions about whether and how they want to participate in rituals and events surrounding a death, is core to treating them like humans.

Society at large also needs to acknowledge and get more comfortable with the reality that children may experience grief very differently than adults, which may manifest in behaviors that, to adults, don't make sense or even cause distress. Young children in particular may be filled with open-hearted curiosity, or a need to work through very literal concerns about matters adults may conceptualize as more metaphysical. What does it mean to die, to stop existing, to leave and not come back? What does it literally *mean* when someone is dead? If their body stops working, why? How?

Responses can be expansive and empathetic, or squirrelly and uninformative; one pathway can prepare children for the larger adventures ahead of them in the world, opening up conversations for children who want to know more. The other, in suppressing curiosity, teaches children to remain silent, to leave things unsaid, to avoid disturbing adults with their emotions. Those kinds of candid conversations also open opportunities for children to talk to each other, whether in the form of structured peer groups or one-on-one on the playground, inviting engagement and compassion for each other.

There is, for some adults, perhaps a sense of terror in the idea of letting children lead, fearing the risk to their tender hearts and a breakdown of their most fundamental responsibility as caregivers, to protect children. Particularly with young children, the impulse to assume that an adult knows best and needs to guide children through the grieving process, rather than moving through it alongside them, can be overwhelming.

This is how humans learn, though, through experiences and reflections on those experiences, and those lessons can feel sour and forced when they arc shaped by external expectations rather than internal knowledge. Adults, after all, might have the same kinds of questions, conflicts, and future regrets, and opening up about them can strengthen bonds with children and increase trust.

Shielding children from death and loss, while it may amount to a short-term protection, is not ultimately beneficial in the long term. These are all things that we have to live, things we come to understand only by going through them, by responding, by adapting. Demystifying death early and often can be a specific form of kindness, one that builds more resilient children.

Particularly at a moment when we are systematically failing to protect children from trauma and loss, it feels twisted, at best, to exert authority over the aftermath. Who are we to claim that we know better? Like children, parents are also learning by doing and through experience. It's impossible to know everything and okay to admit that. Acknowledging this would improve our relationships with children, and the world.

My father should have asked me what I wanted, should have let me bury Sofie on my own terms, should have run the risks that come with letting me see her. But he did learn from the experience, and ultimately, so did I. It's a lesson I've carried forward countless times as I counsel parents with dying pets and other losses in their lives on how to talk about it with their children. The root of Sofie's name, σοφία, means "wisdom," an appropriate word to describe the legacy she left behind. I don't look for her around every corner anymore because I don't need to; she lives within me now.

Chapter 2

Mr. Shadow // Anticipation

It was sometime in the spring of 2010 that I started noticing Mr. Shadow wasn't feeling well. He went to the vet a few times with vague symptoms and came home with various prescriptions, seemed better for a while, then started feeling sick again. It was a summer of wildfires, back when that was unusual, the sky hazy day after day with smoke, the sun burning a bright, angry red against the murky gray. My life felt equally murky, like I was looking at myself through hazy glass.

Mr. Shadow was dumped outside my house when I was in middle school, a friendly gray tabby who loved to curl up on your lap, or next to your head at night, an outgoing cat, a good-natured cat who got along well with everyone. Right before I went to college, he disappeared for a month when we moved, showing up at our old house while I searched frantically for him in my new neighborhood, putting up posters and knocking on doors. After that brief scare, Mr. Shadow was the kind of cat who didn't cause any trouble, until he was around fourteen, and then he did.

It was August when it became clear that something was deeply wrong, and I took him back to the vet for an ultrasound. She found thickening in his intestines, which could be a sign of a variety of things, but probably intestinal lymphoma; lymphoma, according to Cornell University's College of Veterinary Medicine,[1] is the most common form of feline cancer. She offered to do a biopsy and I declined, feeling that an invasive surgery that might ultimately end with euthanasia on the table if the cancer was extremely progressed wasn't fair to him. Candidly, it wasn't as though the outcome of a biopsy mattered: I couldn't afford chemotherapy and radiation, which limited me to comfort care even if I had wanted more, and I didn't. She nodded and told me she would do the same if it was her cat.

The vet put him on steroids and antibiotics, and I took him home, where he slowly began to fade away. It was like watching a Polaroid in reverse, his meow turning thready and stretched, his bones slowly emerging from his once-thick fur. In one of the last photographs I have of him, he is thin, coat dull, lying across a book in the sun, body awkwardly hunched, eyes a million miles away. My other cats, Loki and Mr. Bell, began to ignore him, treating him almost like an inert object, something already dead, and I felt, somewhere deep in my traitorous heart, the same sense: that he was there but not there, dying but also dead. We sat in bed together and watched James Bond, and I set him up with a pillow in the window so he could watch the birds, but part of me was already grieving a loss that hadn't even happened yet.

He started taking buprenorphine for the pain and, for a

while, seemed better, more comfortable. He was no longer active and playful, but interested in attention, and I had to cobble together a pile of boxes so he could get onto the bed, since he was too weak to make the jump.

One morning, he avoided me and hid under the bed, and I thought to myself, *This is the day,* but then it wasn't. I waited too long, I think, to euthanize him—a common sentiment among pet guardians. The vet came to my house with her tech, and had to give him extra Euthasol, despite the fact that his radically reduced self looked like it could have blown away in a light breeze. They said sorry and let themselves out, and I sat with him for a while. Loki sniffed him once or twice, and that was that. I put him in a box and drove him to the crematory, which I had nervously called just the day before, speaking in hushed tones about their opening hours and rates in case he heard me, in case my very words summoned the end. Perhaps they did.

Pulling away, I felt strangely empty, kind of like the moment when the last person leaves the party after things had been winding down for a while, the initial chaos settling into a few people hanging out on the couch and talking in low voices before they finally pack up and leave and the door clicks shut behind them. There was an undeniable absence, and a sense of an end, but an expected one, in some senses almost a relieving one. At least it was over.

Years later, I heard the term "anticipatory grief" and suddenly had language to describe the surreal feeling of mourning him while he was dying, of trying to explain to friends why I didn't seem gutted, overwhelmed by his death—the first death of a pet in adulthood, a rite of passage in its own way. I was sad, of course, and thought of him often, and hated having to tell people he was dead, being reminded each time that he had died and wasn't coming back, but the opportunity to mourn him while he was still alive had offered a chance at turning the idea of acceptance over in my mind, and I felt that through the feelings that came after. They were also intense, albeit a slightly different flavor. Anticipation had not served as a cheat code to avoid post-death grief, but as a way to put his death in a clearer context.

As is often the case when people find the words to describe something, there was a sort of validation in knowing that I wasn't alone in this feeling, wasn't broken or monstrous. A society that expects silence around grief cultivates these feelings in mourners, making them feel at odds when they do not experience "normal" grief as projected by the culture that surrounds them. If grief is something to be boxed up and left by the curb for collection, living in your feelings can seem aberrant, questionable. The griever is caught in a vicious cycle of feeling like they are doing something wrong, fearing the consequences of reaching out, and thereby missing an opportunity to form community in grief.

For the expectant griever, the inevitability of loss is tinged with the emotions that come with being forewarned, including guilt around feeling those emotions in the first place. Impending death is hard news to receive, to break, to share, to understand, to be reminded of anew every day, every time you talk to someone about your loved one. There is a sense of helplessness in facing a terminal diagnosis: You cannot fix or cure the dying, and the impulse can be to shut down in response. To sit, to pause, to acknowledge that something is happening even when you cannot do something about it, is a learned skill, not an innate talent. That moment of rest, a beat of stillness, can be hard both to give and to ask for in the face of anticipatory grief.

The clinicians who are often the first to break this news do not receive as much training as they should in how to do it, and what kinds of conversations to have around it. Instead, they pick up a sense of what they should do long before the first day of class.

"There is a socialization process that happens long before people go to medical school," says Dr. Jillian Tullis, a professor of health communication who focuses on death and dying at the University of San Diego, where she also directs the biomedical ethics program. "Depending on where you go to medical school, you might get really exceptional communication training. If you go to a med school that focuses on patient-centered or biopsychosocial health care, you might get really good training about how to communicate, listen to patients, ask questions. You might go to a program that's very different."

It turns out I'm not the only person who likes to plan ahead, and prefers more information to less: Evidence shows patients actually want to have these conversations early,[2] rather than at a crisis point, but the medical system is still poorly equipped for this, and the slow shift in medical education is only scratching the surface[3]—and, of course, this left prior generations of doctors figuring it out on their own.

Until very recently,[4] medical students did not get the support in medical education to learn the skills they needed to communicate with dying patients and their families, whether they are managing their own feelings of grief and guilt for patients who die in their care or trying to grapple with delivering a terminal diagnosis that may be accompanied by weeks, months, or even years of living with the shadow of death. While therapists often recognize that they too need therapy for processing the things they're exposed to every day, the same isn't necessarily true for doctors. In fact, doctors may be actively discouraged from seeking therapy: Applications for medical licensure include questions about mental health that doctors may fear could be a strike against them, and as a result, they may avoid seeking mental health care.[5] In an era of burnout for so many medical professionals, barriers to mental health care are very concerning.

Anticipatory grief, or anticipatory mourning, is a reaction to an expected death, a social, cultural, personal processing of events[6] that may be negative, positive, or something in between. Often this is in the context of a terminal diagnosis, but it can also be associated with aging and the natural changes bodies and lives begin to go through with the passage of time. The pet who moves a little more slowly and stiffly. The grandparents who stop traveling, start spending more time at home, get tired more quickly, break bones more readily, with skin thinning and bruising more easily.

"That period where someone is inevitably going to die is always tough, and the funny thing about that is we're all inevitably going to die. It reminds us of that period between, where there's a liminal space between life and death," says Cat

Dorman from Dead Pet Girls, a project celebrating the pets we love and lose, when I speak with her and cofounder Steff Boulton about their experiences creating a safe place to talk about pet loss.

Anticipatory grief is a frequent flyer in their mentions, and they say they're proud, and grateful, that they have created an environment where people feel comfortable talking about their fear of future losses. Clearly, people following an account about the deaths of the animals they love are a very specific audience, but even among people who are more comfortable talking about death, there is a vulnerability in admitting that sometimes you look at living beings and imagine them dead; people fear that death and are already, in some senses, grieving them and also thinking ahead to how they will memorialize them.

"It's magical to share," says Steff, adding that "more people are very much wanting to prepare for that time than when we first began."

Anticipatory grief is a complicated, weird emotion. While one doesn't want to play grief Olympics, in some ways, for some people, it can feel worse than an abrupt loss, a slow-rolling nightmare accompanied by an unclear end date. While we all understand abstractly that our lives are finite, watching someone's life wind down with the looming shadow of death is a sword of Damocles situation, death suddenly made visible. And it can be accompanied by feelings of guilt about simply wanting it to be over, about being tired of hovering in this strange place of uncertainty.

If there is no one way to "do" grief in general, that holds especially true for anticipatory grief, which can sometimes make it challenging to talk about. There's also no clear, universal experience to point to and—frustratingly for those who like to medicalize grief—it can't be precisely boiled down to a set of signs and symptoms to check off. It is not a diagnosis but more of a process. At the same time, acknowledging the proximity of death can seem like calling it into the room, potentially causing distress for dying and mourner alike, or intimates who are uncomfortable with these conversations, the ones who live in denial, who don't want to think about it, who turn away from conversations about what's happening and what happens next.

The clinical evidence on anticipatory grief is, to put it politely, extremely mixed, illustrating the incredible variability of this social phenomenon. In a 2017 study[7] in the *Journal of Hospice and Palliative Nursing* exploring anticipatory grief in nursing contexts, author Julie Johnson and her colleagues concluded: "Some argue that anticipatory grief may lead to a prolonged grief reaction, whereas some argue that it aids recovery from the grief process after death, and others that it is not related to post-death bereavement."

Hope that clears things up.

In a sense, all these things are true, sometimes even for the same person, because loss is so intensely personal while being tinged by so many factors, starting with the nature of the death and the griever's relationship to the deceased. An out-of-order death, like that of a child diagnosed with a terminal illness, can feel different from that of an elder who is rapidly approaching the end of their life. There isn't a hierarchy of death, with one worse than the other, but understanding and processing those events is likely to look very different. One may feel cruel, unjust, unacceptable, a crime robbing someone of the opportunity to learn who they are and lead a full life. The other may spark a time of sadness, but also reflection and retrospection about a life well lived. In all cases, it is important to understand that anticipatory grief does not indicate that something is wrong with the griever, that they are being heartless or insensitive to the situation they find themselves in.

Not experiencing anticipatory grief is *also* not a pathology.

Many mourners report similar emotions—depression, for example—in both anticipatory and post-death grief, but one set is associated with expectations around the loss, while the other surrounds the loss itself. Fears for the dying, the future, and the unknown are understandable human reactions to news about an impending death. The medical establishment largely agrees with this, though it may differ on the role of anticipatory grief or what kinds of grief reactions within this context are "normal" and how long it will take to "return" to some sort of equilibrium, revolving around functioning and "impairment scales"[8] and a restoration of productivity.

Anticipatory grief is not just for surviving mourners. It also affects the process of dying for people facing terminal diagnoses. Patients too can move through markedly different manifestations of this phenomenon, some of which may contribute to acceptance and growth, others of which can be traumatic. In popular parlance, when we say "at least she went quick," we imagine that a death was made better by the truncated nature of the illness, the limited window of pain, suffering, and psychological distress associated with impending death, in contrast with the dreaded "long illness," but both come with their own distinct forms of grief. The reactions of the dying person can color the feelings of the mourning, and vice versa: This is a path people walk together. It can be a stressful one for both when they cannot speak to the elephant in the room, name the feelings that they are having, talk about the possibility of a changed world where one is dead and the other is still alive.

Anticipatory grief may help people move through or with grief,[9] a concept I much prefer to "recovery" or "getting over it" or "healing from" when it comes to mourning, because the goal should be to integrate that loss into a new version of the world, not erase it. There is nothing to "return" to, because the place that once was is gone, akin to arriving at the shore of a reservoir and knowing that drowned houses and roads lurk beneath the waters. Sometimes that weight is heavy, but as the poet Hanif Abdurraqib puts it, "grief makes a home within us if we allow it to."[10] Grief can be someone we live alongside, a neighbor we welcome to dinner rather than report to the cops for making us uncomfortable.

Facing an anticipated death is a source of stress, but for some, it can manifest as "eustress," a reaction to stress that may be beneficial rather than purely negative. Researcher Hans Selye, who explored stress in myriad forms across his career, appears to have coined the term[11] in the 1970s in the context of his work on the physical and psychological effects of stress. This concept acknowledges that challenging events do not necessarily have to be negative or cause negative outcomes—though it is important to note that one cannot overcome stressors by the sheer power of positive thinking. Moving to a new city is a form of stress, for example, but an adaptive person may respond to that stress by making new friends, pursuing an interesting job, seeking out activities, responding with emotional growth rather than negative feelings about the change. Eustress around death and dying in particular can be integrated into the process of moving with grief as people develop coping skills that serve them[12] and their fellow travelers. When grief acts as a teacher, it encourages emotional growth and resilience. Sometimes the only way to learn a lesson is the hard way.

Anticipatory grief is also more easily carried with community, whether it be informal gatherings of friends and loved ones, peer support groups, or more structured supports that help mourners grow with grief. Without community, it can be, as it was in my case, incredibly isolating, carrying a simultaneous weight of grief and guilt over that grief. In companionship, it can instead be part of the process of working through grief together, finding common ground with others, seeking and offering support in accordance with capacities and needs. Critically, the ability to simply talk about that grief and explore how it feels, rather than attempting to conceal it, can allow mourners to start growing and adapting to the changes happening in the world around them.

Spirituality and commonality through shared beliefs can also play an important role, no matter the nature of one's spiritual traditions or lack thereof. I remember once being told that, as an atheist, I must not fear dying in the way that my interlocutor, a Catholic, did. To the contrary, I responded, if there is nothing at the end, if death is an absolute void, a vanishing, a nothing, it is terrifying in an entirely different way: being snuffed out, like a candle, denied a second wind in the afterlife. My only spiritual continuance is in the memory of those around me.

Spiritual supports, whether they come from religious officials, people who share the mourner's faith, texts, or other sources, don't just affect psychological growth through grief. Lack of support, or a poor understanding of the way faith traditions influence the way people think about loss and death, can intensify suffering. In clinical settings, where spiritual suffering affects mental health, it can also affect physical health; the sick are made even sicker by their isolation and misunderstanding of their spiritual journey.

Honoring anticipatory grief requires that we cultivate our listening skills.

Sometimes anticipatory grief is made more complex by denial, the steadfast refusal to engage with the reality that death is coming. In a sense, this overlaps with the very American cult of positive thinking, documented with particular zest and cutting criticism in journalist Barbara Ehrenreich's book *Bright-Sided,* which chronicles positivity culture in America. Prior to her iconic book, her 2001 essay "Welcome to Cancerland,"[13] exploring the topic in *Harper's,* was a searing Ehrenreich classic, a skewering of the Pink Industrial Complex that she was thrust unwillingly into when she was diagnosed with breast cancer, a quintessential anticipatory grief for patients and loved ones.

The path is littered with cancer warriors and people expected to fight until the bitter end, rather than explore an acceptance of death. To embrace death, or at least be open to the inevitable, is to "give up," as evidenced across media and pop culture, where dying people are told "Don't give up on me!" If only you could try a little harder to not die. For some, this becomes an important part of their identity, as they view themselves in the midst of a battle, while for others, like Ehrenreich, it could be alienating. She didn't necessarily want to die of cancer, but she also didn't want to be surrounded by positive rhetoric that overlooked the obvious—though in fact, Ehrenreich didn't die until 2022, in hospice care after a stroke.

Everybody wants to be happy: No one wants to talk about death.

Paradoxically, at the same time, there is a robust market for death memoirs—think Paul Kalanithi's *When Breath Becomes Air,* Cory Taylor's *Dying,* Henry Marsh's *And Finally.* And an even larger market for memoirs about death, written by surviving mourners, from inspirational schlock to deeply considered meditations on the interaction between mourner and deceased, such as Nicole Chung's *All You Can Ever Know* or Sonali Deraniyagala's absolutely devastating *Wave.*

"What unites all these posthumous memoirs is the hunger we bring to them as readers," writes journalist Kristen Martin for *The Baffler*, of readers seeking transformation and the secrets to life from these texts.[14] "We expect koan-like wisdom on what matters in life, an enlightened perspective gained from being at or near the end of it."

Perhaps readers do crave guides to dying, especially if they are facing loss and grief, or their own deaths: *Surely, if I read just one more book, I'll understand what is happening to me, and why, and how to do it in the right way.* Or possibly, the books serve as glimpses into a world that feels far away, abstracted, removed, something interesting that happened to someone else and will definitely not happen to them.

Who tells these stories matters, and historically, the authoritative voices in these conversations were not themselves dying, and so not in touch with the immediacy and intimacy of being in a state of active transition. Now dying people are explicitly retaking control of their stories—many thanks to the democratizing nature of the internet, where anyone can start a social media account with minimal barriers—with patients finding equal footing with the funeral industry, religious figures, and medical-industrial narratives that have traditionally dominated conversations about death and dying.

It should seem obvious, but conversations about representation in pop culture should include the dying, who have a unique and valuable perspective on what it is like to die that cannot be fully encompassed by those who are not facing the immediacy of death. In an era of fraught conversations about diversity, equity, and inclusion, we should be foregrounding lived experience as expertise, and also noting that intimate knowledge can come with professional expertise as well, as in the example of Brandeis professor Morris S. Schwartz, a sociologist who taught a class about his own death, as chronicled in Mitch Albom's memoir *Tuesdays with Morrie.*

This is an era in which many people want to share their lives—and inevitable deaths—on social media, where the barriers to entry for participants are quite low. Anyone can quickly set up an account and start reaching followers, democratizing the experience even further and adding tremendously valuable commentary and experience to conversations about dying. Watching people on social media chronicle their deaths in real time is a deeply fascinating illustration of anticipatory grief—and, for those who have already died, a time capsule of their end days.

There's a lot of waiting at the end, with the experience of a slow-rolling death. There are long periods when it feels like nothing at all is happening.

At other times, it can offer unique and intriguing opportunities, for this is a rare moment when it is possible to grieve together with the subject of that grief, to explore and make mutual meaning in a moment that is still very sad. In this sense, it is a sort of opportunity that some people may view with jealousy, denied their own chance to have those critical final conversations with people who are dying, to clear the air or express their feelings, perhaps to settle some business. To know that even as someone is dying, they know how much they are loved and cared for, have a sense of their mark on the world. It is a wondrous opportunity to, as the saying goes, give people their flowers while they are still alive. These shared experiences can tighten community ties too, vital for the period following loss, which can be lonely for some.

Anticipatory grief also provides a more pragmatic, logistical opportunity—one in which people can make concrete plans together, discussing what they want from end-of-life care as well as how they want to be honored after death. These deathbed conversations are sometimes extremely illuminating—discovering that someone wants to be cremated instead of buried, for example, or learning that someone wants a religious ceremony, or nothing at all.

It is possible to have these conversations while we are all still here, to say the things that we need to say to one another, if we make space to do that.

The idea of a "living funeral" isn't new, although it definitely had a cultural moment in the 1990s. In Japan, the actress Mizunoe Takiko held her own *seizensō* on live television in 1992,[15] seventeen years before her death, to celebrate herself but also, just as much, honor the people around her. It also featured extremely memorably in a very brief scene in the 1995 cult classic *Empire Records,* in which the characters hold a living funeral for Debra (Robin Tunney), one of the employees of the titular record store. They set the stage with heavy drapery, candles, and arrangements of Christmas lights in a very earnest 1990s scene, complete with funeral bier. Viewers see Debra laid out, her shaved head nestled on a white pillow, clad in a hoodie.

"We're gathered here today to pay our last respects to Debra," says Corey (Liv Tyler), a high school student who plays a prominent role in the chaos of the one day in the record store's fortunes chronicled over the course of the film. "She left us and never said why. But I'm really going to miss her, and I wish I could have known her a little bit better."

"Dogshit," Deb interrupts, adding that she "hates this funeral" as the other characters chime in, turning the funeral into a shared confessional and storytelling moment that is earnest, vulnerable, and funny, ultimately sparking Debra to bring the conversation back around to herself, the subject, by talking about her suicide attempt with a "lady Bic," her mouth twisting wryly as she describes the struggle to get through her skin and her eventual failure.

It is a very nineties' emo moment that naturally spoke to the very depths of my soul as a death obsessive, but there was also something slightly magical about it. If the film itself was an ode to 1990s bands, with deep cuts throughout for music nerds, it was also a very intentional depiction of disaffected Gen X youth attempting to cover up their very real struggles with dark humor that occasionally accidentally tripped into authentic expressions of love and loss. The start of the scene feels like a very classically ostentatious goth moment, one the viewer is almost prepared to laugh at, but by the end, it has acquired layers.

I cannot be the only person who watched and started planning out my own living funeral.

While I never fulfilled my living funeral dreams (not yet, anyway), they are becoming a more common element of life and culture in the United States, as they should. Making conscious space to recognize and honor a death can feel like an act of surrender and trust for mourners in a culture where acknowledging a stopping point is interpreted as giving up, and it is also a powerful moment to actively engage with their shared sadness. It's a chance to participate in making sense out of death in a conversation with the dying that captures the reality of the experience together. While it may sound trite, it is also a chance to clearly share feelings of love with dying people, to explore their impact on our lives while they are still living.

It is also radical for dying people, especially in the mainstream United States, where a long tradition of bootstrapping and individualism can translate into not wanting to be a "burden" to family and loved ones, leading to decisions that are ultimately stifling. Sometimes this manifests in not telling people about a diagnosis, or downplaying it, or restricting knowledge to a small circle of loved ones. It can also turn up in a reluctance to have conversations about death and dying in these moments, which in a sense deprives the people around a dying person of autonomy and a chance to make decisions for themselves about what might be burdensome or too difficult. Missing opportunities can spark unsettled feelings that last a lifetime, the sense of being robbed of something.

And death doesn't have to be a family-and-friends-only project. It should be a collective project involving a community of people close to the dying. Death doulas, nurses, funeral directors, and other end-of-life professionals, sometimes called death workers, can be a critical part of guiding people through the emotional and logistical processes of dying. Their experiences represent an incredible gift: While each death is unique, people who have gone through this experience before as witnesses and helpers have valuable skills to bring to the conversation, whether they are helping with paperwork, explaining what to expect during someone's final hours, or simply sitting with people so they aren't alone.

Offering that kind of support in anticipatory grief may involve thinking about individual capacities and comfort levels, but it also provides an opportunity to grow closer, to think about what the dying mean to us while they are still alive, to find strength in interdependence. It can be difficult, but it can also be surprising, revelatory. Deathbed confessions, after all, are a staple of history, coming at a moment when the dying have nothing else to lose.

Refusing to say the *D*-word despite the obvious can have truly devastating consequences for dying people and mourners. In conversation with Sarah Chavez, a leader in the Death Positive movement, we spoke about her pregnancy loss: the worst nightmare of every pregnant person and a topic of considerable silence, almost as though it is contagious. For Sarah, this period in her life was emotionally harrowing, and one reason was that seemingly no one wanted to talk to her about it, including the people who were supposed to be providing her with logistical support. Like many people facing something frightening and uncertain, she wanted answers—not abstract, theoretical answers about the meaning of life, but more basic ones about what happens in death, what to expect when she was no longer expecting.

"I got passed around to six different doctors," she said. "Nurses in labor and delivery didn't answer my questions, basic questions about things. The people who were supposed to be taking care of my health and well-being were not doing that, I wasn't able to get the care or the answers that I needed at all. And then afterward, the people that you can kind of expect to support you through grief and the process, that was also just more silence."

Her incredibly isolating time had a profound impact on her that influenced the work she does in death spaces: "Really not wanting to have anyone go through that experience, not have their grief or their pain acknowledged, not have the answers and information that they needed to make informed choices about what was going to happen."

Why do that alone when you can instead do it in community?

It is also critical to engage with the reality that anticipatory grief doesn't mean a free pass from any other form of grief, a hack that will allow someone to find the light at the other end of the tunnel more quickly. Anticipatory grief is not the PSAT, as it were, a chance to practice or take care of some prerequisites. As a form of grief work,[16] it doesn't replace post-bereavement. It should rather be viewed as one iteration of an ongoing process that may last a lifetime, one that deserves more space and recognition as a component of a larger experience of loss.

"Whenever I'm working with someone in anticipatory grief, I always give the caveat that yes, we can discuss practices, we can explore what you feel is important to do now, and yet, when this person dies, there will still be grief," says Kat Primeau, also known as the Good Grief Doula. "There still may be a great deal of it. And it still may hurt in a whole new painful way."

Knowing that a loss is coming, bracing for that loss, having deep conversations that may be informed by social or cultural or spiritual beliefs, is not the same thing as going through that loss. But that knowledge can open up opportunities for making conscious choices about activities to share with the dying, whether that means taking a final trip together, bringing children to a deathbed for a chance to interact with a loved one, or simply making more time to spend with both the dying and the people around them. Those events may come with mixed feelings, including even finding joy in these small moments, but they may also turn into something to be held and cherished in the future: a "huge gift," as Primeau puts it, that isn't accessible to everyone, even if in the moment that feeling of anticipatory buildup may not feel like much of a present.

Anticipatory grief has the capacity to transform fear into curiosity, abject dread into acceptance, to take advantage of an opportunity so many of us have been denied: one more minute with the deceased, one last time to say things before it is too late. It is a chance to make plans together, to laugh together, to cry together, to find companionship in the process of dying and mourning.

But it requires a social sea change, not just when it comes to cultural attitudes about approaching the end of life, but the very capitalist framework in which we are all trapped. Bereavement policies, for example, are already limited enough, but they also tend to focus on post-death. The Family and Medical Leave Act of 1993 covers approximately 56 percent of American workers who need to take time off to care for family members, including dying ones, according to a report prepared for the Department of Labor,[17] but it does not include explicit protections for bereavement, and it only protects access to leave itself—it doesn't mandate that workers receive pay. Some states have moved to add protections for bereavement, but not many—just five in 2023,[18] with three more considering similar laws—and most are limited in scope. Moreover, some communities are more likely to be able to access FMLA protections than others, creating inherent inequalities in who can spend time with dying loved ones. Low-wage workers and workers of color are less likely to qualify for FMLA,[19] and many lead more interdependent lives, with hosts of "uncles" and "aunties" who do not qualify as such under the law. They are expected to push through it when their hearts long to be somewhere else.

Get back to work, Stacey!

Anticipatory grief also forces a difficult reckoning with the realities of unjust deaths: that some communities live in a form of suspended anticipatory grief because their bodies and lives are politicized, and they are more likely to witness death earlier, and in preventable circumstances, whether they be disabled people acutely aware of their fragility in the medical-industrial complex; people dying of preventable illnesses caused by poverty, pollution, and other human factors; Black, Latina, and Indigenous trans women knowing that they are targeted for acts of violence; or the families of people on death row aware that their loved ones are about to be murdered by the state in a retaliatory burst of violence that does nothing to remedy the harm they caused—if, in fact, they caused it at all.

Anticipatory grief can and should be a valuable liberatory tool to claim space for mourning, expanding the definition to include those who experience it on a spectrum that transcends life and death. That shift in attitudes must involve a framework that meets everyone where they are, wherever that may be, and surrounding them in community, recognizing those who may be in a state of anticipatory grief and in need of support, alongside those who process grief and loss differently. Perhaps mourning would have gone very differently during that wildfire summer if I hadn't felt like I needed to conceal the realities of living with a dying pet, including the sorrow but also the sensation of a living death and the frustrations and the guilt over the same. Going days without talking to anyone other than the vet made it both challenging to cope with anticipatory grief in the moment and difficult to relate to friends who didn't fully understand what I was going through. How could they, when I didn't tell them? And how many others in the same position had no idea that there were others like them, that they might be able to find community?

Chapter 3

Mr. Bell // Sudden

My neighboring town, the village of Mendocino, California, has an infamous Fourth of July Parade. There was a time before commercialization, before the tourist industry, before the cost of living crisis, when it was a town filled with artists and creatives who held an annual freewheeling parade with wild floats because it was a place where you could get by on the money from waiting tables at night or clerking at a bookstore, you didn't need to be independently wealthy to survive; there was time and space and room for making art, especially if you were young and still finding your way in the world.

The parade tended to be a glorious, raucous, fun expression of that artistic spirit—what some might call bohemian or counterculture but what was, for me, simply part of life for many years. The floats in the parade would be the talk of the town for months, and entrants competed fiercely for being the most weird or delightful, the most colorful and provocative. It was a unique expression of personality before the soul got sucked out of the town and replaced with Airbnbs and antique stores, tasting rooms, and quaint boutiques—a kind of death in and of itself.

Nowadays, the parade has turned sanitized: a procession of fire trucks and emergency vehicles, tame floats from local businesses, people politely handing out candy and reminders to wear sun hats, everyone getting burned in the sun anyway, old friends reuniting in the streets, dogs nosing around every corner.

But in the last year I went, a long time ago now, the parade's creative spirit was still in full bloom. I parked at the cemetery like I always did and walked into town with camera in hand, weaving my way through the crowds to capture the magic and chaos. My annual parade posts were a big hit on my blog, with comments from readers all over the world as well as those who were nostalgic for home.

Usually I stayed for the post-parade festivities at Friendship Park, but that year I didn't, pulled back home by a sensation of something wrong, and that sensation was accurate. Mr. Bell, my childhood cat, hadn't been feeling well for a few months, although it wasn't clear why. Almost entirely white, save for a gray mark on his head that looked like the thumbprint of a priest on Ash Wednesday, he was known as Smudge in the shelter. We adopted him several years after Sofie died; my father later commented that he put off having another cat because he didn't want a repeat of Sofie, but he caved to the reality that you cannot protect a cat-loving child from the inevitable. Mr. Bell lived with me in Caspar as a child, but also in Oakland and San Francisco as an adult, and he came with me when I moved home for good. In his early teens, Mr. Bell developed squamous cell carcinoma on his ears, leading to a bilaterial pinnectomy, leaving his ears cropped like a teddy bear's, a distinctive appearance that made him a big hit on my social media. In his senior years, Mr. Bell enthroned himself in a desk drawer that came to be known as "the cat drawer," where he would curl up in a tight ball while I worked—his pillow still occupies that drawer, still with a faint sprinkling of his short hair.

On that Fourth of July, not long after I got home, he crawled out of the cat drawer and had a seizure. Shortly after that, he was dead, leaving Loki and me behind.

"Died on the Fourth of July," I quipped to friends as I struggled to break the news about the cat I had spent most of my childhood and my early adulthood with. This sudden death meant that death hadn't been on anyone's radar, it wasn't a quiet undercurrent in the way I had talked about him over the previous months as it can be with animals who die after an illness; his minor health problems seemed like normal senior cat issues. Everyone wanted to know what happened: Did I euthanize him or did he die on his own? Was it painful? Had I noticed any signs? Everyone wanted to tell me how good he looked the last time they saw him at dinner or game night or afternoon tea. On social media, everyone wanted to tell me about the rainbow bridge and their special white cat, sending me pictures without thinking that perhaps I did not want to look at images of other people's cats at that moment.

Having no time to prepare and grieve for myself, it felt like his death spiraled quickly out of my control, becoming something that was no longer mine even as I was struggling to understand that it had happened at all. I was also besieged by "It's just a cat" comments, with people failing to comprehend why the loss was so disorienting and upsetting: How could I still be sad a few days, a week, a month later? And when was I going to get another cat?

Each conversation was an opportunity to relive the death all over again, and the abrupt nature was overwhelming. Part of my brain insisted that he was still alive, that he would be waiting in the other room when I rounded a corner, and his absence was jarring. Loki roamed the house looking for him, pawing at the laundry basket and behind every door. Waking up in the morning to an empty place on the bed where he used to be felt like he was dying again. I tortured myself, trying to remember if anything had seemed odd when I left that morning, if he had finished his breakfast, if I could have prevented his death through some magical sequence of actions, if this was, fundamentally, my fault. Lacking a necropsy, and therefore not knowing precisely why he died, these are questions I can't answer. Maybe they are answers I don't even want to know.

What does it mean, to die suddenly? Dishes left in the sink, sticky note on the mirror to remind yourself to buy toothpaste, papers stacked on your desk to get to tomorrow, unsaid words hanging in the air. There is so much you needed to do and now someone else needs to wrap it up while also coming to terms with the fact that you are dead. They can't ask you about the cryptic note in your top drawer. If you didn't leave a will or have clear conversations, they don't know your plans for the first editions on your shelves, your wants and wishes and desires for the remains of your life, let alone your own remains.

A sudden death requires survivors to process a lot of information and emotion, all at once. The shock is so jarring that the world feels unreal, like this is happening to someone else, sometimes creating a sense of numbness. It is overwhelming to try to understand the how and why while also trying to deal with the administrivia of death. I remember standing in the living room, fixated on and frozen by a pressing question as I realized the crematory would not be open on the Fourth of July, the weather was hot, and the freezer was full of ice cream: What was I supposed to do with the body? This was a problem that needed to be solved now, not contemplated and addressed at some point in the future.

According to CDC statistics,[1] two of the leading ten causes of death in 2023 were sudden and unpredictable: "unintentional injury," such as traffic collisions and drug overdoses; and stroke. Heart disease, which can be silent until it becomes a sudden killer, was also on the list. Even if someone is aware that they or someone they love are at risk—a smoker, a driver, a person with high cholesterol—they may not connect that risk with their own immediate reality. They may think that death will pass them by, be startled by the end of the road. It's nice to imagine these things won't happen to us or people we know, but unfortunately, people are going to encounter sudden death in their own lives, whether it be a loved one, friend, coworker, or another potentially important person in their lives.

This sudden wrenching from the norm—being alive—is disorienting for everyone left behind, but the *nature* of a sudden death can shape how it is felt and, in turn, how survivors process it.

A ubiquitous form of sudden death is the freak event that forever changes our lives: the riptides and falls, the heart attack while mowing the lawn, the senior cat who has a seizure after a brief period of feeling unwell. These events can upend our lives, and fathoming them may be a deeply personal matter; those around us may even shy away from spending too much time thinking about these kinds of deaths, fearing that their everyday nature is a reminder that they, or someone they care about, could be next. This abrupt crossing from life into death creates a swirl of emotions, all at once.

It's a baffling experience. Everything was fine, until it wasn't.

"I remember feeling so bewildered," Nicole Chung says of her father's sudden death. "Like there was a broken connection in my brain between me and reality. It was such a hard thing to wrap my head around."

Chung's father had ongoing health issues, so she wasn't unaware that his life might be shortened by his illness and interactions with the medical establishment. She was also struggling with living across the country, feeling distant from her parents and wanting to support them, see them, have her children grow up with them and know them. Her father's death was also made more complicated by financial stress. And while she understood that his chronic health problems would contribute to his death, she also viewed it as a kind of "negligent homicide" caused by structural problems with the health care system.

"I couldn't picture a world in which my father wasn't alive anymore," she says, and then, very suddenly, she had to navigate this huge, sudden loss on both an emotional and practical level, from across a huge literal and metaphorical distance. Such a distance can become a massive gulf between you and the people around you, and sometimes it even creates gaps within yourself.

"There were weeks," Nicole told me, "a couple of months that feel scooped out of my memory. . . . We moved during that period—our lease was up, we had to find a different place to live. I don't remember packing."

In moments like these, being surrounded by supportive people who are willing to show up for the mourner during their period of disorientation and beyond can make a profound difference in how the mourner integrates that loss into their life moving forward. Mourning a sudden death is traumatic, and it can mark the body and mind in deep ways that demand empathy and care from those around us.

To get a deeper understanding of the way trauma interacts with our experiences of the world, I called David Emerson, coexecutive director at the Center for Trauma and Embodiment. He focuses on PTSD and complex trauma in his work, and although he does not specialize in grief, he is very familiar with the interactions of trauma and grief in his clients, given the fact that they are ever-present themes in our lives. He says that "our basic sense of self and bodily integrity are threatened" when we experience trauma, and that can include trauma around loss.

Grief is both a psychological event and a somatic one,[2] especially when paired with trauma, and in the case of sudden death, the rapid onset can be a true overload. That can manifest in familiar emotions: anger, sorrow, confusion. But it can also cause physiological events. People in mourning may lose their appetites, develop disruptions in cortisol levels, and have issues with cardiac health that increase the risk of death.[3] Surviving spouses are more likely to die in the first six months after a loss: the infamous "widowhood effect."[4] Survivors of people who died by suicide are also more likely to interact with stigma,[5] which can further complicate their responses to that loss.

"Trauma and survival are lonely experiences because they're very overwhelming experiences," Emerson notes. That feeling of being overwhelmed, of sensory overload, can take over your whole body in a way that bystanders may not understand. It can express itself surprisingly; for some people, perhaps, it looks like lying in bed, feeling unable to complete even the most basic tasks of daily life. For others it may emerge as emotional volatility, outsized reactions to very ordinary events or stimuli. Some people may behave uncharacteristically. Others may act to push these feelings away by flinging themselves into work or administrative tasks associated with sudden death.

Traumatic deaths—as is often the case with sudden deaths—are associated with a greater incidence of grief reactions that can become severely disruptive;[6] some might refer to them as "disordered," though that term carries notes of pathology that do not provide space for the varied manifestations of human emotion. It can also cause permanent changes to the brain, a profound marker of the deceased's legacy in our lives. Sudden death is associated with an increased risk of developing post-traumatic stress disorder,[7] for example, a complication with big implications that can result in symptoms such as hypervigilance and fear that add to the emotional distress of the loss itself. Healing, Emerson says, requires "reconnecting to the self," something that can be very challenging when there is a sense of abstraction or distancing, as in the case of sudden death.

Imbalances following a loss are not necessarily wrong or bad—any traumatic event deserves a pause, says Emerson—but sometimes they do rise to the point of concern,[8] suggesting that a griever may need more structured care—not to be fixed, but to be supported. Disruptions in grief can make it difficult to get through basic tasks of self-care and activities of daily living, such as cooking, bathing, and dressing. Someone who has severe insomnia, for example, is at risk of a variety of physical and mental health consequences caused by lack of sleep, and intervention, whether in the form of informal support from friends and comrades, moderated peer support, therapy, or other means, might be merited to help them manage their reaction to a loss, to find a new baseline to build upon. There is no minimizing the loss itself or the associated trauma, but there is a world of difference between perseveration and feeling stuck circling a series of events and growing into and with grief.

But sudden death is not an equal opportunity visitor. For some people, the risk of sudden death is much higher thanks to systemic social inequalities that affect our experiences of daily life. Sudden cardiac death, for example, is more common in the Black community[9] for a variety of reasons, including medical racism. Structural inequalities such as occupational segregation[10] determine who is more likely to work in dangerous professions. Suicide is more prevalent among LGBTQIA+ youth, especially those of color. When grief is tinged with an awareness that the death was preventable and linked with larger social inequalities and injustices, it adds a layer of difficulty to an already troubled time.

The larger societal tragedies, those that could have been prevented through policy decisions, advocacy work, and cultural shifts in the way we think about the world and each other, carry a heavy weight. These are the worst of the violence humanity can inflict upon each other. "The cruelty is the point," Adam Serwer wrote in *The Atlantic,*[11] coining a phrase that became absolutely and noxiously ubiquitous in talking about the policies of the Trump administrations, but it applies more broadly to the world we live in. Society is cruel, sometimes on purpose, sometimes as an unintended consequence, and that creates, inherently, "bad deaths": those in which dying and mourners alike lose control of their stories and lives.

How do we reckon with sudden deaths that feel profoundly unjust? Writer Meg Bernhard, who attended an International End of Life Doula Association (INELDA) training for *n+1* magazine in 2024,[12] found herself struggling with this very question after she became curious about death doulas and the Death Positive movement thanks to posts on social media that felt energizing and inspiring to read, filled with people she'd "want to be friends with," a world of death influencers.

At the training, and in her subsequent reporting, she struggled with a larger question: How do you situate sudden, violent, traumatic, unjust deaths within the framework of the popular perception of a "good death" movement? Death acceptance, an understanding of mortality, and an awareness of the inevitable feel very different when a death is sudden and unjust.

"INELDA's ambition is to create the conditions for a 'good death,'" she wrote. "It's a noble and palatable image, but it cannot accommodate so many tragedies of modern life: deaths by accidents, or guns, or police brutality, or overdoses, or suicides. . . . Maybe end of life doulas can only make bad deaths better."

She struggled with this essential conflict in the training and in conversations with fellow attendees, experiencing a sense of a cultural gap. In the experience of planning for her own death, a required part of her training, she found herself fixated on what it means to die young and suddenly, wondering if the death of her friend Haley in her teens had hardened her, perhaps even made her cynical, in the midst of conversations about dying in old age or after long illnesses. Her experience made her realize that talking about death is important, but so is acknowledging that death is not a "great equalizer."

This distinction is both a point of tension and an important one. We cannot guarantee everyone a good death or mourning period, and shying away from that is a disservice to the very communities who need that honesty and clarity most. Supporting the diversity of mourning may help to "make bad deaths better" by acknowledging, from the start, the shocking or political nature of those deaths, the added note of fury that comes with knowing a death was preventable or came so abruptly that there was no time to prepare. Knowing in your bones that something is unfair and having that unfairness spoken aloud by a witness can be a profound moment.

The increasing incidence of deaths in climate catastrophes, such as hurricanes and wildfires, illustrates a kind of bad death, a cruelty born of policy choices and a refusal to engage with how we are causing these events, and the legacies they leave behind. I have a vivid memory of the fall of 2018, when for days I would wake every morning to a dusting of ash across my yard, so thick on my windshield that I had to wipe it away in order to drive: the fallout of the Camp Fire, which claimed eighty-five lives and nearly obliterated the town of Paradise, California.[13] At the time, I thought of how I was wiping away the remains of people's houses and lives, inhaling the combusted remains of fellow human beings who died for a host of reasons related to societal inaction, not a freak act of nature: a utility's failure to maintain its infrastructure;[14] runaway climate change contributing to hot, dry summers; barriers to evacuation for people in a community where officials bungled the process of evacuation notifications and coordination,[15] leading to confusion and panic.

These deaths are sudden and at times feel inevitable—the cost of living in wildfire-prone areas, for example—but they aren't. Every death in unprecedented flooding, a devastating wildfire, or sudden tornado is a tragedy for the family and loved ones. It is also one that weighs heavy on society as a whole, challenging us to think about our own role in these deaths, our sense of helplessness at feeling powerless to effect the change needed to stop them. These deaths contribute to the collective trauma of the communities where they take place, to the sometimes absurd conversations we find ourselves in as we watch the same events repeat themselves over and over again: Which wildfire year was it that Janice died, again?

There are also the sudden deaths that are considered inconveniences, as when someone dies by suicide in a subway system, a death forces the temporary closure of a job site, or an employee dies suddenly with work undone. Many of the complaints about these deaths and their impact on day-to-day business can be traced back to the pressures of capitalism, turning a death into a problem that cuts into the bottom line and, therefore, becomes a source of anger. Commuters are upset about delayed trains, workers fear the consequences of missed days in their paychecks, bosses are irritated by paperwork and inspections and other repercussions of on-site deaths. The death turns into a problem to be solved, a mess to be cleaned up.

The initial selfishness of responses to such deaths is an indicator of something deeply broken in us. For surviving loved ones in such cases, these callous expressions of irritation and inconvenience can be extraordinarily cruel and violent, making the trauma associated with the sudden loss even more acute and leaving survivors with even more to process as they see firsthand the cold indifference of the surrounding world.

After an Amazon worker died in December 2022, for example, colleagues came forward to claim that there were boxes stacked around his body[16] as they were ordered to keep up with the holiday package rush, ensuring those Prime packages arrived on time, aware that even small delays in the supply chain can have huge ripple effects. That same year, a truck driver struck and killed a farmworker in California, and her comrades were ordered to keep picking carrots while her body lay in the field—despite the fact that one of them was her daughter.[17] To know that a loved one's death is a footnote in a capitalist hellscape is a grim thought.

These kinds of sudden deaths, those that highlight inequality and injustice, can coalesce into rallying points to express rage, call for change, or find solidarity. They can become a nexus of collective grieving, as seen at George Floyd Square in 2020 after police officer Derek Chauvin kneeled on the eponymous Black Minnesotan man's neck for over nine minutes, asphyxiating him in front of a crowd of horrified onlookers.[18] His final words, "I can't breathe," ignited a spark at a moment when most of the nation was sheltering in place in the early months of the COVID-19 pandemic, resulting in widespread protests across the country. Many Americans were acutely aware of inequality and already on edge, deprived of opportunities for socialization and living under the shadow of a poorly understood virus. Floyd's murder became a tipping point.

Those protests had a profound impact, driving numerous companies as well as the federal government to respond to the nationwide calls for racial justice by incorporating more explicit diversity, equity, and inclusion practices into their operations, though many of these were rolled back in 2025 under the second Trump administration. Unusually for police killings, Chauvin was convicted of murder and incarcerated,[19] though he was also the beneficiary of a massive fundraiser fueled by supporters; not everyone in America saw what he had done as a crime or something worthy of action.

The paroxysm of sorrow and frustration in the aftermath of deaths like Floyd's may be channeled into marches in the streets, impassioned speeches on the floors of legislatures, and mutual aid to support those most affected. Critically, such deaths force people to come together, not leave grievers isolated, and they have the potential to drive change if people can keep up the momentum.

Communal mourning may illustrate the best parts of ourselves at a moment when we see each other most in need. There is something both powerful and heartening in this coming together, especially when it involves crossing lines of community, culture, and experience, uniting people from disparate backgrounds across a shared event and recognition of humanity. Sometimes people forge connections and build relationships they wouldn't have created otherwise, thrown together by happenstance, finding common ground and building power in the aftermath of a devastating event.

When grief is taken outside the home, it has distinct benefits to both mourners and those around them. Many hands make light work, and grief can be very heavy work when people undertake it alone. Refusing to be silent about grief also forces uncomfortable questions, requiring that society not look away, especially when the expression of grief is unavoidable because, again, it disrupts capitalist systems and the status quo. For example, when people are gathering on the National Mall to spread out the pieces of the AIDS Quilt, or showing up to stage a memorial, they are impossible to avoid; they are taking control of the mourning process and requiring that society see and answer their cries.

"There's evidence that supports that sharing the burden of grief in public invites others to aid in the healing process," wrote Yolande Clarke-Jackson for *Yes!* of the coming together that can occur in the aftermath of sudden death.[20] "It can also allow a stronger social resilience to discuss topics of grief and mourning. And it connects us to community in ways that may be able to enact change. In short, externalization and communal care of grief can be transformative."

Clarke-Jackson views collective, public grief as "revolutionary" for society as well as crucial for individual mourners to find strength and power in grief shared, with mourners who feel called to speak carving out a public space to make their words unavoidable, no matter how painful they may be. These collective moments also provide an opportunity for pause to explicitly acknowledge grief, to say something we don't always say aloud: This is actually happening, and it is unfair. As Clarke-Jackson notes, this can be freeing for mourners, turning grief from an experience of isolation into something with deeper cultural meaning.

But collective mourning is not always an inspirational tale of people banding together in the face of tragic events. In the aftermath of many mass tragedies, we see the #Strong language arising almost immediately, with the site of the tragedy used as a prefix in the hashtag that is intended to express solidarity. It appears on social media, signs that pop up seemingly overnight in front yards, a pile of cheap mass-produced swag, T-shirts and hats and totes and bumper stickers.

It also echoes very American attitudes about positivity and bootstrapping, tasking people in mass mourning with performing strength and resilience within hours or days of a tragic event. While perhaps intended as expressions of unity, they also carry unspoken implications about people who are not "strong," who are not team players, who want to rage and scream and cry, who have very different reactions to sudden deaths. And they require grievers to conform with a program that they may not necessarily have shaped: Attend the mass memorial, add flowers to the growing display, give interviews to the media that align with a message. Do not stand out from the #Strong collective, do not dilute the brand, stay on focus, on point.

Maybe we don't want to be strong. Maybe we want to be soft, to feel the raw sensitivity of the world around us. Maybe we want other people to be vulnerable with us, even though that can be frightening.

And that outpouring of public support can dwindle quickly, leaving the fragile shells of grievers behind, because it's easy to take an isolated action, to donate to a GoFundMe, but a lot harder to stick with people in their sorrow. Grief remains an uncomfortable topic, and mourners who do not move it along may find themselves abandoned by people who are not willing to live with their sorrow, especially when that sorrow is politicized. Staying too long in the shadow of grief may require those around mourners to examine the society and culture we have built that contributed to the death. Grief also interacts with the rapid news cycle and a world in which things are constantly moving, changing, evolving, a culture characterized by being constantly on the go, and one that does not mesh well with supporting people at a time of loss, who take a step outside of time and place to grapple with events whose aftereffects linger long after the news has moved on.

Our short attention spans can feel brutal to those in grief.

The hollow promises of "thoughts and prayers" followed by the disappearance of interest—whether that be media trucks packing up to go home or friends stopping by less and less often, coworkers less and less tolerant about missed work—is a secondary bereavement of sorts. So too is the sinking sensation when a preventable death does not result in meaningful change, when all the strength in the world cannot force society to confront an issue.

And at other times, sudden death tears a community apart. People may argue over how to respond, who is responsible, how to make meaning. It may be politicized, or mourners may be told to keep quiet, with some sudden deaths wrapped in guilt and shame. Sometimes, grief becomes reactive, as it did after October 7, 2023, when Hamas operatives stormed a music festival in Israel, killing 364 people.[21] The Israeli government responded with an unprecedented military assault on Gaza and the West Bank that a 2025 United Nations report determined meets the criteria for genocide,[22] driving Palestinians off their ancestral lands and eliminating their culture. That wildly disproportionate response entrenched a cycle of grief and fury, becoming a rallying point for people all over the world and a topic of global criticism. It was also the end of many professional and personal relationships, highlighting the depths of the schisms that emerged in conversations about the topic even among people who didn't necessarily directly know people involved in the conflict; the mass witnessing of violence such as bombed-out refugee camps and a growing list of dead children became a kind of collective horror that will linger, for many of us, for the rest of our lives, paling in comparison to the suffering of people living through it.

Editor and writer Lisa Goldman, who has covered Israel and Palestine for over a decade, wrote for *New Lines* magazine in 2024[23] about visiting an exhibition commemorating those killed at the Nova festival, seeing a display that slipped more into airing grievances than mourning, and one that felt like a muddied commemoration of the lives lost rather than a collective pause to mark those deaths. The creators of the exhibit were being forced to both process and perform their loss, to view the events of October 7 in aggregate while under scrutiny from the entire world. That is not a good starting point for authentic expressions of and conversations about grief.

"My feeling was that the people who had created this exhibition were not clear about their motives. This is understandable: They are traumatized and grieving. . . . I have seen how dangerous and insidious grievance culture can be," Goldman wrote, describing an event that felt to her more like a commodification of a horrendous event than a genuine effort to remember the dead. The entire carefully curated exhibition, down to evoking emotions with the use of incense in a multisensory experience designed to immerse the viewer while advancing some very specific narratives about the relationship between Israel and Palestine, at times verged closer to nationalism than a shared sense of love and loss, or a space for healing.

Speaking to American Jewish people a year after the killings, writer Elad Nehorai reflected upon the dangers of acting quickly in the wake of sudden death without taking time or space to grieve: "As the news was coming and we were still processing all the details and absorbing the scope of the massacre, we were simultaneously watching people debating, celebrating, calling to arms, mocking, and on and on. . . . What we all needed then was a moment to grieve. We needed to absorb the shock of what we had seen, feel it, and cry together. Despite (or because of) all the urgency of the moment, our bodies, minds, and souls were in an urgent need of healing and collective support. . . . The public events became war rallies."[24]

The rapid response to mass casualty events like this can eclipse the rights and needs of mourners, cultivating a landscape in which people are expected to rapidly take, and defend, sides.

As President George W. Bush put it in 2001 after the sudden and shocking destruction of the World Trade Center in a terrorist attack that also damaged the Pentagon and crashed a plane in Pennsylvania, "Either you are with us, or you are with the terrorists,"[25] setting up an appealing vision of a binary choice, one in which there is a clear right and a clear wrong; notably, the aftermath of the September 11 attacks resulted in the deaths of hundreds of thousands of civilians across Iraq and Afghanistan, another profoundly disproportionate response.[26] These deaths were deemed acceptable, perhaps even necessary, in the quest for vengeance that marked the aftermath of 9/11, against the voices of protesters across the world.

Fear of, and lack of preparation for, death forces people into making lurching decisions they may come to regret in the case of sudden deaths, including when it comes to a politicized death: A mourning family may be plunged into demands to perform the right kind of activism, for example, or workers are forced back on the job to pick things up as they were before, as for instance at that Amazon warehouse where a worker lay dead and pickers were expected to simply move around the body. Without a pause to acknowledge and mark that passage, survivors can be left in a state of unresolved suspense.

People may feel distress around decision-making that feels both urgent and permanent. To bury or to cremate? To hold a memorial or not? Open or closed casket? Which side to take? Navigating these questions under the pressure of a body lying in temporary storage is enough of a strain in any circumstances, but in a sudden death, they can be even more jarring, especially when that death has become a social one too, the death no longer the property of the mourner, in a way. When everyone is jarred by a death, whether personal or political, sometimes the mourners at the core of the event fall out of focus. At a moment when the mourner needs their people to help them, to bring casseroles, to simply sit with them and acknowledge the solemnity of the event, losing control of events or, worse yet, feeling like they need to assure the people around them or take an immediate political stance in the aftermath of a jarring event can be traumatic and frustrating.

Psychologist Susan Silk and mediator Barry Goldman spoke to this when they coined the phrase "comfort in, dump out," in a *Los Angeles Times* article presenting the idea of ring theory.[27] This invites a more collective view of crisis, including that around death, that views it as a community project while keeping those most closely affected in the center of the conversation and the priority for support and care. Silk and Goldman used the example of a patient, "Katie," experiencing a major medical event.

"Draw a circle. This is the center ring. In it, put the name of the person at the center of the current trauma. For Katie's aneurysm, that's Katie. Now draw a larger circle around the first one. In that ring put the name of the person next closest to the trauma. In the case of Katie's aneurysm, that was Katie's husband, Pat. Repeat the process as many times as you need to. In each larger ring put the next closest people."

Ring theory is somewhat imperfect, especially in highly interdependent communities, but it's a powerful shorthand. The role of people in inner rings should not be comforting or reassuring those in outer rings or focusing their energy on meeting the needs and wants of others. Those who are farther out can provide not just emotional but material support to allow grievers space and time; the rings highlight the possibility of varying degrees of closeness to a loss or major event rather than a simple calculus of mourner versus outsider. This concept applies not just to sudden death but loss more broadly: Whether someone dies abruptly or slowly over months or years, the people around that person still need their people. That access to support can make a difference in their grief, can intervene in the loneliness and isolation that some grievers feel as those in the outer rings provide care, while also splitting the duties of that care to ensure that no one person has to be a pillar.

Compassionate supporters who understand this do not have to have all the answers; sometimes, simply being there is enough. The best supporters at a time of loss are aware that they cannot repair the loss itself, that what's broken is broken, but they can make it more bearable by identifying the things they can actually help with. On a deeply interpersonal level, sometimes that does require simply sitting with grievers, witnessing their grief and acknowledging this horrendous thing that has just happened without attempting to make it better. With any loss, mourners may want to talk about it, to tell a story, to turn a series of sometimes upsetting and baffling events over in their minds as they work toward coming to terms with it, and a witness can be an integral part of that emotional process.

Concrete help is vital, and, critically, it often doesn't require any special skills. Picking up or cooking meals, taking out the trash, starting a load of laundry, picking kids up from school, taking a pet to the vet, writing thank-you cards, making phone calls—these are all basic and necessary things that those in the outer rings can do for those in the inner ones. More trusted confidants, or those with particularly applicable experience and skills, can help with those more fraught things: sitting in for a conversation with the funeral home, reviewing wills and other documents, closing out bank accounts and chasing down retirement payouts.

A burst of practicality can be incredibly valuable and useful in the immediate days and weeks following a death, a way for people to involve themselves in a supportive, structured way that can help mourners feel lifted and supported by community. But these are all things that people don't just need in the immediate wake of sudden deaths; they are ongoing and slow rolling. I just closed out the last portion of a friend's estate after almost three years. I went through most of that prolonged process on my own, and finalizing those documents was also its own strange mourning moment, making me feel as though I had truly erased her from the world. But it felt like a thing I couldn't really say to anyone, because hadn't she died so long ago? Her ashes are long scattered and her clothes long sold from the thrift store, so why does it matter that it took this long to wrangle a minor financial matter?

And that practicality can also mask and obstruct necessary emotional engagement with the loss itself. The inability to prepare for such deaths can turn grief perfunctory and transactional, with a focus on getting things done rather than marking passage. The abrupt nature of such deaths may result in tremendous pressure to subvert grief to "get through it" in a society that rewards those who suppress their expressions of grief, leaving open wounds that may continue to seep for years.

Refusing to engage with feelings associated with a loss can leave mourners with a lingering sense of a life and relationship left incomplete that they only begin to confront years later, sometimes when jarred by another life event or reminder; grief loves an ambush. That feeling is far from uncommon, with people navigating grief after sudden death, especially a traumatic one, years later, at a time when their supporters have long since moved on and they are forced to confront the fact that they never truly had an opportunity to explore their relationship to the loss, to the deceased. Time and grief catch up with us all, in the end.

To die suddenly is to leave the world and your survivors undone. To be affected by sudden death is, for many, to balance the ravages of grief against the logistics of responding to that death. For others, it is to witness the way in which close survivors are caught in the undertow of that death without necessarily being aware of it, because they are so focused on reaching goals they or society have set, goals that have sometimes been forced upon them. The culture we live in makes it very easy to attempt to set grief aside, finding other things to focus on in the aftermath of a sudden death, whether it be fundamental logistics, turning grief and anger into activism without an opportunity to pause and fully sit with them, or feeling obligated to press on to serve others, whether they be children, other family members, or people in our lives that are counting on us for support and survival.

You must sell the Jaguar, get copies of the death certificate, testify before Congress, organize a march. Acknowledging that grief after sudden death may be momentarily subverted by shock and the pressure to keep living, to perform the work necessary to survive in a literal and figurative sense, is important to building a culture that's more supportive of mourners.

Culturally, we need to understand that grief may come in waves that can last for weeks, months, years, and it's necessary for mourners and their supporters to be prepared to live through and with that. We need to explicitly create clearly designated space for expressing feelings around a death over the long term, rather than setting limits on how long and how often someone can talk about their feelings around a sudden death. This is an important element of personal healing, but also a culture shift. Embracing grief as an extended community project also makes activism around grief, when activism is a necessary response, more sustainable; that work can drag on over the course of lifetimes. When community support flames out after a brief eruption of shared outrage, fear, and worry, it leaves a handful of dedicated mourners behind fighting powerful forces that resist the revolutionary change they are demanding. Without an awareness of the trauma associated with sudden death and the imperative to stick with each other through that trauma, grief will remain, a lingering thorn, for months or years, one that will occasionally cause a deep twinge of pain, a reminder of a huge life event that remains an elephant in the room until it is confronted. It will haunt the survivors who feel left behind, wondering why they're alone, curdling to bitterness and a sense of feeling out of step, forever baffled by an abrupt turn of events that their minds can't resolve, a drawer forever closed to avoid looking inside and feeling undone by what lies within.

Chapter 4

Leila // Guilt

I adopted Leila from the feed store, where the Humane Society had cleverly installed a cage by the register to bait prospective adopters. I didn't want a second cat, but when she rolled over and gazed at me with her brilliant blue eyes, I had no choice. I took her home to Loki, and the two quickly became infamous for despising each other; for several years, I lived in a literal house divided, with Leila haunting the kitchen and living room while Loki stalked the hall, my bedroom, and the office. Leila destroyed innumerable household items with her penchant for peeing in terror when Loki looked at her, and for years I could not abandon the habit of gingerly touching upholstered surfaces to check for wet spots before sitting down.

People asked why I didn't take her back to the shelter.

Leila had been found in a foreclosed house, left there for an amount of time that wasn't certain, the sheriff having finally showed up after repeated calls from the neighbors about a cat trapped inside. Her medical record from the shelter tells a story of emaciation: She was covered in fleas and infested with parasites, but she was still friendly and outgoing with people despite being abandoned. In the face of that, how could I return her? She had already been left once, and she had chosen me. I owed this to her.

Over the years, age and exposure finally allowed Loki and Leila to tolerate each other, sometimes even warily curling up next to each other on the couch, and it was there one evening, as we watched Netflix, that I found a little lump in her side. The vet determined that it was cancerous, and she had a mammary chain removal—a mastectomy for cats—in the hopes of arresting the spread of the disease. It was an invasive and traumatic surgery that required weeks of recovery and extensive pain management, Leila draped uncomfortably on pieces of furniture while I tried to coax her into eating something, anything, fearing the liver failure that can happen in cats who forgo food too long.

As with Mr. Shadow, I was confronted with a myriad of choices for her care. I could prophylactically remove the mammary chain on her other side, drive two hours to Santa Rosa for chemotherapy and/or radiation, or I could roll the dice, knowing that most of these treatments would be palliative at best: They would put off the end of her life but not forestall the inevitable, and most of the studies I read suggested that these measures would increase her survival time by just six months or less. I could hope that the cancer hadn't metastasized, that she might enjoy many happy years peeing on my couch and worming under the covers with me at night, trying to convince herself that Loki wasn't on the other side.

And for a while, it seemed like maybe the cancer had, indeed, been arrested, until she started breathing more and more heavily, gasping for air, a sure sign of pleural effusion, the membranes between her lungs slowly building up fluid, forcing her to fight against the pressure to breathe. The vet at the emergency clinic seemed relieved when she delivered the bad news and I asked not how to cure her but how to make her comfortable. Leila spent several weeks at home after having the fluid drained, taking steroids, until she was again struggling to breathe. The vet told me it wasn't painful, but I can't imagine that was true. If nothing else, fighting for air is frightening, and fear is a form of pain.

She was still friendly and curious, wanted to play, and was very excited when I took her outside to let her cautiously explore the outdoors in her final days. She loved rolling around on the sun-warmed bricks of my patio, nosing under the ferns along the edge of my yard, but she wanted to drift, to cross into the forest, and I knew what that meant. I steered her away from the edges of the yard, built little fern palaces with her where we lay together in the late spring sunshine, which seemed like a cruel taunt.

On the day I euthanized her, I had to drag her out from under the bed to take her to the vet, who couldn't make a house call. I hated myself in that moment, for causing fear and stress in her last minutes of life. I texted a friend about how unfair it felt that she should fight me even as I was trying to do right by her. Sometimes the spirit is willing, my friend said, but the body is not. Leila did not pass without a struggle at the vet's, resisting the sedation, feeling so alive and vital even as she took fast, shallow breaths, struggling for air as her heart pounded desperately. I took her to Bubbling Well, a pet cemetery three hours away, to be cremated and wandered the grounds, struck by the sheer number of well-maintained graves covered in flowers and toys, even those for pets who had died years, sometimes decades, ago. This was not a place where pets went to be forgotten.

Her ashes came back to me in a cedar urn, and on warm days, the scent of cedar winds through my house.

It took me years to disentangle my feelings about Leila's death. I felt guilty for the series of choices I made, wondering if I should have been more aggressive with her care. I should have been aware of her increased risk for mammary carcinoma because she was spayed late, I should have been more vigilant, caught the original tumor earlier. I should have gotten the second surgery, even though it would have put me deep in credit card debt. I should have considered a short course of chemotherapy, or at least gone to consult with a veterinary oncologist to see if she could take oral medication and my vet could monitor her treatment locally so I wouldn't have to repeatedly drive two hours to the closest specialty clinic. I should have noticed that she was having trouble breathing earlier. I should have had her lungs tapped a second time to remove the fluid again, rather than euthanizing. I should have waited to euthanize her if she was still eating and playing and happy, even if she couldn't breathe. I blocked out the image of her panting after only a few steps.

In cases of terminal diagnoses, there is immense pressure to try everything, to embark on the most heroic measures possible to save the afflicted animal or person. This has long been a trend in human medicine, where incredible advances have allowed us to cheat death. We can transplant organs. We can treat people with a myriad of options. HIV, once a death sentence, can be controlled with medications that make it undetectable and untransmittable, simply a minor part of someone's life, and 2024 headlines demonstrated that we are on the path to outright curing people now. We have incredibly complex and amazing surgical interventions and robots to use in the operating room for precision tasks. We have targeted chemotherapy tailored to individual cancers. We can take advantage of incredible gains in genetics to develop treatments optimized to individual bodies and genes. Some of these things are miraculous developments: An insulin pump can help a diabetic person lead a full, active life, an artificial heart can keep someone alive while waiting for a transplant. Lifesaving measures are transforming what it means to be human, making more and more things survivable.

Animal medicine is rapidly following as the scope and depth of veterinary care improves, with an explosion of veterinary specialties accompanied by advanced treatments that sometimes equal those available in human medicine—for those who can afford to pay. Of course you can't turn your back on the chance of a few more months, can you? Don't you care about your beloved pet? Euthanasia has turned from an expected outcome to a moral quandary rife with judgment.

But some of these shifts in medicine, for animals and humans alike, are more fraught. We can poke and prod the dying seemingly indefinitely, if we want. We forget, sometimes, that just because you can does not mean that you should, and that what is true for you, and works for you, is not universal. Sometimes your life is shorter, but the quality is better, if you aren't pursuing treatments that can be emotionally and physically grueling, focusing instead on basic supportive care. As a former coworker liked to say, "Here for a good time, not a long time."

To decline treatment is to give up, a failure not just for the dying but for those around them, especially physicians. Atul Gawande's *Being Mortal* and the subsequent *Frontline* documentary about the same explored this in thoughtful, vivid detail, articulating the pressure doctors feel to try everything, to be able to say they did everything they could. How many television shows have you seen with a grim hospital waiting room and a tired, disheveled surgeon walking toward the family, surgical cap in hand, to say just that, shaken by the sense of failure and the dread of telling the family that their best still wasn't enough?

Gawande notes that it is challenging to communicate with patients who are nearing the end of their lives and facing choices about life and death in a culture where "try everything" is assumed to be the norm, making it hard for physicians to educate patients about hospice and palliative care options, sometimes leaving patients adrift when they feel that they don't want to continue or pursue aggressive treatment. Even as some physicians seek training and support with these kinds of conversations, patients may be very resistant to them. Why are you bringing up hospice instead of talking about the treatment plan to fix Grandma, your plans for curing our child? These pressures to "keep trying" force physicians to offer treatments and recommendations that may conflict with ethics and common sense: When my grandmother was in a comatose state with no signs of brain activity after a fall, for example, the doctors were suggesting an MRI to determine if her neck was broken, rather than discussing termination of life support, which is what she had explicitly indicated was what she wanted if that very situation arose. Gawande also outlines the grief and guilt physicians feel when patients die despite their best efforts, the struggle they endure when patients indicate that they don't want to pursue every measure in the hopes of a cure or to prolong their lives.

Trying everything comes at a cost. There is the spiritual and emotional cost that accompanies the experience of prolonged treatment, especially in the context of illnesses that people are expected to treat like the Germans across the trenches, to always be prepared to go over the top. That cost extends not just to the dying, but to those around them, to the loved ones who witness these struggles and wrestle with their own emotions, and to the care providers surrounding someone who has a critical or terminal illness, who face love and loss and distress. Choosing to decline or limit treatment isn't giving up and a sign of a lack of will to live, but it's sometimes interpreted and presented as one. Reading the obituaries of people who died after "a long illness" or "a courageous battle," this immense toll lurks between the lines, never making itself known but always present. A hard-fought death is hard for everyone.

And that cost is also monetary, a fact that some may find crude, since talking about money makes people uncomfortable, but the interaction of class and medicine plays a role in the deaths of millions of Americans. Access to that top-tier, try-everything care is heavily rooted in how much money you have, as well as your social status.

Reckoning with the costs of living and dying in America is essential to confronting the role of guilt in our decisions about death and dying. Prior to the passage of the Affordable Care Act in 2009, getting sick, and dying, could be ruinously expensive, to the point that access to health care became an important factor in major decisions—sometimes, for example, the right spouse would provide access to a great health insurance plan, in some cases even driving friends to marry each other to share health insurance plans. On the flip side, people facing high medical costs might have opted for less costly treatment options or been forced to divorce each other to avoid burdening their whole families with medical debt or leaving a legacy of debt behind after their deaths. The ACA had a profound impact on the affordability of and access to health insurance, with transformative effects for many Americans, especially those facing end-of-life costs, which tend to be the bulk of medical expenses over a lifetime.

Even with the ACA, though, health care and end-of-life costs were still high; the GoFundMe for medical, end-of-life, or funeral expenses is a common sight in America, where some hospitals even actively encourage patients to turn to crowdfunding[1] to support the costs of care. Medical fundraisers consistently account for around one third of the site's active fundraisers,[2] and a depressing number are underfunded. The true number is likely even higher, given that people may choose other fundraising categories for medical needs, such as a "travel" fundraiser associated with bringing a family member to a specialist or clinic. Medical debt is a pernicious problem, and it isn't just bills owed to providers and facilities, but personal loans, costs put on credit cards, and other forms of indebtedness as people stretch themselves to the brink to pay for both acute and chronic medical care.

Fear of debt drives people to make medical decisions motivated by cost, not need, as seen in the deaths of diabetics forced to ration insulin because of cost.[3] This "iatrogenic epidemic," as researchers Christopher Su and Scott Ramsey wrote,[4] persisted despite the ACA and takes the form of a cycle: Debt itself is associated with higher mortality, and medical debt entrenches economic inequality, sometimes on an intergenerational level. Medical debt also has a negative psychological impact,[5] becoming yet another burden to carry, with financial strain, including medical debt, a major contributing factor[6] in suicides.

People new to the health care system may not fully understand how much their ability to pay will affect the quantity and quality of care they can access, an ugly discovery when facing a serious illness or terminal diagnosis. They may also be unaware of other limiting factors on health care, including the closure of hospitals and clinics in rural America that is gutting access to health care, especially in the South.[7] Racism[8] and transphobia[9] in patient care are rampant and so is denial of treatment for miscarriage and abortion at religious-owned hospital chains, which control vast numbers of beds across the country. Sometimes all the money in the world is still not enough to get the care you need and deserve.

It is hard not to have feelings of guilt when you make decisions that are driven by money, or when you discover that a loved one's fears about costs had a direct impact on the way they died. In America, a nation where people are very fearful of discussing money matters, these critical conversations simply don't happen in many families—yet another form of things unsaid that come to trouble surviving friends and family. Openly saying that money is influencing health care decisions, whether concerns about the cost of care or the legacy left behind, brings to the surface things that usually pass without comment in

America. The pressure to leave assets and opportunities—not nothing or, even worse, debt—is immense. To sell a house, cash out savings accounts, liquidate other assets to pursue treatment, may be expected in the name of trying everything, but it is also stigmatized: What do you mean by leaving your family with nothing? Do you not love them enough? Are you willing to burden them not just with lingering costs associated with your end-of-life care but also the expense of a funeral? Do you not owe the next generation a better start than the one your parents gave you, your spouse a continuation of the support you offered in life? What do you mean, you're selling the house, why aren't you saving it for the grandkids?

Sometimes these tensions are undercurrents around the deathbed and sometimes they are openly stated, but in either case, they can feed feelings of resentment, guilt, and obligation that may also be affected by social and cultural factors. When these emotions are colliding with grief and end-of-life decisions, they can take on an outsized role. I am surely not the only person who has witnessed surreal and sometimes deeply disturbing arguments at the bedsides of ill and dying people as future survivors argue over who gets the house, the car, the 401(k); or despairing dinner table conversations at home over the prospect of wrangling medical debt, with hospitals and providers preparing to jockey for position during probate, hoping to extract as much as they can from the estate.

Money, the pressure to try everything, and the refusal to have open conversations about these factors even in the face of the obvious are, of course, far from the only drivers of guilt.

Things left unsaid can also become haunting for survivors in the aftermath of a death, especially in a death-negative culture that makes it so challenging to recognize the fact that someone is dying and it is probably time to say those things before it is too late. When it is very clear that people have reached the end trajectory of their lives, it's time to take the plunge into these hard conversations. Perhaps those things unsaid have been simmering for decades, and the inability to clear the air becomes a sticking point in grief; or perhaps people feel guilt over not expressing love or commitment to people while they were alive. "I never had a chance to say . . ." is a common sentiment in conversations about love and loss.

We live in a culture where saying these things to people while they're alive can feel a little awkward, too earnest, perhaps, for many. Perhaps it is a legacy of Calvinism, but expressing authentic emotion tends to be frightening for many white Americans, even in an era of endless media and pop culture about "feels" and "vibes" and "speaking your truth." The WASP stereotype of remaining buttoned up tight and letting feelings pass unremarked and unresolved is deeply ingrained in many lives and deaths. Taking a pause for feelings may be a thing that other people do, alongside spontaneous expressions of emotion; many Americans do not grow up in households where talking about feelings is normalized, so they are ill equipped for these conversations as they grow into adulthood.

This is especially so when they are confronted with the reality of an oncoming death, or a missed opportunity to speak their minds in the case of someone who dies suddenly, or far away, or in another context that makes a deathbed conversation functionally impossible.

This feeling of taking action too late, and sorrow for missed opportunities, reflects the fact that guilt does not travel alone. It often keeps company with regret, as author Nicole Chung told me when we talked about the death of her father, where the abrupt nature of his death colored the grief she felt.

"After my dad died I felt this deep regret—why didn't I know better, plan better? I should have known this was going to happen. . . . It took such a long time to forgive myself. You can have regret, real regret, but that doesn't mean you yourself are guilty. Learning the difference between regret and guilt was an important part of my grieving process. Really sitting with that and grappling with that was part of my grieving process, crucial to understanding why I shouldn't punish myself forever. My father wouldn't have wanted me to."

Humans share an intense fear of making mistakes and second-guessing their decisions, as I did with Leila. These thoughts can become intrusive, contributing to feelings of intense regret—the *shoulda woulda couldas* about things we couldn't have even known about or controlled for, but convince ourselves in retrospect are our fault. We are swift to condemn ourselves for messing up, and slow to give ourselves grace in the aftermath of a death, especially when it involves a fellow being we feel responsible for, whether it be a pet, a friend who needed help, a loved one who counted on us to make the right decisions. The dirty little secret no one wants to acknowledge is that it will always be possible to find fault—sometimes faults that are only visible to ourselves if we search long and hard enough.

This fear and surrounding guilt can feed a quest for absolution in the aftermath of a death, whether religious, personal, or spiritual. The fad for séances and the Spiritualist movement in the late nineteenth century represented a deeply relatable human desire for one last conversation with the deceased, whether it be to settle old scores, convey one last emotion, or find peace that allows people to shed their ghosts. Writing about the Spiritualist movement for *Lithub,*[10] author S. E. Porter, who researched it extensively in connection with a novel on the topic, found that while we often talk about Spiritualism in the context of scammy mediums, the movement was much deeper and much more complicated in an era of incredibly high child mortality and tumultuous social change, from the Civil War to the Industrial Revolution. People genuinely believed, or wanted to believe, in the capacity to contact the afterlife, and these events also posed an opportunity to say things that might have felt impossible in ordinary conversation, with Porter commenting that the medium could become a channel for things too frightening to say aloud: "What if we distance ourselves from our inner voice by calling it a voice from the beyond?"

Even today, experimenting with Ouija boards is a classic rite of passage.

The way we react to grief, and the notion that there is a wrong way to grieve, can also be a contributor to feelings of guilt, whether it's being gutted by the death of a coworker while feeling relatively unaffected by the death of a sibling, or deeply mourning a pet while not feeling as stricken by a friend's death. Differing feelings about loss are a natural part of being human, mediated by our relationship to the deceased, the manner of their death, and numerous other factors, but society can be quick to judge when we fail to live up to expectations for mourners. This is perhaps especially true of outsiders who may not entirely understand what's going on in a situation. There is a sense that you are a bad person if you mourn someone too much, or not enough, or mourn two different losses in very different ways; this creates internal pressure to meet societal expectations that simply exacerbate those feelings of guilt and anxiety. That judgment can also be reflected in the support and empathy people receive in the wake of the loss, the assessments of a mourner's validity and basic humanity.

Shortly before Leila died, my grandfather died after several years of failing health.

I hadn't seen him in over a decade because I am largely estranged from my mother's family, but I responded to the call when my aunt asked and traveled south to join the family at his deathbed. By the time I arrived, he was nonresponsive, already taking on the sunken, yellowing, distant form that indicates someone has entered active dying. He didn't stir when people bustled in and out of the room, or when a collective of us picked up food from an Italian restaurant he had enjoyed and ate dinner in his room. The nurses remarked that it was so nice to see his family gathering around him; for me, it was a surreal moment, being in a room with people I didn't know and who largely didn't know me. As the oldest grandchild, I hadn't even met some of the cousins who were present, and it was clear that my aunts and uncles had a vision of me frozen in amber as a young child, not an adult with my own life and interests; some also held their own ideas about why I was estranged, what I had been up to since they saw me last, checking my arms for track marks, probing to learn what I did for work.

I tend to be a person who is quick to involve myself in administrivia and caretaking, which is what I did. I brought in a case of water for people to drink, sorted out phone chargers, helped with hospital paperwork, and ultimately accompanied my grandfather's wife back to their home that night—a place I had entered a grand total of once before and would have gotten lost trying to find in a maze of suburbia. Their guest room felt like a foreign country, filled with the eclectic things people accumulate when they have lived somewhere for a long time, with photographs of people I was probably supposed to recognize and costly little ornaments from Gumps, a former San Francisco institution, dotted about. I appreciated the water pressure in the shower. The next morning, we ate yogurt and fruit pulled out of a fridge packed with smoothies and boxed meals and an array of things she and family members had purchased in an attempt to get my grandfather to eat in his last days, their expiry dates rapidly approaching.

We went back to the hospital, where the nurses had moved him to a much larger room in anticipation of more family arrivals, but before they got there, he died, alone with me and his wife and my oldest uncle. I can't imagine I'm someone he would have picked for deathbed company, but sometimes that's how death takes you, lying in a hospital bed holding your wife's hand while someone tells you about the tulips blooming in your yard. I was glad that he had comfort and friendly voices around him, but I didn't feel any particular emotional attachment to the moment. My first thought was to remind his wife to take his ring, which we had to wrestle off his swollen knuckle with the assistance of soap from the en suite bathroom.

The death of a grandparent is supposed to be a rite of passage, but it wasn't to me. Some friends got it, especially those familiar with my history, but others seemed surprised that I was more upset about the death of my cat than a man with whom I shared genetics and little else. I got the sense that I was supposed to feel guilty about this, to view myself as cold and uncaring, perhaps. While I was invited to attend his memorial, I didn't, because I had a major surgery just days before; I also didn't feel the need for closure or further engagement, as I had walked away from that side of my family long ago, most of them strangers to me.

I felt guilty over the choices I made and didn't make for Leila, but I didn't feel guilty for not being upset about my grandfather's death. It was simply the *snick* of the final latch of a door I thought I had closed long ago.

It is seemingly not enough to feel guilt over one's relationship with the deceased, over lost opportunities and things unsaid, over choices made that maybe we would make differently if we had a chance to do them over again. For some, guilt can even persist over the decisions we make for people after death, especially in cases where the deceased have not communicated what they want, or where their wants conflict with the personal and cultural beliefs of the people who are arranging their funerals.

In some cultures, for example, lavish funerals and memorials are the norm, and formalized mourning may last for days and weeks, sometimes with multiple ceremonies, as in Buddhist tradition. Failing to observe those ceremonies could create a hungry ghost or leave someone adrift in the afterlife. Being unable or unwilling to pay for or undertake the logistics of these events can be viewed by community members as evidence that families don't care, don't love enough, or are selfishly hoarding money for themselves instead of honoring the dead.

Here again, money anxiety enters the conversation. The costs of a funeral can become wrapped up in someone's sense of how much the deceased meant to them and can also become a final, outward testimony. When a funeral becomes an external performance, it can drive intense feelings of guilt and a sense of losing control. When funeral expenditures become a stand-in for measuring the status and value of the deceased, failure to spend enough can become yet another driver of guilt. Who wants to remember a beloved family member with a cheap direct cremation and a private scattering, even if that's what they wanted and what's within budget, when community expectations to celebrate the life of the deceased are so high? When you want to make good on the things you didn't do in life?

The idea of buying our way out of guilt and remorse is quintessentially American, an expression of a world in which we believe that we can buy everything if we try hard enough. The funeral industry is fully aware of this in the way it markets to mourners, right down to the way caskets are displayed and discussed in a way that encourages families to pick the upgraded option to show their dedication to the deceased, a moment frequently captured on HBO's *Six Feet Under,* where siblings Nate and David Fisher sometimes argue over Nate's distaste for funeral costs and David's desire to increase the bottom line in order to keep the family funeral home running. David is quick to assess the financial capacities of mourners and weigh them against their feelings of guilt with a gentle nudge in the right direction: the more expensive casket, the bigger floral displays.

"As a culture, in America, I think that shame is just so pertinent to the capitalistic machine: If we shame ourselves enough, we will buy more to get them that good death, we will grieve better if we spend more, if we buy the seven thousand dollar green composting; we will not feel guilty because we did that for them," says Colleen of Queer Death Collective-PDX, an all-volunteer community of comrades engaging in radical death care, articulating pressures around funeral choices and noting they can have especially profound interactions with beliefs and attitudes within religious communities, where expectations about funerals can be very rigid.

As Colleen notes, this has also spilled over into the world of "green" funerals in a nation where companies are doing their best to leverage environmental consciousness for money, turning what should be a fundamentally anti-consumer endeavor into one that has run rampant with capitalism. Among the living, people show their commitment to environmental sustainability by buying more things, signaling to those around them that they're dedicated to the "green"—and clean, right—path with a wide array of products that prey upon the understandable impulse and desire to care for the planet. It isn't possible to take personal responsibility for or spend our way out of a climate crisis and environmental devastation, but the parties responsible for that destruction leverage guilt to convince people that they can try.

These costly but virtuous options persist in death, with some "green" burial options more expensive than their "traditional" counterparts, even when not all traditional mourning practices are inherently harmful for the environment. Jewish and Muslim traditions calling for burial in plain coffins or shrouds, for example, are very low impact and a perfectly reasonable way to honor the planet. While alternatives such as human composting or alkaline hydrolysis often come from a good place, an interest in exploring other ways to honor people and their remains, their rapid commercialization is a testimony to the tentacles of capitalism and their talent for wrapping around every aspect of our lives and deaths. Like David Fisher upselling the Titan, funeral directors are quick to pivot to expressed concerns about and desires for a funeral with low ecological footprint, eager to avoid missing a sale.

"Guilt is one of the best friends of shame," says Colleen. "The shame of not doing well enough, not grieving correctly."

In an era in which public shaming is a constant theme of concern for trolling conservative media and people angry about being held accountable for bad deeds, shame occupies an interesting and complicated role in our lives. There is the notion that shaming someone is to make them feel like a bad person for the things they've done (or haven't), which may act to distinguish it a little bit from guilt. Guilt feels like an emotion associated with a specific action: We feel guilty for not latching the door properly, allowing a pet to escape into a busy street, or for not encouraging someone to go to the doctor earlier when they first started showing symptoms of an illness.

Guilt is the turning over of that event in our minds, burnishing it, punishing ourselves for whatever it is we did, or didn't, do. Shame, on the other hand, is the sense of being a bad person, for having done something so heinous that it cannot be forgiven, or for a pattern of behavior. When someone is "shameless" it is an indictment of their character; when someone feels "guilty," it is introspective.

In a way, it strikes me as the difference between the Justice and Judgment cards in a tarot deck. One is about internal reflection, inner calling, an exploration of the self by the self, in which rumination and self-accounting can result in feelings of guilt or, perhaps over time, understanding and absolution. The other represents a more external, social phenomenon. Justice is about cause and effect, finding truth and lies, fairness; it is often represented by the classical Western allegory of justice, a blindfolded woman with sword and scale, waiting to weigh and find you wanting. This is shame.

"There is shame," wrote Sloane Crosley for *The New Yorker* in an essay about the death of her cat and a conversation with a veterinarian friend about the second-guessing that pet guardians have around euthanasia decisions, the same feelings I had as I watched Leila's body fail while her spirit remained. "It comes at the end and springs from the suspicion that, in being so greedy for unconditional love, we have made an awful mistake."[11]

This shame reflects our intense connections with pets but also the external pressures around these relationships and how we interact with others. If euthanasia is generally accepted as a common end-of-life outcome for pets, it is also one that will be nitpicked and discussed in detail with questions about quality of life. In interviews with me, pet guardians sometimes express remorse around feeling selfish or greedy, like Crosley did, for prolonging their pets' lives in the face of evidence that those pets were suffering; they often turn to me for forgiveness, wanting me to tell them whether they made the right or wrong choice.

"Are you keeping an animal alive for you, or for them?" is a question that often comes up in prompts for thinking about euthanasia decisions. Feeling guilt around these very personal choices can tip over into shame when we feel judged by outsiders for those choices, or fear the specter of being judged, sometimes extrapolating from the ways in which we might judge others in our shoes.

Should you feel ashamed for euthanizing an ailing pet right before going on a trip, fearing that they might suffer or take a turn while you are traveling? Should you feel shame for choosing behavioral euthanasia for an animal that simply doesn't respond to any interventions? For euthanizing an incontinent but still mobile aging pet?

These questions haunt the species divide, but they are not limited to animals, because they reflect deeper societal influences on the ways we react to death in a culture where making the wrong move subjects you to judgment.

When it comes to humans and animals alike, should you feel ashamed for feeling a minimal emotional reaction to a death? Or for being absolutely destroyed by a death, still struggling to function for weeks, months, even years after? Or for being more worried about how many death certificates you will need than about the cooling body in the other room?

These feelings can weigh heavily on grievers, and they can also add layers to the grieving process. Shame in particular can contribute to more distress in grief,[12] increasing the risk of depression and other mental health aftereffects following a loss. Shame, and shame about feeling shame, can worm its way deep into the psyche.

The influences of capitalism loom over how these emotions are processed as well.

Anything that makes mourning more complicated, that results in needing to take more time off, to attend more therapy sessions, to spend more time with family and loved ones, is repellent to capitalism. Time is money and time spent on regret, guilt, and shame is time wasted: You chose your choice, now move on. Expressing these feelings is even more forbidden, as they might make those surrounding the griever uncomfortable—could even, perhaps, force people to regard each other with empathy or to reflect on the role of these feelings in their own lives. Thus guilt in response to death is discouraged: We shouldn't feel it and we certainly shouldn't discuss it if we do, even though the thing we may need most is to talk through that feeling with another human being, to feel seen and heard, to find ourselves in conversations, or in reading other people's words; to know, fundamentally, that we are not alone.

Part of coming to terms with Leila's death also required me to come to terms with the role of these feelings in my grieving process. Like Nicole, I had to feel these feelings in order to understand my grief, rather than attempt to stuff them into a box somewhere and not look at them. As long as I left them unaddressed and focused on the next thing, on not missing work, on not inconveniencing others with my grief, they were raw, always bubbling near the surface, ready to explode. I had to recognize and pause with those feelings—while also not falling into the trap of marinating in them, getting stuck in a gyre of emotion that did not serve me or Leila's memory.

That can be a difficult path to walk in a culture that tells us these feelings are not allowed, that we must be decisive in the aftermath of death; if you feel doubts, you must work through them quickly and then assure others that you do not feel guilty.

"I think every emotion is a teacher," death doula Trishia Renee Frulla of Transcendent Transitions tells me when talking about how to allow ourselves to experience guilt, regret, and shame—bad feelings that we are not supposed to feel and must take steps to eradicate when we do. "We just would rather have happy teachers. When I think about how our current world is, and the dominant societies and systems that are in place, there's a reason why there are less tools on how to be brave, how to sit with these hard feelings. There's a reason why 'they' don't want us to know how to grieve, or know how to release these discomforts, or sit with discomforts."

At Frulla's death café events, she says, one of the most cathartic experiences can involve simply sitting in silence, a very conscious moment of pause and reflection in a culture that expects us to always keep going, to be driven, to move forward to the next thing. Consciously shifting outside that path can be uncomfortable and unsettling for participants, but, she says, "quiet can be very loud."

In a society of so much sound and sensory stimulation, quiet can be heavy at first, before settling into it and finding freedom.

Feelings of guilt are a key component of David Kessler's Six Needs of Grieving, an approach to grief rooted in his own interactions with loss, chronicled in his book *Finding Meaning*. Kessler has worked extensively with grieving people, including those who have witnessed traumatic and mass casualty death events, and he also worked on a book with Elisabeth Kübler-Ross, widely regarded for her work on the subject of death and loss. Kessler's needs recognize that grievers have a variety of emotions around death and may move fluidly between them throughout the mourning process as grievers search for meaning.

"Releasing the burden of guilt" is one of those needs. The others include having one's pain witnessed; being able to express feelings around the loss; integrating the pain and love associated with the deceased and the loss; being "free of old wounds"; and finding meaning in life after loss. Meeting these needs, which interact in complicated ways, is a project of community, with many directly requiring interaction with other people in order to be met, even when those interactions may be demanding or uncomfortable, as for example in the need to have a witness to pain and struggle, a witness who many want to fix the griever when what they need most is to simply be heard. It is impossible to release the burden of guilt if you cannot talk about it, explore it, and be honest with yourself and others about where that narrative is coming from.

That spaciousness for acknowledging feelings and engaging with guilt is in critically short supply in contemporary American society, particularly when it comes to grief, and especially when it comes to losses that society doesn't comprehend, doesn't view as important, or doesn't want to reckon with. I think of this as I watch society react to deaths caused by racism, disablism, transphobia, other forms of bigotry and hatred, and the pressure to move along, rather than stop to explore our own complicity. We aren't personally responsible for the harm, we say, so we can look in the other direction, and we do not want to be confronted by the grief of those left behind. When we have a niggling sense of guilt around a death, or interact with grievers who feel guilty, who feel regret, who feel shame, admitting that these emotions are present feels dangerous, inherently unstable, frightening.

But guilt is not a pathology to be fixed or something to feel bad about.

Guilt is the teacher who pushes a little harder, asks you to show your work, suggests that you revisit something. Sometimes that teacher is too exacting, unkind, even cruel, picking away at your edges until you feel like you are going to fall apart. But at other times, guilt is a tough but fair teacher, the one you talk about years later who had a profound impact on your life, who shaped you into a better person, perhaps more caring and thoughtful, more compassionate with others, able to be a teacher in turn to others. After hotly insisting that I didn't feel guilty for my choices around Leila's death, and then having to unpack those feelings later as thoughts of Leila and her last days were a constant in my days and nights, refusing to release their grip on me, I uncovered important knowledge in that guilt: the awareness to make better choices for future pets, certainly, but also to be kinder to others who are suffering, to not be the looming figure of shame in their lives, to open up space for emotions that should be felt, not denied. Without guilt as a teacher, I think those lessons would have taken longer, and perhaps have come at a higher cost, one that no one should have to pay.

Chapter 5

Tab4 // Witness

In the summer of 2017, I found myself stalking the local animal shelter's website after Leila died, "just to see," in between lying in the middle of the living room floor watching termite dust spin down from the ceiling and working out my grief by vigorously attacking the looming blackberry vines that threatened to take over my entire yard. Hot, sweaty, sticky, covered in small cuts, I would scroll through their cats under the lazy blades of the fan, drinking lukewarm tea left over from the morning. When a seven-year-old cat that looked exactly like Leila popped up, I knew it wasn't reincarnation, or fate, or anything other than happenstance, but I still ventured out to their tree-ringed campus on Summers Lane, next to the reservoir. It was a sunny day with a light breeze, a perfect kind of day, and the cats in the Kitty Cottage were enjoying the sun, chasing leaves as they fell across the catio and chittering at passing birds. The cat in question, Lola, had enthroned herself on a ratty chaise lounge and glared at the other cats when they strayed too close to her, raising a paw with a warning hiss.

Lola was a bit of a bitch, honestly. I knew I wouldn't adopt her, or any of the other cats swirling around me, but not being at home lifted a strange weight I hadn't even known was there. I sat out there for hours with the cats, letting the curious ones sniff at my shoes while the shy ones watched me with wary eyes. One of the kennel attendants came by to feed them.

"Do you take volunteers?" I asked, and "Sure," she said.

As soon as the executive director discovered I was a journalist, I was put to work writing up descriptions for the animals for the website, trying to strike a jaunty, friendly, informative tone—which looked so breezy and easy on other shelter websites, but grew much harder when I had to do it myself. The staff distrusted me at first, like most new volunteers, waiting for me to get bored and wander away, or to take an animal home and never return. Some had been there for years, forming a deep connection with the animals they saw every day, doing the messy, hard work that volunteers did not: cleaning and feeding, medicating and monitoring, watching the constant ebb and flow. It took years to win their confidence, to be considered one of them, rather than an outsider.

For the sake of organization, I set up a sprawling spreadsheet, "Adoptable Animals Media Info," each animal having their own row. Was their description done? Had it been updated? When were the most recent pictures taken? Did they get along with cats? Dogs? Young children? Did the staff have any notes? The first tab, "In Care," spoke for itself, followed by "Foster" and then "Adopted," animals moving their way through a happy series of events to the status of "Healthy in Home" in ShelterLuv, the software the shelter uses to keep track of their population. Sometimes an animal would boomerang back, a return, and I would be forced to fish their line out of the "Adopted" tab and sadly plunk it back into "In Care," updating their description with a "returned to us after her owner passed away" or "came back to the shelter after his family was no longer able to care for him."

But then there was Tab4.

Tab4 is for the dead.

Sometimes an animal is too sick or injured to be saved, or the shelter lacked the veterinary resources: a dog with cancer, a cat with a urinary blockage. The vet staff couldn't provide the needed care or the shelter couldn't afford the high cost of getting outside care (fortunate, as a small independent shelter, to have a vet staff in the first place) or the best care was a good death. Sometimes there was a freak accident, like the office cat who shattered his jaw, received thousands of dollars' worth of surgery from an outside clinic, funded by a loving staff, and then did it again almost immediately, betraying a sign of an underlying health issue. It would have been inhumane to put him through surgery again, so everyone gathered around the table in the vet clinic to say goodbye. (While a member of the public was angry that the shelter had opened late that day: "Don't they even care about the animals!" he groused when a red-eyed front desk person unlocked the door.)

There was the dog who had been showing signs of aggressive behavior but then snapped one day and became embroiled in a massive fight that took four staffers to break up. One kennel attendant tearfully recounted hauling desperately on his collar, shouting, trying to get him to let go of a smaller, weaker dog. The dog was euthanized for behavior, a very unpopular decision[1] that sometimes is the best choice, even though no one wants to hear it, with few resources available to support pet guardians, let alone shelters, through the process,[2] although professional guidelines[3] on the topic are becoming more precise and detailed. What do you do when you have a 120-pound dog who is so aggressive that he can't be taken out of the kennel, requires two staffers to clean his space, has to be held at the far end of the facility so he doesn't fence-fight with other dogs as they're walked by? What do you do with a dog who has multiple bite quarantines on his record? Who is becoming more and more uncontrollable the longer he stays in the shelter, driven to abject misery despite the best efforts of staff to provide kindness and enrichment?

Then there was Missy, the sleek, quiet gray cat with a beautifully soft, shiny coat. It was the winter holidays and the staff were working on an abbreviated schedule, the shelter closed to accommodate their need to be home with their families, and the cat staff didn't spot in time, in a world of free-feeding where it's impossible to monitor individual intake, that she wasn't eating. Volunteers, fewer in number and distracted by the holidays, weren't as attentive to changes in the cats either. Missy went into liver failure and died. There was another cat who was simply mysteriously dead on her cat tree one morning when staff came in to clean. The dog with a tumor dangling from her nose, snarled up deep into her sinuses, impossible to remove. The ancient blind, quivering Chihuahua covered in open sores who didn't respond to any treatment.

Shelters inherit the aging, the broken, and what happens next is inevitable.

When an animal dies, I could have right-clicked their row, hit "delete." I could have refrained from looking them up in ShelterLuv to see "Deceased" listed under their status. But it didn't feel right to erase them as though they had never been. Many of these animals were beloved by staff, who sometimes raised money from their own meager salaries to pay for offsite care, who took them home to foster them, who came in after hours to work with them, to give them fluids, who fought for them in the vet clinic and who wept and berated themselves, asking why they didn't do more. Should have taken the dog into foster. Gone to offsite obedience courses. Brought in a behaviorist. Noticed that she wasn't eating, that he wasn't acting right. In the end, all that was left to mark their passage was to pay for private cremation.

Animal shelter workers are not automatons or heartless dogcatchers, as the media sometimes casts them. Like so many of us, they form deep emotional bonds with the animals they care for, thinking of them long after they go home at the end of the day, wondering how they are doing in their new homes, taking home the sick, the lame, the unadoptable rather than leaving them to languish in the shelter. Each of the animals who doesn't survive is duly noted in the controlled substances log that records use of euthanasia drugs; in ShelterLuv; in statistics that members of the public scrutinize, searching for proof of "no-kill" status; in Tab4, the tab I could not bring myself to rename from its default title.

Occasionally, late at night, I clicked over to Tab4, going down the list of names, remembering their faces, their stories. And I knew that I was not alone, because sometimes I saw the telltale signs of someone else viewing the spreadsheet. I once caught the now-deceased shelter manager, a taciturn woman who loved animals ferociously, flipping through the euthanasia records for no real reason other than to look. To remember.

Tab4 was a microcosm of the shelter's tragedy, but it was also a deeper testimony to the sad side of animal sheltering in the United States. No matter where you are, from an underfunded municipal shelter with staff struggling to keep up to a high-end private rescue with ample supports, death happens, because things that are alive inevitably stop being alive, for a whole host of reasons.

In the shelter environment, there is a sense that this death and subsequent grief is displaced, offloaded, outsourced, that society has turned its back on the animals and pushed the pain onto people who are usually underpaid, with limited benefits and few days off. They are not in sheltering for the money, but because they genuinely care about animals, and sometimes they step out into the woods or the alley or wherever is away from the public because they don't want to be seen screaming at the burden that their communities have put on them. Meanwhile, the public has washed its hands of unwanted and uncomfortable decisions, leaving shelters to pay the price, literally and figuratively. And the public doesn't just neglect animals themselves but the people who love them and struggle with life events that make it impossible to care for them.

"Professionalism" does not render someone incapable of feeling pain, distress, empathy with animals—and with the sad stories of the people behind them, like the person fleeing a domestic violence situation who surrendered a cat and returned to the shelter weeks later, when they were safe, hoping the cat was still there. (He had been adopted the previous day.)

The term "moral injury" seems to have first been popularized in 1984 in *Nursing Practice: The Ethical Issues,* a nursing textbook written by Andrew Jameton. It refers to the tremendous moral struggles involved in health care, especially for direct providers such as nurses who form intimate bonds with patients. While it is often applied to human medicine, it fits animal welfare too. Whether you are caring for humans or animals, it is not uncommon to be asked to do things that feel unconscionable or upsetting, to go against your morals, to do things because they are the best option but still not a good option, to sometimes defy what you view as the lifesaving purpose of your work—as for example in mass triage, where medical professionals may have to abandon some people to die in order to save others. In a paper published in 2005, Charlie Reeve and his colleagues described the "caring-killing paradox,"[4] in which shelter workers may be lovingly changing blankets and refreshing water in the morning, then leading an animal into the clinic for euthanasia in the afternoon, an experience of incredible cognitive dissonance and stress that has mental health consequences.

This is sometimes known as "perpetration-induced traumatic stress,"[5] described as "causing trauma as a form of trauma"[6] in the context of acts of violence committed during wars, but it is more broadly applicable to any profession in which people cause harm or violence because it is their job, in the process traumatizing themselves. As licensed clinical social worker and trauma therapist Benji Marton put it when I called to discuss his 2019 paper on loss and grief among animal shelter workers,[7] "You're being traumatized on a day-to-day basis" in shelter settings, and even shelter management is reluctant to engage with that fact. Marton, like me, became interested in the psychosocial world of animal shelters because he worked in one and witnessed the daily struggles of its staff. Working in private practice now, his voice still breaks as he recalls a dog euthanized for behavior or talks about the cat he still has after rescuing it from euthanasia for roundworm.

Shelter staff are also dealing with secondary trauma: On any given day, they are confronted with some of the worst parts of humanity, hearing and witnessing horrible abuses, whether they're animal cruelty cases or people fleeing domestic violence and tearfully surrendering their pets or tenants forced to move after months of harassment by profiteering landlords. Animal shelters are high-risk environments for this form of trauma,[8] and yet it is poorly understood and only recently accepted as a contributor to traumatic stress, with animal shelter workers five times more likely to develop PTSD than the general population.[9] Chronic, long-term exposure to traumatic events weighs heavy on the hearts of shelter workers[10] and is in its own right a form of grief, as trauma is so often interwoven with death, the fear of death, witnessing the aftermath of death in the people around us. Referring to this as "compassion fatigue" isn't the right way to describe it, to my eye: It isn't that people are exhausted by caring or aren't tough enough to survive animal sheltering, but rather that caring for animals in the strained world of the shelter, with nearly daily heartbreaking events that take place behind closed doors, foments existential crisis.

In shelters, as Marton and I discuss, this trauma is layered with the added burden of knowing that society has chosen to place these responsibilities on people who step forward to help the helpless—to, as venerable animal welfare organization Fund for Animals puts it, "speak for those who can't." The public doesn't think about the shelter unless people want to complain or they need something, leaving workers to take on the emotional toll. At many shelters, it's not uncommon for people to surrender elderly, ill, injured animals, or, worse yet, to claim these animals are strays even though they are obviously not, making staff feel like they are doing their dirty work for them as they walk away from the responsibilities they brought on when they took in those animals in the first place, leaving an animal for a few terrified hours or sometimes days on a stray hold before vet staff determine that the best option is a dignified ending.

"It was really hard for us not to be really angry with people bringing their animals in, even if it was for a good reason," Marton commented, speaking to the eternal struggle of shelter staff trapped in a demoralizing, traumatic environment who never have the time or capacity to make space to talk about what they're enduring. In that setting, it's hard to not be angry, to not hate people, to have compassion for those who are also struggling, to simply turn away from someone in the produce section without a word after watching them surrender an animal the day before because they were "tired of it." Yet caring for those people as well as animals is critical to working in animal sheltering, as much as it seems impossible sometimes.

When people offload responsibility, they don't want to hear about what comes next.

The Mendocino Coast Humane Society, where cats like Lola

live waiting for people like me, is indeed what popular parlance terms a "no-kill" shelter, though many, including me, prefer the term "closed-admission," which is more accurate. Everyone who finds out that you volunteer or work at a shelter eagerly wants to know if it is no-kill: "You don't euthanize, do you?" I want to say, "Yes, all shelters do, obviously, because death is a part of life, although closed admission shelters don't euthanize for space." I want to ask, "What would you do if I told you that shelters *do* euthanize?" I used to, but I got tired of having these arguments.

What would you do? Will you take them all home and love them and care for them? Will you pay thousands of dollars for costly surgeries and care? Would you like to let a dog with advanced lung cancer gasp for breath in its kennel, barely able to move, rather than allow her to pass peacefully? Would you volunteer your time and money and skill? Maybe help people fight evictions so they can stay housed with their pets? Lobby for pet-inclusive resources for unhoused people and people fleeing intimate violence? Address the incredibly broken system of veterinary education and care that leads to spiraling costs[11] that are impossible for many people to afford? Vet costs aren't the only affordability issue when wages stay flat and inflation increases the cost of food and pet supplies, housing, and myriad other needs. It's no wonder some members of the public struggle when even shelters are feeling the pinch despite access to wholesale pricing and donated food and pet supplies.

What would you do about the scores of kittens and puppies every spring, sometimes neonates who require intensive around-the-clock care for weeks because people "don't want to spay her until she's had one litter," or "don't see the harm in letting him tomcat around the neighborhood a little bit"? What about those who couldn't find affordable veterinary care until it was too late, or who refused a spay-abort on moral grounds, made queasy by the thought of something vet staffs encounter more often than they are willing to tell the public?

According to Shelter Animals Count, a national database that tracks thousands of partner organizations, an estimated 6.3 million cats and dogs entered U.S. animal shelters in 2019—a year used by many welfare organizations as the last "normal year" of statistics before the COVID-19 pandemic—a number that dropped to 5.8 million in 2024.[12] After 2019's euthanasia count of 765,797,[13] the nation hit a record euthanasia low of 424,620 in 2020, but by 2024, as shelters across the United States started to experience profound overcrowding and an increase in long-stay animals, particularly large-breed dogs, it was creeping back up again: to 606,653, with another 127,202 listed as "unassisted deaths in custody," including three of the shelter's kittens who died over the course of a horrible month of a distemper outbreak: Agave, Caramel, and Mickey.

The media was quick to blame the "pandemic puppy" phenomenon for the increase in intakes following 2020's record low, which, like most things in animal sheltering, was actually more complicated[14] than people simply getting puppies for fun and then discarding them when they returned to the office. The blooming shelter population, for people who actually worked in shelters or bothered to contact shelter directors for more information, had more to do with the mundane realities of living under capitalism. Refusing to engage with these issues is another way of leaving shelter workers holding the bag for societal problems.

When the nation and the world briefly came together in 2020, more animals were fostered and adopted, but also there were fewer lost animals and strays, leading to reduced intake, which clouded the outcome numbers. Financial supports—including increased unemployment benefits, a pause in student loan repayment, and eviction moratoriums[15]—helped families through circumstances that normally might have led to surrender. As these supports dwindled, shelters with municipal contracts—which often mandate an open-admission policy—started to see funding cuts even as they also struggled with staffing problems and inflationary price increases for food, supplies, veterinary equipment, and more, with more members of the public seeking help.

From behind the desk, I saw a marked rise in surrenders associated with evictions and being unable to afford care, findings echoed across the country. It's not that people don't want their pets but that having pets is turning into a luxury for those who have insufficient income to pay for their needs. In truth, these human reasons outstrip animal-related problems such as illness and behavior by three to one.[16] And they have nothing to do with the popular stereotype of treating animals like a fad.

Modern animal sheltering has come a long way from the grim "pound" of old, rows of rusting metal cages for cats and hard, cold, concrete runs for desperately barking dogs, a dark hallway leading to the "kill room" where healthy, adoptable, happy animals are "put down" for lack of homes, dogs wagging their tails to the end, cats purring and reaching out a paw to a scrubs-clad shelter worker. California, Florida, and Texas remain the largest offenders when it comes to euthanizing shelter animals for space because these states are so large, with so many animals, even despite mass spay/neuter efforts, transfers out to rescues and other agencies, and other schemes intended to increase live outcomes. But euthanasia rates have thankfully plummeted overall, and shelters don't see themselves as warehouses for the unwanted.

The no-kill movement, which insists it should be possible for every shelter to have a live release rate of 90 percent, has come in for heavy criticism for many who work in animal welfare for perpetuating myths about animal sheltering and putting shelters in incredibly difficult positions. The popular conception of "no-kill" also hides some uncomfortable animal welfare truths.

At closed-admission shelters, every animal must be held until it can be adopted, placed in foster care, transferred out to another rescue, or assigned to duty as a barn or warehouse cat. That can mean animals lingering for months or even years. Sometimes those animals develop medical or behavioral issues in a shelter or rescue, and in some cases they may experience living conditions that teeter between animal welfare and a hoarding situation. Conditions in overwhelmed or poorly run rescues can be painfully similar to those that would lead to a humane law enforcement action: a house crammed with rescue cats, for example; a property crowded with dogs who don't get adequate yard time because a single person drowning in empathy simply can't keep up; a municipal shelter housing dogs in crates in hallways. Sometimes these organizations recognize the problem and ask for help. Others do not.

In 2019, Leah Fieser, executive director of Brother Wolf, a North Carolina–based rescue, wrote an extremely controversial essay about how "warehousing isn't working"[17] and addressed the problem of long-stay dogs in a frank discussion of when euthanasia is the best outcome. While it was a necessary conversation in sheltering, it also highlighted how love can turn cruel, how caring for animals can turn into simply keeping them indefinitely on-site with no hope for anything else, living at shelters for months or years. To save more animals, Fieser's rescue had to let some go.

"These dogs do not lead lives that any of us would want for our own animals," she wrote. "They spend up to twenty-two hours a day in isolation in their kennels as almost all of them are too dangerous to interact with other dogs, and most of them can only interact with a small group of staff or volunteers with expert handling skills due to their aggression. Most are on prescription medicine multiple times a day to help them cope with the life a dog must endure when sheltered long term."

Is this life better than no life?

The dirty little secret of the no-kill movement is this: High-kill facilities are usually open-admission, which means they need to take every animal who arrives at their doors.

Closed-admission means that when someone comes to a shelter or rescue in need of help with an animal to surrender, if there is no room, they may be turned away. Sorry, we're closed to intake. We can put you on the waiting list. Closed-admission facilities can turn down hard medical cases or those with significant behavioral challenges. They can tell a sobbing, desperate woman who's losing her housing and just wants her two cats to be safe that they can't open their doors to them because they don't have room. When closed-admission shelters transfer animals in from other facilities, they can pick the most adoptable, bypassing seniors, animals with behavioral or health problems, or animals such as the large dogs that tend to linger in shelters; they target, for example, small- and medium-sized dogs who know basic commands and juvenile cats with years of life ahead of them.

Many shelters try to avoid that: They attempt to make room, to set up a foster, to refer to a rescue or another shelter. But when it becomes unavoidable, those animals can end up at an open-admission municipal or county shelter, which is still a better outcome than simply being abandoned on the street, poisoned, or taken home and shot in the head on the back forty. If these shelters have no room, they need to make room.

You've seen them on social media too, posting their "kill lists" as they plead with rescues and the public to spare them a task they do not want to perform, and you've probably heard them subjected to derisive comments: "I would never adopt from a *kill* shelter!" "I bet the city employees euthanize on three-day weekends so they don't have to come in!" "They're not even trying at all at County, it's disgusting!" "How dare the union ask for more pay, those workers are so greedy!"

"I hear about stories where shelter staff or managers get death threats because they're euthanizing animals," veterinarian Kathleen Cooney, senior director of medical education for the Companion Animal Euthanasia Training Academy (CAETA), told me when we talked about this issue. CAETA offers in-depth training on humane euthanasia across the country, ensuring that what must be done is done well. We both reflected on a case from 2022, in which Maine Veterinary Medical Center was temporarily forced to close due to an incredibly high volume of death threats surrounding a dog named Jaxx, whose guardians surrendered him because they were unable to afford care.

Jaxx, notably, was not euthanized but adopted, and the extreme response from around the country highlighted the way animal lovers can dehumanize animal carers. Those public pressures paired with internal organizational ones contribute to immense strain for animal shelter workers, who are first responders but rarely honored like firefighters or paramedics.

This is the dark side of the no-kill movement, a theme that comes up again and again with shelter workers all over the country, from those struggling at small municipal shelters to advocates for those working in shelter medicine. As society offloads responsibility for the animals and outcomes it doesn't want to face, so too do no-kill shelters put off the inevitable. There's always room for kittens at a closed-admission shelter, Marton said wryly, unless they're sick, and then they can go to the county shelter.

This is not to cut open-admission shelters a total break. Some have disturbingly high euthanasia rates and clearly don't engage with their communities; they don't put in the effort to reduce overpopulation and place animals elsewhere. Some straight-up lie when outside rescues ask if they need help. In two states,[18] agencies still use gas chambers, a horrific method of killing in which animals are crammed into a box filled with (usually) carbon dioxide gas to slowly asphyxiate, which can take as long as twenty minutes, while they are acutely aware of their failing bodies. In a position statement on the use of gas, the Humane Society of the United States says:[19]

"If animals are placed in the chamber together, they may begin fighting out of fear and desperation. For several minutes, they may be in the box, terrified, clawing and calling for a way out. They may struggle for air or begin convulsing before finally losing consciousness."

Yet open-admission shelters are a product of the societies they are grounded in, an ugly manifestation of a culture that understands the fundamental need to care for abused, unwanted, and down-on-their-luck animals but is unwilling to look at the natural outgrowth of pushing this responsibility onto others, forced to make difficult choices behind closed doors.

Our Tab4s remain worlds of individual tragedy and sadness. At closed-admission shelters, thankfully they do not include the names of healthy, theoretically adoptable animals who sat in the shelter too long, who fell on the wrong side of a shelter manager's pen as they struggled to make room for a hoarding seizure or an explosion of puppies or a family of three terrified cats surrendered because their guardians were evicted and they couldn't find a safe place to land. But even in closed-admission shelters with that coveted no-kill status, death can be an albatross.

Their "Deceased" outcomes tell their own sad stories; workers know all their names and their stories, as I told an angry member of the public once when they complained about euthanasia statistics for a recent year. I didn't need to open ShelterLuv or Tab4 to identify each of those animals.

This daily litany of tragedy doesn't just apply to the shelter's own animals.

Some shelters also offer owner-requested euthanasia for terminally ill animals when their guardians have nowhere else to turn; a shortage in veterinarians and the high cost of end-of-life care have forced shelters to step up and provide this vital service, which is emotionally taxing for vet staff, even if they know they are easing an animal's suffering. Shelters typically try to book people in before the shelter opens, when the building isn't filled with chaos, but sometimes the timing isn't right. Sometimes someone is crying in the family room while the front desk is knee-deep in phone calls and processing an adoption, while the staff are cleaning hallways and talking about their lunches, acutely aware that everything is audible the next room over.

It is not uncommon for guardians to request euthanasia and decline to be present, leaving staff to pet dogs and cats and talk to them while they die; I once sat on the floor of the clinic with a bulldog, waiting what seemed like an eternity for the initial sedative to set in, petting and talking to him. When I unfolded myself to go back to work after the veterinarian confirmed that he was dead, my hands were black with filth from his indifferently maintained coat. Shelter workers don't know their owners' backstories, what they may be going through, having met them only briefly on a terrible day, but for staff, it is hard to imagine leaving their pets in the care of strangers in their last moments.

It is hard not to judge.

At a dinner party, a veterinarian in private practice told me a story about a terminally ill kitten she euthanized, the owner refusing to remain present, not even wanting the carrier back. She recounted how the staff whispered about him and remembered him at the end of the day, the guy so heartless that he left the clinic before they'd even drawn up a sedative. Only later did she find out, via a friend at the animal shelter, that the man had adopted two kittens after his baby died of a fast-moving, cruel cancer, to give him and his wife something to live for, only to have her, in turn, die in a car accident, leaving him alone in a rattling house with two kittens and unbearable grief, devastated, unable to live through another death.

Any number of famous figures have been linked to the expression "Be kind, for everyone you know is fighting a hard battle," perhaps because it is so universal.

Animal welfare workers are not the only ones who judge. In the early 2010s, at the height of the personal essay industrial complex, a woman wrote an essay about surrendering two senior cats to a busy open-admission municipal shelter, where one was euthanized at intake. When she changed her mind and decided to come back for them, she was infuriated and responded—as so many women in their twenties did at the time—by writing an essay for fifty dollars that exposed her to weeks of merciless public outrage, an incident that sticks in my head perhaps because I was mired in that very industry. The comments were vicious: *How dare you give up on your cats like that! You got what you deserved, I would never have done that! Animals aren't disposable! Do you have any idea how much she must have suffered after being abandoned in a noisy shelter just to be killed?* The essay is lost to the sands of time now, but I still remember another that appeared several weeks later, from a vegan who took a job as a euthanasia technician at an open-admission shelter precisely because she cared about animals and wanted to give them gentleness and kindness at the end. While her essay—it too is lost to the endless media shuffle of shuttered outlets and dead links—wasn't an explicit reproof to the earlier one, it was a story that made people uncomfortable to read. It was an essay about this world from the shelter side, about the rage and sadness at seeing animals like these come in, a read that resonated with shelter workers and volunteers.

We see the immediate consequence of grief in animal sheltering in an employee turnover rate of 38 percent,[20] compounded by a median income of just $29,790 annually,[21] often without benefits beyond those mandated by state or local law. In unionizing campaigns, many animal shelter workers express wishes for only the most basic things: pay that reflects the costs of living, appropriate PPE, mental health supports. Talking with animal shelter workers at Humane Animal Rescue of Pittsburgh, which had a unionization campaign in 2023, I was repeatedly struck by the simple and also highly relatable things people wanted, something as basic as a moment to reflect on a euthanasia, or the feeling that they are playing a more active role in shelter decisions. Instead, they are forced to absorb a sadness and move on to the next thing, to arrive at work after a day off to discover that a beloved shelter cat was euthanized for an illness that was no longer treatable and immediately start caring for an animal cruelty case. Every shelter worker I talk to at every level across the country remarks on the constant high turnover. Administrators are sometimes reluctant to provide support to staff on the grounds that turnover is so high it's not worth it. Employees tell me they are treated as disposable. Municipal shelters, which are usually open-admission, are feeling the strain of a moment when surrenders are increasing while it's challenging to keep enough staff on hand to meet the shelter's needs, where workers are expected to have a high distress tolerance to get the job done. Lack of staff has a cascading effect as shelters struggle to meet the basic needs of animals, let alone provide them with affection and attention; and with length of stay rising, especially for large dogs, the situation can become acute.

We know more about the subsequent mental health situation for veterinary professionals than shelter workers, thanks to growing interest in the suicide and mental health crisis[22] among veterinarians and veterinary technicians. For animal welfare workers, such as kennel attendants, certified euthanasia technicians, front desk staff, behaviorists, and the myriad of other personnel who make shelters run, we have very limited data.[23] These workers, with their high turnover and lower social status, lack the professional organizations that lobby for veterinarians and vet techs, though the National Animal Care and Control Association is trying to change that.

When those staff ask for help, they run into social attitudes around nonprofit work and the belief that caring for animals is a sort of sacred task, one so fulfilling that only a monster would complain about it. This is work for a cause: Shelter workers are supposed to be able to endure harsh working conditions, low pay, and high stress because they are here for the animals. These pressures, journalist Sarah Jaffe notes of nonprofit workers more broadly in her book *Work Won't Love You Back,*[24] aren't "just coming from the top—the culture of 'movement' work also tends toward self-sacrifice," which, "whether swaggering or self-abnegating, leads workers to stay past closing time," and the consequences can be incredibly damaging. This is a thing that breaks you, over time, to have your love and care and passion exploited and thrown back in your face when you ask for fair pay, paid leave, emotional supports, respect.

"This framework is often used in nonprofits," said Jay Cunningham, a worker at Humane Animal Rescue of Pittsburgh when we talked about the organization's fight for a union. "You shouldn't ask for fair wages, shouldn't ask for better working conditions, because you're doing good. It's so hypocritical. We can have good working conditions and still be doing good. If we are continuously showing empathy and compassion and care for all these animals, why are we not given the same? There's nothing wrong with advocating for better."

Board members and members of the public are concerned, as they should be, about the conditions for the animals, the quality of their kennels and access to veterinary care, the food and treats and toys that mark their days. They are utterly incurious about the living conditions for the staff who lovingly care for those animals, and how jarring their comments can feel to people with hands chapped from constant exposure to water and cleaning supplies, those who are couch-surfing because they lost their homes, those who are making difficult choices brought on by the costs of vet care for their own animals.

Poor and working-class people have historically been considered less emotionally expressive, with a narrower emotional range and a higher tolerance for upsetting circumstances: a "thick skin bias."[25] A deep thread of classism and racism runs through the idea that shelter staff don't need mental health supports; there is also a huge lack of recognition that shelters are filled with constant grief, from happy tears to secondary trauma to disenfranchised grief over deaths in care.

The daily impact of grief in all forms is of little interest to many members of the public. They don't see Tab4, only an empty kennel.

It doesn't have to be this way. In fact, there are a number of proactive steps animal welfare advocates could be taking—and are taking—to address moral injury and the slew of griefs large and small that haunt the steps of animal welfare workers. One critical requirement is engaging with the inevitability of that grief, asking not how it can be hidden, but how it can be openly discussed and acknowledged, making animal welfare workers feel validated in their emotions and able to express themselves, and helping communities understand the tremendous sacrifices that happen behind the scenes.

Perhaps, just as medical schools do with end-of-year ceremonies commemorating anatomical gifts,[26] we should be holding annual memorials for the animals who pass through our care. Honoring the lives and deaths of the animals that surround us also connects us to our human worlds, and to each other. Such memorials can also, as they do in medicine, encourage reflection and contemplation on ethics and community.[27]

As Cunningham puts it, "We want to go to a park and cry together sometimes."

I remember a kitten who had become a favorite of the staff, carried around in the hood of one of the kennel attendants, buried under a plum tree that everyone surreptitiously weeded on their breaks. Her memos in ShelterLuv told their own sad story, one of "failure to thrive" or "fading kitten syndrome" and endless attempts to save her life. A few years later, the staff buried Asia, a cranky and much-beloved tortie with a creaky scream-meow, under the same tree and planted succulents over her.

For a long time, shelter staff kept cremated remains and pictures of some beloved shelter fixtures on a shelf behind the front desk. In the kitchen, a kennel card for a shelter cat who was deeply loved and died in an incredibly traumatic, upsetting way was taped to the wall, yellowing, its corners curling. When the staff had to completely strip and clean the kitchen during a ringworm outbreak, it reappeared, freshly printed, though no one would claim responsibility for it. These mementos send a quiet signal to members of the public who pay attention: The sense of duty and care to animals does not stop when they die. Workers learn from and honor all the animals who pass through the shelter doors, even if briefly.

Creating an explicit space to honor grief also requires honoring the mixed feelings that come with positive outcomes, whether they be transfers to specialty rescues, success in a foster program, or adoption. These emotions can feel taboo for animal welfare workers and may be poorly understood among the public as well. I was not the only one, I know, who lingered over the "Adoption Updates" bulletin board in the hallway, seeing familiar faces in their new homes, romping on the beach, chasing wand toys, snuggling with human family members. I was pleased to see them there, to know that they were loved and happy, but part of me also missed seeing them, knowing the perfect spot on their backs to scratch them, greeting them with a goofy nickname and watching their tails wag.

Annual commemorations and memorial walls are, of course, not enough to support the emotional needs of shelter workers, just as pizza parties will not fix low wages.

In shelter settings, argues Marton, there should be a counselor or social worker on staff or retainer to create space for time to breathe and talk about euthanasia as well as the grief that comes with good outcomes, the happy tears seen when a beloved animal finally makes a perfect match. In some shelter and clinic settings, social workers are in fact providing services to staff as well as the public. Kelly Bremken, a veterinary social worker at Oregon Humane Society, is one among a small and growing cohort who are representing veterinary social work, with the University of Tennessee's Veterinary Social Work program providing an early trailblazing path in the field. Her work across multiple Oregon Humane Society locations spans a huge variety of staff and public needs.

"I want people to understand the weight and the pace of the work, to see us and value the expertise we have, not just 'the pound' or dog kennel cleaners. The respect, care, and empathy staff give to each other, the pets, the public. I wish people had more compassion for the work," she says, speaking of facilities where on any given day she may be mediating an employee dispute, developing mental health programming, training vet staff on power imbalances, helping a member of the public access food assistance, or debriefing after a traumatic euthanasia. This programming must be customized to workers and the shelter environment, led by someone staff members trust and feel comfortable with. This deeply grounded desire for respect goes hand in hand with the need for public support, and both are necessary for the public to understand that grief in shelter settings is much more complex than it might appear at first glance.

This is also a moment for frank conversations and transparency about euthanasia decisions that involve shelter staff more broadly in the process, helping people understand how and why these decisions are made, and offering them opportunities for a more participatory role. That conversation is necessary at closed- and open-admission shelters alike, and it must engage with the highly stigmatized role of euthanasia in animal sheltering, with an eye to including public education so animal welfare workers feeling grief over euthanasia don't find themselves condemned by the community for the work that they do. Euthanasia shouldn't live in the shadows. It is part of the work of treating animals with respect. There is sometimes joy in a peaceful ending, as uncomfortable as this makes some people feel. Ending suffering is part of the work of animal welfare. Dr. Cooney, who provides euthanasia at a local shelter in addition to leading CAETA training, remarks of the shelter environment: "When I go in and see firsthand the quality care that shelter staff are able to provide these animals during euthanasia, it does my heart good."

There will always be a need for sheltering. In an ideal world everyone can afford housing and care for their pets; no one faces catastrophic life events such as intimate partner violence, illness, or death—and if they do, a friend steps up for their animals; every animal is a right fit for their household; every large dog has room to run; and every cranky cat who hates children sleeps under the sewing table in a home blissfully free of resident or visiting small humans. Animals are immortal and untouchable, never struck down by cars or eaten away by cancers. Until then, we need animal shelters, and we need to value the people who work in them. And we will always need veterinarians and techs, dog trainers and cat behaviorists, people who provide needed care for animals and inevitably carry grief with them as well.

The future of grief in animal care settings recognizes that the grief will always be there. Sharing our lives with animals, and forming deep bonds with them, perforce means sharing deaths with animals too.

There will always, inevitably, be a Tab4, but leaving it shrouded in silence serves no one. The grief of animal shelter workers is diverse and an example of institutional, structural suffering caused by a society that is often unwilling to face the uglier parts of life. Everyone loves cute puppies and kittens, but no one wants to talk about the owner of two senior cats requesting euthanasia; or the dog everyone at the shelter adores with a broken leg requiring thousands of dollars of care that the shelter cannot provide and no pro bono vet can offer; or the grinding daily reality of witnessing human and animal suffering.

I think of the tremendous daily weight when I interview animal welfare workers, from kennel attendants to veterinarians at academic medical centers. It is made even heavier by social attitudes around the work they do and a round rejection of their grief. It is souring to think that a profession marked by compassion and commitment is devalued by a culture uncomfortable with the realities of their daily work, with a focus on euthanasia choices that may be forced by factors such as resource scarcity as much as they are by terminal illness or extreme injury. That focus elides the other distressing aspects of animal welfare work and their corresponding emotional weight. Someone must take these burdens on, even at a high personal cost, and the pain of moral injury is only exacerbated by lack of compassion from outsiders. Tab4 will always be with us: Deciding how we want to commemorate those rows of animals and the people who care for them is up to us.

Chapter 6

Loki // Performance

I euthanized Loki on a Monday.

On Wednesday, I was on a plane to Chicago to speak at a conference of LGBTQIA+ health providers and researchers, where I would talk to attendees about how to interact with the media, accumulating a stack of business cards and distributing promises to follow up. Between sessions, I wandered numbly through downtown and down to the lake, staring out across the endless water, my phone lighting up periodically with texts from friends that I ignored. At night, I sat in the dark in my weirdly capacious bathtub, staring at nothing.

On Friday, I pitched my editor at *Rolling Stone* a story I'd been longing to tell, waiting for the right moment, feeling crass even as I knew that events recur cyclically in the news whether or not I am considering writing stories about them: What happens to the survivors of mass shootings? The country was still reeling from the deaths of sixty people and the wounding of hundreds of others at a music festival in Las Vegas—events I had watched unfold on Twitter as I sat in the lobby at the emergency vet, waiting, in a funny twist of fate, for the same vet who had told me Leila was dying five months earlier to come out and tell me the same thing all over again, this time looking at Loki's X-rays, Loki's lab values.

I wanted to tell the stories of those "hundreds of others," of the "and some-such-number wounded," of the people who looked into the face of evil and lived, sometimes with lasting physical disabilities and emotional distress, to remind people that mass shootings are not just killings, but mass disabling events with a ripple effect. To remind people, also, that these mass-mortality, mass-disabling, mass-mourning events are preventable, but we choose to leave people and communities with a legacy of violence.

Yes, my editor said.

On Sunday, I flew back to California, where the skies had turned orange and reeked of smoke, fires like jewels scattered below the plane under our final—very late—approach to SFO. Road closures trapped me at friends' houses in the Bay Area, where I did reporting crammed into guest rooms; perched in the branches of someone's lemon tree to get a better signal, with their children sliding slices of cheese under the guest room door because I "looked sad"; in my car on the curb while a friend went to Berkeley Bowl, shocked that I would pass up an opportunity to peruse my favorite commercial grocery store produce section, a veritable wonderland of fruits and vegetables that must be enjoyed at least once in everyone's life. Not even for rambutans would I get out of the car that day. Even without the ring of fire that kept me from my home, I didn't even really want to go home: There was nothing for me there anymore.

I talked to emergency room physicians and PTSD specialists and survivors of mass shootings, who generously spent time with me telling stories they'd told over and over before, answering questions they'd received innumerable times, putting themselves on the line for advocacy just like they did after every mass shooting. I frenziedly crammed academic papers and watched people shooting ballistic gelatin on YouTube, tracing the explosive and destructive impact of bullets, imagining them slicing through the bodies of terrified festival goers who just wanted a night out to listen to music, only to have their entire lives upended. A survivor of the Gabby Giffords shooting told me about the shrapnel that still lived in her body, a constant, lingering reminder of the day she decided to take her child to a Congress on Your Corner event, thinking it would be an educational event and instead finding herself turning into a human shield to protect her child.

"My cat just died," I blurted awkwardly in the middle of one conversation, immediately flushing with embarrassment that my source couldn't see over the phone as I broke the rules of detached professionalism that I was supposed to be following, the imperative to be an impassive gatherer of facts, not a fellow human being.

"Oh," she said after a pause. "I'm so sorry."

"It's okay," I said. "So, tell me more about your hospital bills . . ."[1]

Working as a freelance journalist means that you are constantly moving, with no room for rest or error. To fall into stillness is to watch bills accrue while savings dwindle, and it is also to fall out of the eye of editors seeking prospective writers to commission. I had to keep working or perish, to keep filing stories and developing pitches, conducting interviews and promoting my work on social media, navigating around the inability to go home to my own house and my own bed, using my phone as a mobile hotspot to work on edits on the train. Go, go, go, faster, don't fall behind. Even as I was reporting on the gun violence story, I was doing preliminary interviews for a feature on phalloplasty at VICE and, oddly enough, final edits for a longform personal essay at Longreads about Leila's death. ("Sorry I'm late with these edits!" I said in an email to my editor. "I was picking up Loki's ashes at the crematory.")

The year 2017 was a strange one in America, especially for journalists covering politics, as I did at the time, with news moving so quickly and chaotically, stories unfolding in such wild and unexpected directions, that my waking hours were spent glued to my phone or computer, scrambling to catch up, my inbox bursting with messages from advocacy groups and legislators' offices and ordinary people desperate for someone, anyone, to listen to them, to tell their story, to make the world make sense.

"Not," I joked to a friend over cocktails, wearing an ill-fitting pair of pants I'd bought at Target because the two pairs I'd taken to Chicago in my carry-on were in the wash at my friend Tristan's house, "a super-great time for my cat to die."

Loki's death was sudden, and shattering: One minute he was sitting in his bed on my desk while I interviewed a disabled fashion activist for *Teen Vogue,* the next he was staggering through my office, howling, as though something had broken inside him. He screamed all the way to the emergency vet in Santa Rosa—two hours away—where I felt like my internal world was falling apart even as I was, yes, glued to my phone, refreshing Twitter as reports started to come in about the shooting, following innumerable hashtags. Everyone around me was fixed in their own internal world, that place of deep darkness you find yourself in at the emergency vet in the small hours, because there is no good reason to be paying VCA $1,500 just to walk in the door at 10 p.m. I couldn't even bring myself to tell anyone I was at the emergency vet, because it felt selfish in the grand scheme of things all around me, even as my throat clenched at the sight of a pile of euthanasia authorizations the receptionist was painstakingly scanning into files, something to do in the off-hours, a rote task that carried with it untold sorrows.

My brain didn't even really process what the vet told me, and I left at three in the morning to make the long drive home with Loki mute beside me, a bag of opioids between us, me thinking, foolishly, that we could have more time together.

He was just a cat. But also, he was a whole world.

If pet loss is a form of disenfranchised grief—which we will be exploring in the following chapter—it is also a kind of grief that highlights very specific societal expectations around who is allowed to grieve and how, a stark reminder of how we are expected to perform even as it feels like the world is ending, this vast, searing nothingness inside of us threatening to open up and swallow the world. Those expectations do not begin or end with the deaths of our animals.

Society has very clear expectations of grievers: You're allowed to be sad for a little while, maybe post some maudlin pictures on social media, a little video compilation, but you'd better keep it moving. Definitely don't talk about it after more than a week and keep that grief to yourself, it's icky. Be sad but not too sad, attend a tasteful "celebration of life," spend a night looking at some old pictures, go to sleep, roll out of bed, go to work, clock in. It's all in the past now. Remember, no one likes to hang out with someone who's still talking about their dead even weeks later, and you want to make sure editors will think of you as one of the good ones, always on deadline, always responsive to edits, never any trouble, thank you, please come again.

Do not, under any circumstances, allow yourself to drown in a wave of grief. Do not stop for one minute to think about the enormity of what just happened, let alone directly integrate loss into your work. It would be dangerous to admit that you are a human being with a life, as Jamie Loftus did on her podcast *Sixteenth Minute (of Fame)* in a summer 2024 episode ("grief, part whatever") that she put together in the whirling weeks after her father's death, doing what so many professional artists do when faced with grief: talk about it, write about it, paint about it, and—I am not speaking for Jamie, but for me—subvert it, squash it down (the reason I reach for my laptop instead of a friend at moments when my life is imploding). There is a sense of distancing involved when it becomes a topic to be put on paper, smoothed and soothed through multiple rounds of edits, requiring the ability to step back lest you sink into it and never escape.

"At some point you will have a library hold that will outlast your father," she said at one point, with a levity teetering at the edge of the abyss as she talked about being forced to sum up her father, an enormity of a person, in "three sentences" for an obituary or conversations about him. I thought about my own library holds, the fact that I was thirty-seventh in line for Joan Didion's *The Year of Magical Thinking,* which I wanted to reread for research, three unanswered voicemails from my father sitting like smoldering bombs in my inbox.

How do you sum up someone you've spent your whole life with in three sentences?

Jamie knew her father was sick and spent time with him in his last days, revealing that she had been working on episodes of her podcast in places that felt achingly familiar to me: in cars, outside waiting rooms, lodged in strange places, plunging forward without a break. For her, the process was clearly cathartic, but it was also a sobering reminder for listeners that podcasters are acutely aware that a missed episode is a missed opportunity, a break in the release schedule a violation of expectations, and, sometimes, a contract. "grief, part whatever" might have been a departure from her usual fare, but it was, in my opinion, one of her best episodes, a raw look into her interior life, a testimony, a memorial, a constellation of words that went far beyond the three prescribed sentences society told her she needed to use to tie her father up in a bow when talking about his impact on her life.

It isn't just that grievers are expected to move it along here in white America, to compartmentalize so that their loss doesn't bother anyone, but that the small window of tolerance for grief covers only a particular kind of grief. The wailing and screaming of my Greek childhood: right out. On the flip side, finding joy in grief and room for play: also out. Relief? Definitely out. Anger or betrayal? Guilt? Keep those feelings off main, please.

This is how it goes: There will be a death.

You will be sad: The amount of sadness permitted will be dictated by a black box formula that cross-references the nature of your relationship to the deceased with your race, socioeconomic class, employment status, and other factors, but no one will be able to tell you precisely what they are, only that you are getting it wrong.

You may perform your grief for a set period of time that the formula will also helpfully spit out, but you definitely need to wrap it up after the funeral, memorial, or other ceremonial event. You can tuck the prayer cards or programs or poetry chapbooks into a drawer full of things that you should not look at again, lest they remind you of the person (or animal) you once knew. You will be allowed a handful of "She used to love it when . . ."s before your punch card is used up.

You will work through it, move past it, get over it, get another one. As if it was that simple.

In some media and pop culture, we see a particularly sharp illustration of this, as characters move quickly through death, grief, and a return to status quo because extended grieving does not fit the storyline. Think of the truly wild heart-wrenching deaths of the week on soap operas (or *Grey's Anatomy*) that are forgotten again almost as quickly, subsumed by the steady flow of drama. Or of the deaths that open each episode of *Six Feet Under,* a show about a deeply fucked-up, repressive family of funeral directors who deal with death constantly and yet live in a world of ornate denial about grief and how it shapes their lives.

That doesn't mean pop culture always fails us when it comes to conversations about death, of course, as things like *The Year of Magical Thinking* and a long list of other mourning memoirs, autofiction, and straight-up fiction can attest. Some instances stick with you.

Buffy the Vampire Slayer's "The Body" is a stellar standalone episode about death in a show filled with death, a reminder that the ultimate enemy is no vampire or monster from beneath but the slow march of eternity. In "The Body," the show follows the aftermath of the previous episode, which ends as Buffy's mother, Joyce (Kristine Sutherland), dies in a perfectly ordinary, unremarkable way, discovered cold on the couch, not falling in battle with a demon or saving the world. She's simply a mother, who is dead.

There's an aching scene where Anya (Emma Caulfield), a vengeance demon with hundreds of years of experience in the world, is completely baffled by the situation and attempts to talk through it, as is her wont.

"Are we going to see the body?" Anya asks, in her trademark blunt, almost childlike style.

"What?" Willow (Alyson Hannigan) responds, looking shocked and disgusted.

"Are we going to be in the room? With the dead body?"

The scene is stiff, awkward, consciously not scored, so the sounds of rustling clothing and shuffling feet are audible under the dialogue, the actors held tense in the mundane world of panicking over which sweater to wear to a memorial. It is almost viscerally uncomfortable in an episode where viewers are offered limited relief from the aftermath of a death that feels more immediate and relatable than anything on the series.

"Are they going to cut the body open?" Anya continues, clearly struggling to comprehend their collective loss and seizing on anything concrete. Willow snaps at her, berating her for "the way you behave." Anya, looking for some sort of guidance, always feeling out of place in contemporary human society, responds, "Nobody will tell me!"

"Because it's not okay for you to be asking these things!" Willow says.

"But I don't understand," Anya answers, sobbing. "I don't understand how this all happens. How we go through this. I mean, I knew her, and then she's—there's just a body, and I don't understand why she just can't get back in it and not be dead anymore. It's stupid! It's mortal, and stupid. . . . I was having fruit punch, and I thought, 'Well, Joyce will never have any more fruit punch, ever, and she'll never have eggs, or yawn, or brush her hair, not ever,' and no one will explain to me *why*."

In that moment, Anya reveals her depth of affection for Joyce and her confusion with social expectations that run unspoken, with everyone expected to navigate loss in a prescribed way that is never openly stated. Friends Willow and Xander (Nicholas Brendon) appear chastened by her speech as she speaks, in a strange way, for viewers who are themselves contemplating death—maybe Joyce's, maybe someone else's.

Anya's voice is so many of ours when she plaintively asks, *"Why?"*

What makes *Buffy* stand out is Buffy's and her sister Dawn's continued mourning for Joyce, a mourning that affects their decision-making well through the end of the series. Joyce's death doesn't end with "The Body," becoming instead a constant that they carry with them, a refutation of the way we are "supposed" to grieve, in discreet bites and stages; Dawn is so bereft that she even attempts to raise their mother from the dead, evoking the longing we experience for lost loved ones in a very immediate way. That same longing, and Dawn's feeling of isolation as the sole survivor of the Summers family, comes up in the following season, when the group of friends successfully resurrects Buffy herself after a dramatic sacrifice—one that itself echoes the role Joyce fulfilled in Buffy's life.

One of the most influential discussions in the West of how we grieve—and how we should—comes from psychiatrist Elisabeth Kübler-Ross, whose foundational 1969 text, *On Death and Dying,* explores grief and loss from the perspective of the dying patients she worked with; if you've read or heard about one book about grief, it's probably this one. The stages she described—denial, anger, bargaining, depression, and acceptance—have been represented as a sequential model for "working through" grief. Kübler-Ross herself made it clear that they were not intended to be viewed this way,[2] but in a society that craves order and quick resolution, it's perhaps not surprising that people interpret them to mean that there is an order to grief, a checklist to be followed. Furthermore, the stages are applied to grievers in general, rather than the unique and specific experience of dying with a terminal illness, which was the actual focus of Kübler-Ross's book, though her broader body of work explored many experiences and expressions of grief.

This is a problem with serious consequences, not just an academic matter of radically misinterpreting someone's work. Kübler-Ross has become the go-to touchstone well outside the field of psychology for talking about grief, and she is frequently included in pop psychiatry books about loss, with most laypeople able to name at least a few of the stages, even if not necessarily in the presented order. The stages are also constantly represented in social media slideshows and videos with very confident creators making sweeping and authoritative statements that are often very seductive in their simplicity, simultaneously pursuing the laudable goal of talking about grief and bringing these conversations out of the shadows while also presenting a clearly codified guide of what to expect and a reassurance that grief is something to get through, to fix. Meanwhile, psychologists, sociologists, and other researchers have built out innumerable additional models of thinking about grieving, as well as challenging Kübler-Ross's work itself.

"Inaccurate portrayal of the model may lead to bereaved individuals feeling that they are grieving incorrectly," researchers wrote in a 2021 study in *Frontiers in Psychology,* which felt like a direct shot across the bow at any number of online grief "resources," with the title "Stages of Grief Portrayed on the Internet: A Systematic Analysis and Critical Appraisal."[3]

While the researchers were quick to acknowledge that Kübler-Ross's work has played an incredibly valuable role in how we talk about death and dying, they noted that her work wasn't designed for and shouldn't be viewed as a playbook for loss. "Clinicians have pointed to potential negative consequences for bereaved people who do not 'conform' by going through the stages but who think that they should be experiencing them," they wrote, an example of the performance expectations that weigh on people in grief and can make the process of engaging with that grief even harder than it needs to be.

The internet has exacerbated this as a world in which information quickly becomes flattened, distilled into tiny snippets for distribution in cutesy inspirational slideshows and authoritative videos, in which things are stripped of context and subjected to an endless game of telephone that whittles away at their core meanings. Thanks to the rise of "artificial intelligence" based on large language models, some of this content isn't even created by humans but by algorithms taking a stab at defining and describing human experiences after sucking up and digesting people's words. There is something darkly funny about losing our humanity in this way, about thinking that a computer can do what thousands of years of people have not and find the key to unlock *Grieving for Dummies.*

In a world that longs for a quick fix for things, and also for instructions on how to cope with life, that calls for "an adult" even when you yourself are the adult, it's nice to think that there are "stages" we can step through, akin to the promotion ladder at work. Sometimes you might get a little stuck or fight with a manager, but in the end, you'll get there, new and improved, healed. As a process-oriented person, I understand the appeal. Like Anya, I feel unmoored without clear directions. But that is, unfortunately, not how grief works.

Several social factors compound to create expectations around what kind of mourning is appropriate and who is allowed to do it. One is the simple cultural hegemony of white supremacy, which sets very clear expectations around the processes involved in dying and mourning, many rooted deeply in the Protestant belief systems that have influenced the United States since North America was colonized. Death and grief are positioned as personal tasks to overcome, things to "work through" and "move past," and they must be performed in "traditional" (white) ways, like so many things in this world. In this case, the performance of grief is part of the ritual of grief, the expectations of performance sometimes overriding the actual experience of grief.

There is a deep suspicion of more expressive modes of grieving and commemorating the dead. A funeral—or, better yet, a memorial without the body present—should be tasteful and quiet, everyone dressed in somber colors and talking in hushed tones. Perhaps there will be some funeral baked meats, as Hamlet says, a little potluck "back at the house" for intimate friends and family who will disperse at the end of the night. A funeral should not be noisy, disruptive, expensive, flashy, and this is often applied in particular to funerals in Black, Indigenous, and Brown communities that have different beliefs about death and mourning. Their funerary practices may be treated by white culture as a cultural oddity, such as the second line parades or "jazz funerals" of New Orleans. Similarly, the ornate homegoings of the Black community or the lavish traditions of a Mexican Catholic funeral are outside the bounds of appropriate behavior, sometimes used as evidence that these communities are "wasteful," especially when it comes to the practice and tradition of an extended family and community gathering to help to pay for such funerals. Why can't you memorialize within your means? Or they are exoticized: Noble savage myths surround the funeral practices of Indigenous people, especially closed practices where outsiders are not welcome.

I explored the racialized pressures surrounding mourning practices in a conversation with death doula Nina Bailey of Melanated Mourning. Bailey's work focuses on support for Black mourners in a climate where "everything is going to seem like anger most of the time because our feelings are suppressed"—a reflection of common social attitudes about Blackness, especially for women, who can be caught in the "angry Black woman" stereotype for simply expressing themselves.

Bailey's work integrates ancestral connections and the need to honor mourners and the dead alike with dignity and respect, while foregrounding the performance expectations around Black grief, many of which are rooted in centuries of racist beliefs about Black emotions and lives.

"I think Black people have had enough of people telling them what they should be doing, how, what, where they need to go," she says, explaining that she works to create safe spaces for Black mourners to process and express their feelings "to be their full human selves," rather than complying with demands to follow a blueprint of remaining quiet and not upsetting others. Her work also explores themes of surrender and trust, both challenging things to do in a culture that is very focused on control, whether we are imposing it on ourselves or others.

"We can't dismiss people's emotions because you're uncomfortable," she concludes.

It's not just racism that dictates how and whom people may grieve. There is also a deep streak of disablism in how we engage with grief, something autistic writer Marianne Eloise noted when writing for *The Conversationalist* in 2024.[4] Perhaps fittingly, she too frequently revisits the depiction of mourning on *Buffy,* seeing herself in Anya's outburst.

"I do not handle grief well. Autistic people, much like ex-demons, are often assumed to have no feelings at all—but the reality is the opposite: We often feel things very deeply, on a cellular level that affects every aspect of our functioning. Because of this, it can take us a while longer to process things, or even just to express them outwardly. Death and grief are no exception," she wrote, talking about the anticipatory grief she felt as her grandfather was dying, followed by the devastating reality of that death. "My grandad was here, and then he was sick, and then I could no longer call him to talk about the birds in his garden. I couldn't accept it."

Some people interpret this struggle with acceptance and fixate on questions like "Why?" as evidence that autistics—and other neurodivergent people—are innocent, childlike.

Expectations around how we should behave in grief are deeply rooted in larger neurotypical beliefs about how people should behave in general. Neurodivergent people are sometimes stereotyped as cold or brusque when sometimes what we are is deeply wounded and confused: This thing is not *fair.* It doesn't make any *sense.* We ask questions in an attempt to make sense of it, to find people who feel the way we do, in a world where everyone seems to expect us to feel differently. Must we be so alone in this moment? Our expressions of pain make people feel awkward and uncomfortable because they are so vulnerable, and also sometimes because we are asking the questions many other people feel but have been taught not to ask out loud.

There is also disablism wrapped up in responses to particular kinds of deaths, in which the general assumption is that disability is indicative of suffering, that we should be happy that someone is "in a better place" when the best place for them was here, with us. In this framing, dying with a disability is a form of freedom—encompassed in things like endless mawkish editorial cartoons after the death of Stephen Hawking, all depicting the late physicist rising from his chair to meet heaven's representative. In death, the implication was, people will finally escape their disabilities, will no longer be wheelchair bound or trapped in a broken body, and thus our period of mourning should be suitably short and peppered with gratitude for an end to a life of suffering.

Let us gather to be inspired by the ultimate triumph over disability: death.

Another factor in the pressures of performance is, of course, capitalism, a powerful specter that mediates how long and in what manner you are allowed to grieve. People who are grieving are not productive. If you are not productive, you are not contributing to society, so what value do you have? If you are not productive, you are also not providing for yourself or your family, death pushing you closer to the brink of financial crisis; few people can afford to take time off to acknowledge a loss, let alone deal with the myriad administrative tasks that crop up—and that's if they are allowed to take that break at all.

Bereavement leave is still not a legally-required right on the federal level in the United States, with only a handful of states offering protections for mourners who need time off[5]—unpaid, of course. Workplaces may offer differing amounts, if any, and they are usually restricted to specific relatives, with a set number of days doled out for a sibling, a parent, a grandparent; only the most generous of employers provide partial or full pay for those missed days. For those grieving close friends, teachers, lovers, lost pregnancies, pets, and others who do not fit into this framework, there is no allowance for mourning; I was reminded of this in 2021 when I was working in the depths of the nonprofit industrial complex, grieving for Ember, and only two close coworkers commented on it, while another member of our team received paid leave and an outpouring of sympathy after a death in her family. The sense of resentment that bubbled up in me wasn't fair: It wasn't her fault that she had suffered a loss, that people were kind and tried to be supportive, that her loss was recognized by her colleagues and employer, that the loss of a pet was regarded as more or less a nonevent at a moment of *so much death,* 2021 being simply a sea of funeral notice after funeral notice; but it still stung enough that I used a week of PTO to escape.

Avoidance of societal complicity and discomfort is another contributor to our very strict pressures around the performance of grief and the pressure to avoid drawing attention to a death or highlighting the way in which it affected survivors and members of the deceased's community. When griefs are mediated by social factors, as they often are—as, for example, in the case of disability icon Carrie Ann Lucas, who died in 2019 at just forty-seven[6] after battling with her insurance company for months over basic benefits she needed—engaging with those deaths and with that grief is also a voyage of self-examination that may come with extreme discomfort. Why are some of us allowed to survive the society in which we live, while others are not? How is it that I am here writing when Carrie Ann Lucas, when Erin Gilmer, when Stacey Park Milbern, when Stella Young, when Lisa Egan, when Alice Wong, are dead?

Society also struggles with differing forms of loss in a culture that often views loss as very literal: a death, with a body to go with it. Grieving for missed opportunities, big life changes, and other events is alien and strange, and people are discouraged from sharing those feelings. Think of the promises to write, to "keep up," from people moving apart who know, deep inside, that "keeping up" will probably turn to a few emails a year, perhaps to nothing, that this is a relationship that will be forever changed. Speaking about these kinds of losses is challenging, with the mourner having nothing specific and collectively understood as a loss to point to.

Pauline Boss, a professor emeritus at the University of Minnesota and family therapist with forty-five years of experience, describes a particular form of death-adjacent loss cultures struggle to reckon with: "ambiguous loss," a term she told me grew out of work in the 1970s around "father absence in an intact family," where she found that "a father could be physically present but psychologically absent." There is no death to grieve here, and yet it is still a form of loss. Ambiguous loss, explains Boss, is "a loss that never had a name before." Her work also includes research with families of soldiers missing in action, another form of loss in which someone is absent but not definitively dead either. She's seen laypeople apply the term to the losses associated with climate change, missing children, the loss of limbs, of cognitive capacity.

She was initially surprised by the widespread interest in the term, expecting her colleagues in the field to be interested but noting that "ordinary people catch on to this theory almost immediately." This is, in a sense, a democratizing of psychology, meeting grievers where they are with language that feels intuitively familiar. Boss's work, unsurprisingly, involves considerable exploration of what happens when it's challenging to pinpoint the exact moment of a loss: Her book *The Myth of Closure* tackles the common societal expectation that grief follow a trajectory ending in a definitive "closure," which allows the griever to resolve the situation.

How should the parent of a missing child experience and express "closure" when this implies that a loss is finalized? When, perhaps tomorrow, there will be a new lead? This is amplified in entire communities who are subject to widespread and systemic ambiguous losses, such as the Indigenous people across North America living in the midst of an epidemic of missing and murdered Indigenous people. These loved ones are missing, causing irreparable harm to their families, but this is also a loss tied to colonialism and subjugation, one with knockdown effects that hollow out entire ways of being. If that doesn't provoke a collective scream of grief, I don't know what should.

An ambiguous loss can be an ongoing, slow-rolling source of grief that society does not know how to cope with, an ulcerated wound that resists even the most stubborn efforts at treatment—precisely the kind of emotional experience that makes most people uncomfortable.

Nearly everyone I talked to for this book included some version of a comment about our drive to fix things rather than live with the world we are in when it comes to expectations around how people perform grief, raising the question of why we continue to believe that grief is fixable. If so many of us recognize this attitude as toxic and unhelpful and think it is a bad thing, why are we here? It is painful and upsetting to live through any kind of death, and it is also deeply unsettling to be in the presence of someone who is mourning, to take their feelings as they come, to acknowledge their validity. Being confronted with loss conflicts with our innate fear of being unable to help, to make it better, to deal with situations in which there is no polished outcome. Our response to things we cannot cope with is often to shut down, or shut them out.

Performative pressure is deeply rooted in the individualistic nature of the society we live in, where grief is personal and something to be kept quiet, since it is not something that can be repaired and put back on the shelf. Our distrust of things that cannot be explained or fixed conspires with the bootstrapping so quintessential to white American culture: Just deal with this on your own terms. You can expect your ten minutes of sympathy, but no more than that. To grieve more deeply, more publicly, is attention-seeking behavior, and no one wants to see that. Everyone hates a pick-me, someone who cannot leave their baggage at the door. A public expression or manifestation of your grief is a direct confrontation, a cry that no one wants to hear. *See me. Witness me. I am here.*

This is a marked departure from grief and funerary ritual as social enterprises, as they have been in many communities throughout history. In Jewish tradition, for example, the practice of sitting shiva after death creates a framework for a family to temporarily step outside of society to mourn, and it is accompanied by expectations of visitors who will come to support the family, taking on some of the burden of grief.

Sometimes, as an individual or a collective, you just need to cry, and crying, like other displays of painful emotion, makes people uncomfortable; it should, instead, be viewed as something that can lighten a shared burden, with everyone in a community agreeing that a loss is deep, irreparable, and also integrated into shared history, community, and culture.

Under this framing, performance and expressions of grief that deviate from expected norms are indicators of pathology, of doing it "wrong," as for example in the cases of people who feel a sense of freedom at a loss. This includes a variety of emotions considered questionable, tacky, or inappropriate, such as relief upon a death.

But is relief not a natural sensation to have, sometimes? Relief is not necessarily joy or celebration or happiness, but it is an acknowledgment that the status quo has changed, that someone you love is no longer suffering, perhaps, and also that a period of uncertainty or strain has ended. We may experience relief, for example, when a beloved senior pet dies because we no longer need to litter the house with pee pads and fear urine-stained sheets, a sensation quickly followed by a sense of guilt: How can I be glad, in this moment, that I get to put my house back in order, that I no longer have to worry about what's waiting behind the door when I come home from work?

We may feel relief at the death of a loved one after a long and lingering illness, and sometimes even before: relief at a definitive diagnosis, the knowledge that someone's time is limited in the near future, not the abstract; that we have an answer, even if it is not a good answer. Relief that a tortured, complicated relationship is over and we can move on.

Sometimes we have giddiness, joy, laughter, humor in the absurd. Death is, in some ways, sometimes very funny, and sometimes we whistle in the dark, laugh to avoid crying. Sometimes grief looks like picking up a stranger at the bar, taking them home, fucking them to feel something, anything at all, feeling filled with self-loathing and disgust in the morning—or maybe not feeling anything at all. Or it looks like anger, apocalyptic, destructive, unstoppable rage, breaking things and storming through life, for how could death take someone like this? How is the world still progressing, every turn of the globe a turn further away from the time when that person was alive? Or it looks like not knowing how we should feel, a sense of numbness and confusion as we search for meaning in the unknowable.

There's a vast industry around performing grief correctly—entire shelves in the bookstore are dedicated to texts with saccharine promises of "grief recovery" if you follow the right steps and believe hard enough, like you can positive-think your way out of something that has irreparably altered the world around you. This interior breaking is the thing society most wants to avoid in the griever, exemplified by the uncomfortable body language of Xander and Willow when confronted with the pure confusion and sadness that Anya is trying to express.

That *Rolling Stone* story, "What Happens to Survivors of Mass Shootings like Las Vegas?," remains one of my favorite clips, even as I can't bear to read it now because it is so wrapped up in the grief of that moment—both my own and the nation's, twisted and snarled beneath the surface of the story. I reject the idea that writing from a place of pain makes work better, that artists must be tortured in order to produce their best work; but it is an inescapable fact that a story born from trying to understand the unexplainable, trying to comprehend that which is so far beyond our ken that it will remain forever alien until it happens to us, is one of the best I ever wrote, tying my own pain with those of the people I interviewed, with the clinical language of those who care for us. Though I do not include my personal story in the piece, which would have been a violation of journalistic norms and expectations, it was, in its own way, a form of catharsis, even if that took the form of forcing readers to witness the ongoing grief and pain that can come with survival, of asking the reader to consider many forms of loss and to explicitly engage with them as something that affects all of society—something, therefore, that we should all experience together.

"Survivors may deal with a lifetime of acquired physical disability thanks to bullets that cannot safely be removed," I wrote, but the story was also about the emotional fallout of surviving a mass shooting and the lifetime of distress it causes, to live through something like that. The echo of a mass shooting cannot safely be removed, and, like other mourners, survivors are expected to perform their grief in a particular way.

As I talked with survivors about their advocacy, I was struck by the way in which societal expectations of grief shaped their initial responses to the events that brought us together, and the responses to seeing their trauma play out again and again on the national stage, their willingness to relive it over and over again for nosy parkers like myself. One told me about the network of survivors that quietly visits the latest members of their club, the one no one wants to belong to, while they are recovering from their physical injuries: visitors to hospital rooms and family homes, who talk with people about what they can expect not just from physical recovery but from emotional recovery, and society's reactions to their experiences, to the attitudes that build up around survivors-turned-activists.

We have a moral imperative to spare each other suffering, to build a world in which people do not die at the hands of the state or one another. But we also have a moral imperative to recognize that death is an inevitable constant in life, and our responses to death and our expressions of grief are inevitably also going to be very different and also need to be allowed to unfold on their own time and in their own way.

Death hits differently depending on your relationship to the deceased, on the circumstances around you, on your own personal beliefs and life lived. If it doesn't strike us uniformly, it seems patently absurd to suggest that we should process the aftermath uniformly, conforming to rigid expectations about how we should look while mourning. The push to pathologize any kind of grief that involves discomfort for others is a reflection of a society that doesn't want to witness distress, and responds to that not by mediating distress but by telling people to be silent about it. Out of sight, out of mind.

Grief is not something with a neat and tidy end date, one to follow like a paint-by-numbers. First this color and then that, slowly layering until the painting is done and then you can throw it away, the work complete, the final product of no real interest beyond a brief once-over. It is repression that creates lasting wounds, and the harm we do to one another in telling each other how to grieve is insult added to injury.

Several weeks after that story ran in *Rolling Stone,* I received a card in the mail with an unfamiliar postmark, the return address smeared, although I thought I recognized the first name. My post office box was and is a matter of public record on the "contact" section of my website, so occasional letters or packages aren't terribly surprising. I wriggled my finger through the flap to open the envelope and pull the card out as I waited in line to pick up a package.

It was a simple cream-colored card, bordered with a black stripe.

"In Deepest Sympathy," it said, and I opened it to a note from the survivor I'd interviewed all those weeks ago, the one I'd told about my dead cat, a woman who took time to track down my address and send me a kind note in the midst of a very busy life of gun violence advocacy and ongoing recovery from her injuries, a friendly voice across the void.

I hear you. I see you. I witness you.

Chapter 7

Ember // Disenfranchised

Ember, a polydactyl tortie with quick, soft paws, died in a night of chaos and unpleasantries in early June 2021, the windows still open to capture the cooling breeze after the heat of the day. She had been "doing poorly," as the unhelpful diagnosis goes, and I had been in and out of work dealing with her health problems over the previous month, fighting a shortage of veterinary care affecting the entire country[1] that made it nearly impossible, at times, to access what she needed, with the emergency vet two hours away focusing on urgent cases, not a cat who simply wasn't herself.

Ember died at a highly unfortunate moment on the global scale, in the midst of the early COVID-19 pandemic, when mourning the death of a pet seemed disrespectful, even frivolous. According to a diligently maintained and very popular COVID-19 dashboard hosted by Johns Hopkins, 600,000 people had died in the United States[2] by the time Ember jumped out of her bed, seeking a place to hide, a place I wish she had found so that the last few hours of her life were not pain and terror, trapped in a car, her least favorite place in the entire world.

In the face of such human devastation, how could I be sad about a cat?

I was hit by a double minimization of my grief: the sensation that I inherently wasn't allowed to be sad about the death of a pet—a common feeling in the aftermath of pet loss—compounded by feeling as though this small death didn't matter in the context of what everyone else was going through at that particular moment. I also felt a tinge of guilt over my close connection to an animal, deeper than some of my human connections, with a loss that felt more intense, perhaps disproportionate to outsiders, and, therefore, something suspect, possibly even unacceptable, like something that shouldn't be mourned at all.

I am not alone in feeling like a bad person, or a cold one, for being more affected by the death of an animal than that of a human. In a striking 2019 essay for *Gen*[3] that captured many of my own feelings about the divide between pet and human loss, Meghan Daum wrote about the contrast between mourning her father and her dog, Phoebe, and the guilt and discomfort that came with feeling like perhaps she mourned her canine companion more than her father in a world where expressing such a thing is very difficult.

"My father's death makes me feel like the ceiling of the world has been lowered," she explained. "I've learned to get by in that constricted space, constantly ducking my head to avoid hitting that ceiling. But Phoebe's death is a different proposition somehow. Phoebe's death makes me feel like someone has come along with a giant eraser and rubbed out my face."

What she describes is a tale of two griefs, but it is fundamentally the tale of a grief denied: The being she is most connected to in the world, who has accompanied her and comforted her through huge life changes—who, critically, was a more constant companion in recent years than perhaps anyone else—is dead. Her father, an independent adult with his own feelings and agenda who played a huge role in her life and helped shape who she was, died after a short illness, following the expectation that beloved parents grow old and die before us. It's not that she didn't mourn her father, but she had a framework for it, as well as social supports that acknowledged the death as meaningful.

That description of being utterly poleaxed and undone by a loss and unable to convey that without sounding like a horrible person is highly relatable.

With animals like Ember and Phoebe, pressure to keep your grief in the corner, to "take care of things," is overwhelming. In my series of 2023 interviews with pet guardians about nontraditional memorials, many expressed feelings of disenfranchised grief; those interviews turned into confessionals as people felt like they finally had someone who listened to, and cared about, their grief—a grief they hadn't been able to speak aloud, in some cases for years or even decades.

These feelings, the pressure to button grief away quickly, resolve any outstanding threads, and not discuss it, are not limited to pet loss. Many deaths, as well as other kinds of losses, are accompanied by a dictate: Do not acknowledge your grief, do not expect others to do that either, do whatever it is you need to do quietly and in a place where it will not bother anyone. Do not become the kind of person who cries on the subway because you are so overwhelmed by this horrible thing that has happened to you that you cannot contain it, must cry out so the world can witness you. Do not, under any circumstances, look the animal that is grief in the eye. Do not let it chase you. And if that loss is one that society doesn't view as significant, those dictates are even more forceful.

What I went through that summer, what Meghan went through, is what's known as "disenfranchised grief,"[4] a term introduced by Dr. Kenneth J. Doka in 1989. It is more or less exactly what it says on the tin: grief that feels unacknowledged or lesser, sometimes even taboo, something to be held close, privately and in secret, not talked about and certainly not publicly mourned. Any kinds of deeply personal losses behind closed doors are more likely to tip into disenfranchised grief because people around the griever might not even be aware of it.

Because no one talks about them, they can become stigmatized. It is often grief that cannot be adequately processed or confronted for a variety of reasons, ranging from feelings of conflict about the decedent to being a loss that other people don't register as a loss within the context of their own beliefs about what constitutes "loss"—because it isn't a death, or it isn't a death that you should be close to, such as the death of a celebrity you didn't know personally. It can also be grief for a loss that people are unable to simply mourn because it has become politicized and taken out of their control, no longer theirs to experience for what it is.

Even as someone who knew what disenfranchised grief was

at the time, I still felt mired in it, and through the looking glass, I was struck by the way in which my own grief mirrored that of those disenfranchised by the pandemic who felt like they were unable to mourn. It does not go without notice that Doka framed the concept at the height of the HIV/AIDS crisis, when for some communities grief was a constant, aggressive, unrelenting part of daily life, while the world spun on by without them—and sometimes even spat in the face of their grief, minimizing it even further. Deaths in these instances were haunted by a pressure to keep grief silent, private, to avoid upsetting others and live instead in secrecy and shame.[5]

The reflections sparked by the alienation I felt around Ember's death[6] gave me a deeper opportunity to think about who has access to which kinds of grief, and how disenfranchisement takes many forms, whether people are grieving human or animal loved ones or more abstract losses. To live through loss during mass mortality events like HIV/AIDS and COVID is to be carried on a wave of disenfranchised grief that also offers a little window into other people's worlds, a thin sliver of opportunity: If you relate to this on a deep, cellular level, what other kinds of losses around you are disenfranchised? Who else is suffering in silence? How can you ease—or intensify—their experiences of loss?

At the same moment during the pandemic when Ember and I were flung to a destination neither of us expected or cared to visit, it seemed like we might collectively be at a tipping point in terms of discussing disenfranchised grief openly and challenging the social norms that reinforce it. The media was alive with discussions about disenfranchised grief, introducing the concept to broader audiences hungry for reassurance. NPR's *Life Kit* offered a "how to cope"[7] while *The New York Times* explored "Disenfranchised Grief in a Year of Pandemic Losses."[8] In *Catapult,* Nora Feely wrote about "grieving when you can't gather"[9] and what the pandemic stole from families mourning loved ones.

"Not being able to say goodbye, express love, gratitude or forgiveness, and not having the memory of seeing a loved one's physical decline and death, complicates the grieving process," wrote journalist and mourner Lena Sun in a *Washington Post* feature about the world of loss we were experiencing, viewed through the lens of her mother's death.[10] Readers were clearly hungry for it, finding common ground with losses of their own that felt disjointed, isolating: It racked up hundreds of comments within days, including many deeply heartfelt, intimate ones.

"Grief is different from grieving—how we learn to navigate life without our loved one," Sun wrote, articulating the fact that grief is an active process, not a passive one, a verb that the mourner must move with. "Social isolation and the sheer quantity of deaths during the pandemic made this process even harder."

The inability to visit bedsides, to hold rituals and ceremonies, to gather at a home after the funeral, turned death into something unreal and strange, at such a remote distance that sometimes we lived in suspended disbelief. We were deprived of access to rites and community around death, humans and animals alike. We were alone, together: We didn't have to search quite as far for someone else who gets it when it felt like everyone knew someone with COVID, or to see loss as more complex than death at a moment when we were isolated from each other and cut off from community for our own safety and turning to the internet, letter writing, other forms of communication, to find each other's humanity. Experiences of non-death losses—such as instructional loss for children who missed months of school—opened up an opportunity to talk about loss in broader, more empathetic terms.

It felt, for a moment, as though the pandemic had opened a door into a conversation about how we mourn, one that could have been transformative for so many people searching for empathy and kindred spirits, not just over pandemic-related deaths but life's losses more broadly. With so many of us experiencing grief, the feeling became strangely universal and relatable; we could extend feelings about our own losses to the way we viewed other people, and expand our sense of what it meant to experience loss. But that door quickly closed as we collectively suppressed memories and reinstated the status quo, treating this brief time in our shared history as an exceptional one that didn't offer any instructive lessons for life writ large: Loss is personal, some kinds of losses matter much more than others, and either way, you shouldn't talk about your loss because it might upset people or destabilize the world we live and work in.

We disenfranchised ourselves from our own conversation about disenfranchised grief, as we've done many times before at moments of mass loss and trauma. Rejecting a possible future where we engaged with and explored loss openly was a tremendous disservice to ourselves and served only to underline societal expectations about how to mourn.

Disenfranchised grief is sometimes a tangle of mourning and anger that grief cannot be expressed, even if that anger is subverted and a griever doesn't fully recognize it. It can also curdle into resentment as people with more socially understood griefs receive attention. Mourners feel their pain on a very intimate, sometimes embodied, level, but they witness differing pressures and societal expectations that are affecting the way they are treated. An intellectual understanding of what's going on—a recognition that they fit at the bottom of society's hierarchy of grief, and that's why they're not being provided with support, and that's not fair—doesn't change the fact that they feel disregarded. Loss is not a competition, but it can start to feel like one, with the disenfranchised griever fighting to be allowed on the playing field at all.

And society's tolerance for even sanctioned and understood grief has its limits, with culturally defined bounds set on all forms of grief. The widow, for example, may be granted access to more public mourning initially, but if she does not begin to return to normal and seek a new partner, she will be judged for it. The Netflix series *Dead to Me* captured this perennial tension, as a bereaved wife flails through mourning her husband, befriended by a woman with some big secrets: The viewer is supposed to see the widow, Jen (Christina Applegate), as slightly unhinged, her anger and sorrow making her act out in wild ways. This is a dark comedy, so the scenes teeter on the edge of recklessness and hilarity, but they have a sharper, slower, sadder edge as viewers read her behavior as deviant, unacceptable, the wrong way to express grief. She is fighting against a sense of disenfranchisement in a way that invites viewers to think about why her behavior makes them feel uncomfortable.

That kind of pressure has been associated with death and dying for a very long time, especially when it comes to "lesser" losses, as though there is a finite point to reach, after which the mourning will be over and people can move on, and the clock runs out more quickly for some losses than for others. At times, there is a question as to whether a loss is one at all in the judgment of people around the mourner, which can lead those in grief to question their own experiences, adding to the psychological burden of loss.

There are material consequences to disenfranchised grief. It is very hard to experience post-traumatic growth in general, but it is especially so when that trauma is not even recognized as such, when the person who is experiencing it may even be explicitly told that they shouldn't experience it as a loss. This is not about cursory expectations to "move on" but the deep psychological need to build resilience and honor experiences of trauma while also growing through and with them. Failing to do so can contribute to a harmful theory of mind and a wary interpretation of the surrounding world, as the wound splits open again and again, with no meaningful opportunity to heal.

Those feelings can boil over, sometimes in very ugly ways, with the griever lashing out at those around them—or carrying a long-standing grudge that affects the way they interact with the world. These are feelings that can last a lifetime, that grievers may in turn transfer to other mourners, perpetuating the cycle.

If grief should move like a river, ebbing and flowing, encountering obstacles and rapids along the way, disenfranchised grief becomes a log fallen into the stream, a dam, a block. The water cannot flow and instead mills, confused, in a growing pool that grows deeper and colder, water stained with dead leaves and leaching rocks. The rocks in the riverbed below develop crusts of dried mud, the plants wither away and die altogether.

The inability to speak in the moment turns into a block in our lives. Mourning these losses is challenging because sometimes we feel like solitary mourners, with no one to carry the weight with us, and we are disciplined if we attempt to talk about our losses or process them in community. We are already isolated, and society isolates us further. That log in the creek bulges and expands, blocking even the smallest trickle of water. There will be no relief until someone removes it and the water bursts past in a destructive rush.

This is the sharp pain of disenfranchised grief, which comes with an acute awareness that it may never be acknowledged, something that rots from within in a way only we can feel. It is hard to function, let alone have compassion for others and grow and change, when we feel like no one is listening to us, like we never had an opportunity to surface our grief and are constantly biting our tongues. The people living in these griefs hidden from public view are fighting battles no one can see, acutely aware that talking about those battles may be met with hostility.

Disenfranchised grief is not just painful for the mourner but also for other grievers. Those who feel unable to express themselves may begin to blurt out their grief or insert it into conversations where it is not welcome, seeking empathy anywhere they possibly can, longing for commonality and affirmation attached to the griefs of others. It is the ultimate "What about me?" in a search for common ground; we cry out our own mourning, both because we seek to be seen and because we think that perhaps this is a moment where we will be allowed to talk about our grief too.

"If we had our own support cups full, we wouldn't need to hijack grief," grief counselor and author Megan Devine told me when we talked about this issue, speaking to the culture of loss that surrounds all grief, but particularly disenfranchised grief, where grievers facing no space to express their feelings sometimes find themselves in a kind of grief Olympics, inserting their personal experience into someone else's stories without necessarily realizing what they are doing.

Understanding disenfranchised grief also requires revisiting what loss is. Expanding an understanding of loss opens up more opportunities for empathy, but it can also serve as a reminder that many people are experiencing some degree of loss at any given time, and these losses can compound each other. Dr. Doka's exploration of the topic extended to forms of grief beyond death and into the marking of larger passages and huge changes in life. For example, losing a spouse may also turn into losing the family home; and while one of these things is recognized as a tragedy, the other may be considered administrative or transactional: Of course you have to sell the house! That's just part of wrapping up the end of someone's life! This is the kind of loss you are not allowed to grieve and society will not acknowledge, instead expecting silence and offering up platitudes to those who may attempt to express their feelings.

The same holds true for a broad swath of non-death losses, such as the splintering of a community in the aftermath of a fire, something the residents of Altadena expressed to me in 2025 in interviews about community organizing after a fire ravaged their Los Angeles neighborhood. Many shared a feeling of deep loss over their displacement, not just the loss of their belongings and familiar surroundings, aware that many outsiders might see their burned-out homes as a loss but struggle to understand how it feels to be ripped away from their sense of place and the people in it; outsiders might not have empathy for those fighting not only to return but to ensure their neighbors could return as well. "At least you're alive" and "At least you found a house in another neighborhood" are fundamentally dispassionate responses to people in that kind of grief.

Some losses are verboten topics because there is a belief that they shouldn't be viewed as losses at all, that compassion for the mourner should be overridden by the mourner's misdeeds or unacceptable relationship to the decedent or another object of loss.

"Death ceremonies formalize grief. By silently going through this, your grief may feel even more uncontained than it would were you able to grieve publicly at his funeral,"[11] advised *The Guardian*'s Philippa Perry to a distraught letter-writer seeking advice on mourning her secret lover. An affair partner, like the woman who wrote to Perry for help, is not allowed to publicly acknowledge their bereavement. Speaking about it at all may be viewed with hostility, as taking away from or appropriating the grief of the "real" partner of the deceased, stealing not just the affections of the cheating partner but the experience of loss.

Ambiguous losses can be disenfranchised too. When there is no death or clear loss to point to, no shift or clearly definitive ending, survivors may be denied mourning rituals as well as full social status as grievers. Talking about the experience in the context of grief may also be frowned upon, evidence that someone is being fatalistic or losing hope—another case where society rejects the mourner's experience as a true loss.

When society repeatedly tells you not only that your loss is lesser and shouldn't be compared to more serious losses, but that it isn't actually a loss at all, that deep denial of reality stings. How could it not? And that feeling makes it very difficult to talk about that experience and challenging to seek out spaces where you feel like you will be met with respect and kindness, rather than disdain or judgment.

I find another category of disenfranchised grief particularly interesting because it's often not recognized as such: grief associated with politicized losses, which can carry a double weight of anger and sorrow about the loss itself, but also grief about the way the loss played out and was treated by society. People in this situation are unable to mourn the very real and immediate loss of loved ones because those deaths have become wrapped in something larger that doesn't belong to them anymore. These kinds of deaths are all around us, and sometimes it is hard for us to remember that a prominent, widely discussed death also involves very real people who were close to the decedent in a culture that projects a variety of things onto these deaths.

When I visited the Emmett Till Memorial at the National Museum of African American History and Culture, it highlighted these tensions for me. Till was just fourteen in 1955, a child, when he was kidnapped and lynched in a violent punishment for talking to a white woman. The Chicago-born youth was in Mississippi to spend time with family over the summer, something that should have been a treasured memory of adventure and new places and new people, not the end point of someone's life.

Mamie Till lost a son, but his funeral turned into a political commentary, one that resonated for me standing in front of his recovered and refurbished coffin, displayed at the request of the family just as his mangled body was prominently featured in the media at the time of his death as a sobering illustration of the impacts of racism in Jim Crow America.

In a mingled room of predominantly Black and white visitors, we related to this visual representation of profound grief very differently, drawing upon our own distinct cultural backgrounds. Seeing images of the anguished Mamie Till at the coffin and her son's funeral blown up to larger-than-life size on the walls, I thought of her dual losses: of her son, and of the ability to mourn on her own terms, grieving in such a public way and under pressure to relate her son's death to the larger civil rights movement, after a killing that ultimately had a profound impact on American history precisely because it was politicized, its shocking nature a rebuke. As the attendant reminded us not to take pictures at the request of the family, I was struck by their attempt to exert some control, taking back a narrative that had been wrenched from them when Emmett became a symbol.

This kind of personal-turned-political loss also shows up with pregnancy loss. Given how common pregnancy loss is—according to the National Center for Biotechnology Information, 10 percent of recognized pregnancies and 26 percent of overall pregnancies in the United States end in miscarriage[12]—it should be a frequent topic of discussion and acknowledgment, but this is not the case. Instead of being accompanied by supports and conversation, pregnancy loss usually occurs in the shadows, which can be devastating for expecting parents who feel like they can't talk about it and at times are in fact explicitly told not to talk about it because it makes people sad or uncomfortable. Many people who experience pregnancy loss say they feel treated as radioactive, dangerous, infectious, as though just talking about pregnancy loss is what causes it. These are classic conditions for feeding disenfranchised grief, by blocking any opportunities for making it part of the conversation.

But it can also quickly evolve into politicized disenfranchised grief as the griever's humanity is erased in a larger political conversation about pregnancy and bodily autonomy. When an expected happy event that may have been a topic of general conversation ends in sorrow, it can be hard to communicate and talk about, especially in a culture where pregnancy has become such a loaded event, and people fear feeding into political narratives when they are talking about their own personal experiences with pregnancy loss. Could talking about it feed into anti-choice narratives based on considering a fetus morally equivalent to a living person, justifying restrictions on access to abortion care?

"I realized that I was referring to my miscarriage in traditionally pro-life terms. I talked about 'losing my baby' and daydreamed of kicks and contractions. Typically it's pro-life activists who argue that life starts at conception, not pro-choicers like me. But my baby had certainly felt alive to me," wrote Julia Pelly,[13] who went through conflicted and intense emotions during her own pregnancy loss. "I felt guilty both for supporting women's choices to end their pregnancies and for feeling so sad about the end of mine. . . . I felt a great internal pressure to choose between seeing my baby as a baby or as a ball of cells, as a life or as nothing at all."

In this charged climate, pregnancy loss is not only pregnancy loss, but something the political right may try to take advantage of, without acknowledging or engaging with the very real grief of the parents, no matter their political or personal beliefs. Mourning an abortion, as some do, comes with added complexities, particularly with later abortion and terminations for medical reasons such as severe fetal abnormalities incompatible with life, where a wanted pregnancy may have been a matter of public knowledge and discussion. For unwanted pregnancies, not all people who choose abortion mourn the pregnancy, but some do, and they can feel immense pressure around how they talk about loss, turning their personal experience into a political moment. If you are sad about terminating a pregnancy, wanted or not, and you say so, some suggest you will be propping up right-wing narratives about abortion regret or fetal personhood, thereby undermining abortion access. Choosing to mourn pregnancy loss while also firmly supporting everyone's right to make the best choices for themselves is a struggle.

Threading the needle of mourning pregnancy—and, for some, relating on a personal level to a fetus as a potential life, a baby, while not wanting to dictate how other people relate to their pregnancies—is incredibly challenging in a nation where abortion became a hotbed issue after *Roe v. Wade* asserted protections for abortion access in 1973. Republicans fought viciously to undo it, succeeding in 2022 with the *Dobbs* decision. Their aggressive advocacy for more and more restrictions on abortion created a mythos around pregnancy that was incredibly dangerous: treating a fetus as a person whose rights may override those of the pregnant person; mandating burial of fetal remains; pushing for required reporting of all abortions and miscarriages; criminalizing abortion care; and at the same time undermining the safety net pregnant people need to carry a pregnancy safely and raise a child.

Some who choose abortion, particularly later abortion, rage at this as they tell their stories, to humanize the face of people who opt for pregnancy termination in defense of access to this very basic and private right, and to create space for people who may have very different feelings about their own personal abortions. Their willingness to speak, to expose themselves to sometimes hostile public comments, is a testimony to how firmly they want to defend this right, to shift the conversation to make room for more people and experiences.

In "Rivers of Babylon: The Story of a Third-Trimester

Abortion,"[14] T. S. Mendola wrote for *The Rumpus* about terminating a wanted pregnancy, addressing a deeply taboo subject unflinchingly and in graphic detail.

"Monday was the day we had to kill the baby," she said, describing the moment when she felt the baby awaken and start moving, shifting away from the digoxin injection. "I told him, please, please go to sleep. We have to do this for you now." The essay is starkly personal, while interweaving commentary about the political moment and the feeling of a somatic journey undertaken ultimately alone, even with a loving partner. She is disenfranchised because of the stigma of pregnancy loss and the silence that surrounds later abortion, as well as politics and the trajectory of the abortion rights movement, which "steals my right to say without fear of legal reprisal targeted at women like me that what happened next did feel like dismemberment, it did feel like desecration, like mutilation, that I did want his body intact."

She wrote also of being disenfranchised by her Judaism, and the limits set on funerary and burial rituals for infants or pregnancy losses: "There is no middle space of mourning beyond that; it is simply as if the child never existed to the community." For those who find refuge in faith, what an aching experience, to be abstracted from your people at the moment they are needed most, the pregnancy a leaf blowing on a swirling wind.

These political tensions have amplified the discomfort of talking about pregnancy loss, leaving grieving parents unsupported and sometimes actively pushed aside. They are not allowed to take time off work like they would have if the pregnancy had been carried to term and the baby had been born and then died. They are expected to grieve behind closed doors; they may have been the only ones to know about the pregnancy, and it feels awkward to announce that one is pregnant and also no longer pregnant at the same time. The mourning rituals of people who lose later pregnancies and experience stillbirths are viewed with discomfort: Spending time with a deceased child, taking photographs and footprints, marking the passage of a potential life that mattered very much, is to hold a shared grief for a moment, not move on as expected. This is something icky, and also frightening to some: If this person can lose a pregnancy, anyone can, and the griever becomes a black spot. Those who are trying to get pregnant may shy away, while those who are also experiencing pregnancy loss or struggles with fertility may have trouble connecting with fellow mourners because they do not even know they are mourning.

Everyone is an island ringed in blood.

A brief review of Reddit's "Am I the Asshole?" highlights another form of disenfranchised grief that can occur with pregnancy loss and infertility, an iteration of grief hijacking where the hijacking is coming from inside the house: What happens when expecting parents find themselves pushed to the side by their own family members and friends? Perhaps it was someone's parent, for example, who was eager to be a grandmother and treats the pregnancy loss as her personal, intimate loss, broadcasting her grief to the community. She may be feeling very legitimate, sometimes intense grief, but her failure to center the mourning parents can be devastating.

Posts from grieving parents trying to understand why the

people around them have coopted their grief are abundant. Mourners may sometimes find themselves pushed to offer emotional support to people who are not at the core of the loss. Aware of the way people react to pregnancy loss, some parents choose to conceal pregnancies until the last possible moment, to live in secrecy so that they do not have to manage other people's feelings, even as that isolation cuts them off from potential supports in the event of pregnancy loss. Nobody wins.

I had a brief conversation with a pair of parents when I brought by some food after their pregnancy loss, and they told me that they were shocked and disgusted to hear people talking about their pregnancy loss much like they had discussed the death of the family dog (it was a rough year) a few weeks earlier: You can always just get another one, right? Just try again!

Populations experiencing sustained mass traumas are also reckoning with politicized disenfranchised grief and the feeling of being abandoned by society—because if society recognized and cared about their trauma, there would be a bigger push to put an end to these cycles. Black communities face an epidemic of deaths caused by social inequalities within the frame of a white supremacist culture that expresses outrage and distaste for their expressions of grief.[15] Nearly a thousand people died trying to cross the harsh U.S.-Mexico border in 2022,[16] but the families of people from Latin America and elsewhere risking everything in the arid landscapes of the Southwest may not even have bodies to mourn,[17] and they are grieving people the U.S. government has dehumanized for decades. Thousands of Indigenous people are missing and murdered across the United

States,[18] their relatives fighting for recognition and investigative resources. Disabled people face a steady mass drip of deaths caused by violence within the medical complex and are told that these deaths are inevitable: She was very sick, after all—it's certainly sad, but there's no need to be *angry* about it. This experience of death and loss as a social and political identity is explored in Achille Mbembe's *Necropolitics,* which probes "the capacity to define who matters and who does not, who is disposable and who is not."

Decisions about how to respond to these kinds of deaths can be heartbreaking and stressful. Making decisions about how to leverage the political weight of a death while the body is still warm can feel crass, unseemly—the same thing the Till family must have grappled with while under the pressure to move quickly.

"It was necessary to take to the streets, to become not just mourners but militants. How else could one honor the dead, and prevent further deaths?" wrote Hannah Gold in an essay exploring what we owe both mourners and the dead for *The Baffler*.[19] For some people and bodies, existence is inherently political, and the fight to stay alive is an act of resistance, which turns death into something larger than themselves and the experiences of the people grieving them.

"Who is afforded a non-politicized death? Who is afforded a non-politicized life?" she asked.

These questions haunt some disenfranchised grievers facing pressing decisions about how, and if, to integrate a loss into a larger social and cultural conversation.

"It feels dirty to plot like this," Gold continued, "to utilize the real and present grief of others. But in this moment of urgency, it seems we are not above it. Maybe in a generation, I think, these dead will be able to rest." She was speaking to the realities of a world where the dead cannot rest because they are political symbols too, and their mourners share their losses with the world in a way that feels like losing autonomy and control.

Death comes with sharp edges. Who deserves, as Judith Butler has asked,[20] to be mourned, and how? If we acknowledge that disenfranchised grief is real and complex, and that people should be able to mourn the things they experience as losses, there's still a secondary question of how and whether they can mark those losses, what kinds of rituals and ceremonies are considered appropriate, and how much space they can take up in their grief.

That's perhaps exemplified by the ongoing debate over paid leave, one that many people are not even aware of until they need that leave, expect it, and are unpleasantly surprised. Pausing for a loss disrupts the machine of capitalism, requiring society to not just admit that something is a loss, but provide time for mourners to grieve that loss. As states have begun to explore mandates for not just protected but paid leave for mourning, which is a great start, the inclusion of chosen family is also essential, especially for people from communities where chosen and extended family are an important part of culture and values, such as the LGBTQIA+ community and communities of color—two groups disproportionately harmed by disenfranchised grief. Asking for leave from work, or trying to figure out the sheer logistics involved with loss, becomes so much more challenging if you are not among the category of workers codified as mourners. If a beloved cousin who was as close as a sibling dies, for example, a griever is supposed to keep their distress minimal, one friend told me as she endured precisely that situation, denied access to something as simple as paid bereavement leave and the accompanying access to solidarity, fellowship, and ritual, the ability to even attend the funeral.

Disenfranchised grief is not just about a loss—a death, a passage—but also about being denied access to emotions, sometimes in association with a loss, sometimes in association with a larger cultural context. Aside from the very concrete time people may need in the form of space away from work or the demands of daily life, mourners also need to feel like they can express themselves and talk about their experience, not just in the midst of immediate grief, but over the long term; it's unhealthy to suppress conversations about loss, to reject attempts at memorializing losses long after the fact, and unfortunately, Americans do just that. It's imperative to let people mourn on their own timeline and in their own way, and if it feels uncomfortable to witness someone's pain, imaginc how much more uncomfortable it is to experience it and to have that pain denied.

Under this framing, conversations about grief cannot be taken literally as conversations about death, and death cannot be interpreted as an individual issue, not least because everyone who dies knew numerous people, touched their lives in different ways. Loss affects us all, deeply, and some of us are feeling disenfranchised grief without even being aware of it. Expanding our understanding of loss and subsequent grief to realms beyond death and understanding that disenfranchisement often plays a role in non-death losses alongside stigmatized and politicized deaths are both key elements of better grief.

It is also important if we want to understand one another and treat each other with compassion; if disenfranchised grief is about invalidation, the opposite requires respect for and acknowledgment of a loss—even if it is something that we would not personally describe as a loss, something we don't see as a significant grief event, or something we cannot relate to because it is so far beyond our experience and imagination. Challenging disenfranchised grief asks not how you feel about someone's loss—a home that burned down, a pregnancy, mobility, a career, a death—but rather how you can view someone's loss with empathy and create space for it. Perhaps that's time off from work, or bringing casseroles, or commiserating with someone who is going through a huge life shift. Sometimes it is just listening, saying "I see you." It is not about questioning a loss and the emotions that come with it. Those are conversations we push outward, to people less affected.

Acknowledging disenfranchised grief may bring us a step closer to creating space for mourners to express themselves and work through and with their grief in a way that suits their individual circumstances, but that also requires engaging as a society with the reasons why some people (and animals), mourners, events, and deaths are devalued. It is not enough to put up a #BlackLivesMatter sign. We must think beyond the moments of individual deaths and into their structural implications: What can we do to address preventable deaths, so people don't have to fight for acknowledgment and the right to grieve on their own terms? How can we shift cultural frameworks so that when deaths and traumas occur, people are able to experience grief, rather than feeling pressured to suppress their feelings and move on to the next thing? Can we stop running from grief and the specters it raises—that we and everyone around us will die—and be in community with grievers instead? How can we respect cultural rituals and traditions around death and support those who practice them? Which other factors might be interacting with the way we approach grief? What happens when that grief is intensely politicized?

In a harsh helix, people experience disenfranchised grief because society minimizes their losses, sometimes by telling them to be silent, sometimes by thrusting them unwillingly into a spotlight that deprives them of their grief as a personal event. Those who cannot mourn because they are supposed to remain in silence or perform for society at large get stuck. We are all of us waiting for the real memorial, the funeral, the gathering, frozen in amber that is freezing and fracturing as it becomes apparent that these validations will never come, for an end to the ongoing trauma that dogs the heels of some grievers: The loss is not over. We see each other in passing, something about the eyes that is familiar, and we nod.

The notion of being "stuck" in grief is sometimes referred to as complicated or prolonged grief, a subject we will be exploring in more depth in a future chapter, and it raises uncomfortable questions about when grief is pathology, when it is a natural human response to loss, and when it is potentiated by feelings of disenfranchisement and the sense of being unheard, unaccepted. But it is undeniable that some people do find it difficult to figure out how to move forward with grief when their grief itself is rejected.

The way forward lies in honoring griefs, in viewing them as a plural that transcends death—and asking grievers what they want from those around them, recognizing that needs and wants may shift from day to day, year to year. Grief is not over once the body is neatly disposed of, the rubble of the house has been taken away in dumpsters, the final fit on the prosthesis is done, the gun control law is (ever?) passed and withstands legal challenges, the permanent peace is brokered. It is an ongoing shift in our relationship to the world and one that deserves attention and care as well as time and space to be among fellow mourners, to whom we do not need to justify or explain ourselves, for they understand where we are. There must be something better than disenfranchised grief, this experience that slowly erodes the sense of self and place in a society that feels cruelly out of step.

So much of disenfranchised grief is an "I hadn't thought of that," a lack of empathy for people cultivated by a culture that very much does not want people to "think of that," to recognize sorrow and loss and struggle in each other. We don't understand it until we experience it, suddenly thrust into a world where it's clear that people don't think about us or our grief, don't acknowledge that what we are experiencing is grief, that our losses are very real and weigh heavily on us, that they do not end on anyone else's timeline. We struggle culturally to stop for grief and allow mourners to express themselves and live in their feelings, as complex and challenging and hard as they can be, whether they face the perceived "insignificant" loss of a pet or a death that occurs on a global stage, all eyes hungry for details, the mourner obscured in a cloak of headlines. Without creating that space, we will forever be caught in a logjam of sorrow.

Chapter 8

Ash and Tricycle // Inevitability

In the original earliest iterations of this book, when it was still a series of half-formed ideas jotted in a notebook, this chapter had a different title: "Ash and Ember."

Ash and Ember were my fire cats: In the fall of 2017 when wildfires raged across Northern California, animal care services in many areas were overloaded with strays and evacuees, crates piling up in hallways, dogs housed two to a kennel, and for open-admission facilities that had to take all comers, that sometimes forced difficult conversations about how to make room for incoming animals that urgently needed help.

Loki had just died and I didn't want another cat just yet, even as my house felt echoing and strange, empty but for me for the first time as an adult. My luggage from my trip to Chicago was barely unpacked, but every time I opened the internet, I saw a gaping maw of need, a desperate competition for resources. I knew that I couldn't fix the larger structural issues of climate disasters on my own, but maybe I could make a small difference in two lives.

I walked into Mendocino Animal Care Services, our county's open-admission shelter, with two cat carriers and asked for whichever two cats they were having trouble adopting, which is how I ended up with Ash and Ember, huddling in their carriers on the way home, cautiously poking their noses out when I opened them in the living room. Watching them carefully explore my house and argue with each other to determine who should be in charge (Ember), I promised myself something: I would prepare for their deaths in advance, knowing that those deaths would be coming whether I was ready or not. Through Ember, I learned that all the preparation in the world cannot stop you from being ambushed by loss, but it can make navigating the logistics of loss slightly easier and less terrible, less alien and frantic, with less scrabbling to figure out what to do and more ability to sit with loss, to embrace quiet, to be still, to feel a form of comfort in knowing that you have a plan for what to do, even if you have to live through it.

"Ash and I have been alone since the summer of 2021, and his hostility toward other cats makes it likely to stay that way," I wrote in my book proposal in the summer of 2024. After I sold it, I adopted another cat, a nameless orange kitten who came into the shelter with a rear leg so shattered that Dr. Clare decided to amputate it. I watched the surgery, fascinated by the way she parted flesh and tendon, moving swiftly and surely; it looked, if I am going to be honest, somewhat like deboning chicken.

The vet staff named him Tricycle and I took him home, attached to him in a way and for a reason I couldn't really articulate, which I feel is the process through which most people acquire new cats. I was afraid that Ash would despise him, but instead, he was immediately curious, gentle, playful, like a tolerant uncle with a rambunctious nephew, and within days they were curling up together on my bed, Tricycle purring ferociously. Perhaps it was because I had already gotten a look at Tricycle's inner workings, but I looked at him and thought about the words of Joslin Roth of Resting Waters, a pet crematory in Seattle, Washington, when we had a conversation about pet memorials: "If more people paid attention to skeletons as a whole, they would see how much beauty is in them as works of art."

Under my hands, Tricycle's tiny ribs felt like matchsticks, they were so delicate. The shape of his skull under my fingers when I scratched between his ears felt familiar and solid despite his size. It was hard to imagine death for something so small and vibrantly full of life and curiosity, fascinated by a world full of new things; I could see why so many people shy away from thinking about the end-of-life at the beginning of life, which made it feel all the more urgent to confront the inevitable. As his custodian, and the person ultimately responsible for the quality and level of care and love he will receive throughout his life—which could extend for eighteen years or even longer—I have a duty of care to him to think about his future needs in a moment when I can do so with a clear head, not in the moment when facing bad news and hard decisions. While you cannot plan for every eventuality, you shouldn't be thinking during a crisis about what kinds of medical procedures and treatments you are willing to pursue, what living the good life looks like, what intractable pain and suffering look like.

Preparing to make decisions about the end-of-life in advance may be uncomfortable, but it frees grievers to focus on the process of spending time with their loved one through their transitions, instead of making wrenching choices without enough information, or spending time scrambling for logistics when they are trying to mourn. For those tasked with the care of other living beings, this too is a form of care, and one to be approached with respect and kindness as part of the responsibility we have taken on. And for everyone, advanced planning and communication can be a powerful gift for loved ones that goes much deeper than practicality.

These conversations about death and our wishes, for me, are deeply grounded by my experience as a disabled person. The disability community has a long, deep history of feeling connected to each other through and beyond death. Many of us die early, not just because of underlying impairments, but because of the disablist society we live in. Death is an ever-present companion, as disabled icon and cultural force Alice Wong wrote of her "shadow partner" in *Time*.[1] While it's impossible to generalize across all disability spaces, in mine, conversations about death are very normal, whether we're whistling in the dark or mourning a comrade or clearly communicating our boundaries and wishes to each other. And we honor and celebrate not just our disabled elders but our ancestors, as well as the wisdom they pass down that lingers in our lives.

In a conversation about death and disability, the wise voice of my friend Sandy Ho says: "I know this is a conversation we have a lot amongst our friends, especially in our upper thirties and forties folks, checking in: Do you have your person? If it's not a family member, have you written the things down yet? There's a very particular disability part of this. And I think how incredible it would be if nondisabled folks would also take this approach—like, the labor of grief comes in so many different forms that I just wonder what it would look like to actually have infrastructure or support around that beyond just leaning on your friends or family (and even that is such a privilege)."

Inevitability should not be confused with universality. Death is inevitable. Each death is completely different, not just on an individual level but a cultural one, and context is everything, informing both what one wants in the broader sense and how that connects to community. By extension, this also affects planning for it—which makes the things one maps out ahead of time especially important. A tragedy isn't lessened by knowing that the deceased wanted to be cremated, but knowing that someone wanted to be cremated alleviates some of the stress for mourners who don't have to agonize over the most loving and respectful disposition of the remains.

The death of a loved one in hospice is very different from the sudden, sharp shock of a medical crisis or car accident, a death of despair or a death driven by white supremacy or disablism. Understanding the inevitability of grief for all of us necessitates a shared understanding that while death comes for us all, grief manifests in very different ways across people and lives and is deeply informed by the manner of death.

In Matthew 10:29 (KJV), the reader is asked, "Are not two sparrows sold for a farthing? and one of them shall not fall on the ground without your Father." The verse is commonly interpreted to mean that this god cares about every death, no matter how seemingly trivial and small. But this sentiment feels hollow in an era when some deaths are considered worthy of attention and care and others are not, an attitude that carries over into how we think about these deaths and their accompanying needs—such as the acute, immediate, unexpected, and sometimes very costly[2] need for funeral services when a young Black person dies due to pregnancy complications or a disabled person goes to the ER for a dislodged G-tube and leaves via the loading dock.

If a life doesn't matter, if god turns an eye away from a particular sparrow, it is inevitable not because this is the human condition, but because society has made it so, and that complicates both planning and mourning. Undervalued lives may end in silence or a collective scream, but this is not necessarily a cultural reflection on the circumstances of their inevitability. In fact, sometimes the deceased are blamed for and denied control over their own deaths, as in their lives.

Thinking about whose deaths are considered grievable and worthy of any kind of social pause, Sarah Chavez, one of the founders of the Death Positive movement, tells me: "There's a version that's racist and gendered and prejudiced, saying that people aren't worthy of our grief because their lives didn't matter. We see this play out all the time, we see a lot of discourse about the murder of Eric Garner at the hands of police and then passing all these judgments about the victim—he was a criminal, shouldn't have been selling cigarettes, should have been compliant. Or deaths of immigrants in ICE detention centers, almost all of which were preventable, blamed on their decision, their choice to immigrate: 'They did that to themselves, they were asking for it.' The list goes on: the West's indifference to the deaths of Palestinians or transgender women. We see this play out in deeply disturbing ways throughout the pandemic, people refusing to wear masks, making statements about 'the old and disabled.'"

Shouldn't have worn that. Shouldn't have broken the law. Should have known better. So many obituaries and social narratives around these fallen sparrows focus on finding fault in their lives and persons, focusing, for example, on the fact that someone was a sex worker or had a minor criminal conviction on their record. But the deceased isn't the one who should be held responsible for existing in the world: Society has chosen those deaths.

How do you plan for the inevitable when that plan is tinged with infuriation resulting from the acute awareness of the fact that while death itself is inevitable, so many deaths are untimely, out of order, unjust? What parent wants to look on an infant and ask themselves whether they will be burying their child after a freak bike accident or terminal cancer? Why should Black parents have to have "the talk" with their children about interacting with police, fearing the specter of what should be a benign encounter turning into another statistic, when white children are not offered a corresponding talk in resisting racism and abolishing policing? Why should trans people have to gather to mourn murder after murder? Why should disabled people have to watch filicide after filicide and hear from the media that parents were "overwhelmed" by the "burden" of their disabled children, that they were justified in their heinous actions?

In these circumstances, the call to think about pre-planning doesn't carry quite the same ring as it does when talking to an adult facing a terminal diagnosis of cancer, or an eighty-year-old wanting to focus on treasuring time with people in their remaining years. But that pre-planning is not a concession, a shrug, a giving up, a sense that people should stop trying, and it shouldn't be interpreted that way.

This is not the only arena in which conversations about what we might want from our deaths and subsequent ceremonies are not universal and require cultural and social context. The recent flowering of conversations about what a "good death" should look like, for example, have also included more encouragement of planning ahead, but sometimes that encouragement is compounded by expectations of what a "good death" should be that may be very rooted in a very specific lived experience, spilling over into conversations about the end-of-life, imposing particular ideas onto deeply personal and cultural beliefs. How and where people want to die, what they want to happen to their remains, how they want people to mark their passage—these are all very intimate questions with answers deeply informed by who we are.

Some, for example, are rejecting extensive medical interventions, viewing this as part of a good death. Atul Gawande's book *Being Mortal* sparked significant conversations in this arena, spurring readers to think about the extensive and sometimes very expensive treatments available at end-of-life, balancing those against what they might want socially or culturally. Medicare data, which provides a wealth of information about health care spending in general, but especially at end-of-life, finds that a huge percentage of spending occurs at the end. A study in *The American Journal of Hospice and Palliative Care* in 2019[3] (the last "normal year" used to establish a baseline because the disruptions of the COVID-19 pandemic are still settling out, clouding the numbers) identified a range of somewhere between 13 and 19 percent of health care spending involving patients in the last year of their lives. The same study also introduced important questions about the quality of that care, noting that "more effective use of palliative care and hospice benefits offers a lower cost, higher quality alternative for patients at end of life." In a capitalist society, end-of-life spending is sometimes considered a problem to be solved,[4] rather than a symptom of a system that may be broken; but in this particular case, spending less and refocusing that spending on care, not chasing cures, may actually result in a better outcome for some.

For others, though, all possible measures are an important part of their values, for a variety of reasons, ranging from cultural beliefs to an acute awareness of a history of medical discrimination that has condemned many marginalized people with entirely treatable conditions to death or hastened the deaths of the dying. For them, advocacy around death and dying carries an intergenerational, traumatic weight of knowing that fierce self-advocacy is necessary to stay alive, as Serena Williams testified in a 2018 *Vogue* cover story,[5] talking about how she, a highly educated athlete and one of the most renowned women in the world, had to fight to stay alive when she experienced complications in labor and delivery with her first child. When Williams detected the early warning signs of a blood clot, medical staff at first didn't trust her knowledge of her own body. Had she not persisted, she would have died. If a wealthy, powerful woman with access to high-quality care can risk dying because she is Black and pregnant, one can see why some communities might distrust pressure to forgo "extreme measures" in end-of-life care. What one person might view as extreme could be routine and lifesaving for someone else, or personally and culturally important to them, even when outsiders may not agree with their decisions.

If planning around a "good death" and subsequent "good grief" is presented within a very narrow framework, rather than an open conversation, it can do more harm than good. And it can be difficult, at times, to separate our own motives and desires in these conversations, to decenter what we want and actually listen to a loved one telling us what *they* want. I think here about my own resistance to heroic measures in medical care for myself contrasted with the very valid fears of many other disabled people who fear abandonment, abuse, and disablism in the medical-industrial complex, pushing for all possible treatments because they know how many of us have died through neglect, through societal attitudes that our lives are not of value. I may choose a DNR for myself, but I should trust other people to make their own informed decisions; my personal values are not universal ethics, nor should they be. If asked what I want for myself, I will offer it, but I will not tell someone else how to feel.

The growing interest in "green" burial practices designed to limit environmental impact is another example of a conversation that can, at times, disregard cultural traditions and set forth an expected way to mourn at a time when people are already struggling to balance the conflicting expressed wishes of decedents and loved ones. Colleen of Queer Death Collective-PDX, a community that supports dead and dying people, reflects on this tendency as they talk about working with Black families.

"Look at embalming! In Black culture it's really important, because the families are so spread out. In my experience, I have supported people who are like 'I have to get my grandmother embalmed because I have family coming from Atlanta.' And then we have people who are like 'That's dirty, that's bad for the environment.' That is just part of that culture, we have to honor that. They have to get across the country because we've pushed them out."

Embalming may be viewed with distaste by some green funeral advocates, but when it is an important part of a community and culture, pressuring people to forgo embalming is merely repeating a long history of telling others how to live and die. For some, it's not just a question of ensuring that everyone in the family can attend visitation with the deceased but also a larger part of the cultural practice. People *want* to embalm as an expression of love and care for the departed. To *not* embalm is disrespectful.

End-of-life conversations and planning should start with storytelling. The first question isn't what you want done with your body but what kind of life you've lived, and how the values you've formed have influenced your experiences. What are you proud of? What do you regret? What is important to you? That storytelling is just as much a part of the conversation as a frank discussion about disposition of effects and the body; if you loved animals, your values might include directing your estate to an animal welfare organization, for example. This shouldn't come as a surprise when you die!

Talking about end-of-life wishes doesn't have to be a huge, singular, serious conversation, and it should in fact consist of many smaller opportunities to talk. These should reflect the spirit of the person at their core, because planning is about capturing values key to their identity and way of moving through the world, alive or dead. The more you discuss, the deeper and more thoughtful those conversations can become; or maybe you are the kind of person who wants to get to it right out the gate with directions to the grove of trees where you want people to scatter your ashes.

The best time to have conversations about what you want in death are when it's not pressing. Instead, you can offer the people around you a gift, settling matters that they shouldn't have to decide in the heat of the moment. Taking time to communicate about what you want also allows you to investigate logistics: Make sure that what you want is possible, that people know how to set your wishes into motion. The tradition in the funeral industry of pre-planning—meeting with a funeral director to establish a very clear plan for your funeral and prepay at the same time—is valuable for a reason: It allows your loved ones to know exactly what you want. And this level of detail doesn't have to be limited to a formal agreement with a funeral director. If you want your body cared for at home, for example, understand applicable state and local laws, potential barriers to that care, and the willingness of the people around you to care for you in that very intimate way. What do you want if your body sustains significant trauma that makes home death care challenging or impossible? Know your options and your backup plans.

I think of five big questions in these conversations.

The first is more of a "who" than a "what": **Who do you want involved at various stages of your dying processes and in the rites that follow?** For some people, this may seem like a question with an obvious answer, but for others, it's a lot more fraught, and an important one to answer before considering the next four. The people you love are not always the people you trust. The people you are supposed to love are not always the ones you consider to be your family. Not everyone you trust can be trusted with all things. Making sure that you understand who you want to be involved has big stakes, especially if you belong to a marginalized community or are helping someone who does, someone who may have very real fears about what might happen in a medical emergency and to their remains.

Some abridgments of rights can continue even into death, stripping people of autonomy over their bodies to the bitter end. For trans people, for example, misgendering and abuse in death are unfortunately all too common; if trans people struggle to access affirming and competent care in life, it is perhaps no surprise that this happens in death as well, from the treatment they receive at funeral homes to how their deaths are spoken about. We may be misgendered or deadnamed—referring to us by our prior names, rather than the ones we used at the time of our deaths—in obituaries or on headstones, sometimes due to carelessness and at other times due to malice, trans people may face barriers to trauma-informed death care such as gendered end-of-life services that require them to closet themselves to access the care they need. When people are buried under the wrong names and the death certificates and the identifications they leave behind reference the wrong name and gender, it is another kind of death. Trans and otherwise gender nonconforming people are weighed down by these fears and considerations, so the assurance that people are looking out for them and won't allow them to be erased in death can be a comfort, an important element of a good death.

The same can also be true for people who have left or joined faiths, and may have religious considerations around their death and final rites: If you have left a faith, you may not want your care entrusted to a family member who has fixed, religious ideas about your end-of-life. If you have joined a faith and your family hasn't accepted it, they might deny you the rites that are important to your faith identity.

Maybe "who" is an easy socially and legally answered question: a spouse, a parent, an oldest child. Maybe it's not, and you should make sure that the people around you know that, and that your wishes are clearly expressed in a fashion that's legally enforceable. That legal backing can be powerful for the people you trust with your care should they encounter resistance to their role. Take the time to make sure you understand the law when it comes to not only who can make medical decisions for you but who can take charge of the disposition of your remains, since in some regions the law draws a distinction between these parties.

You need to know if the people you are entrusting with these decisions agree with you about your wishes, will support what you actually want, and will be able to make decisions aligned with your values and wants if something goes off the rails. You also want to make sure that those people don't live with regrets or fears that they didn't live up to your expectations and needs in death. If you don't have people in your personal life who can fill that role, that doesn't mean you have to be left out in the cold, whether that means working with a death doula, a designated third party, an advocate from hospice, or another death worker who is comfortable with being your advocate.

What are your quality-of-life considerations? Thinking about end-of-life on a continuum, rather than a binary divide, opens up greater possibilities but also more unknowns. In the capitalist, disablist society we inhabit, assumptions about quality of life are very common: For example, many think that life with a "serious disability" is not worth living, and they express that in their advance directives and with friends. If you fear a life using a wheelchair for mobility, using a ventilator to breathe, why? Are there factors that might change your opinion about the kind of life you want to live, such as access to services and supports to help you thrive?

Sara Goering, a philosopher and bioethicist, is a professor of philosophy and core faculty in the University of Washington's Ethics and Disability Studies Program. She focuses on disability through a feminist lens, and she cuts to the heart of this issue when I call her to talk about disability ethics around death and dying.

"Thinking about a life worth living," she says, a disability "might be challenging in a variety of ways, but it doesn't have to be life-ending. Many people jump to conclusions that I think are really ableist without fully understanding what such a life would be like or could be like, because of course the world is deeply ableist."

Goering, like me, also worries about the context in which quality-of-life conversations happen because "we're not providing realistic or high-value other options" to people facing life with significant impairments. People faced with a lack of resources—or limited exposure to disabled people living fulfilling lives, who might model ways to live and thrive with disability—may feel backed into a corner. If I were asked to choose between rotting in a bed in a nursing home and death, I might choose death; but if I knew that I could be out living in my community, that if I developed pressure sores they would be treated rather than left to fester and kill me, I might feel differently. A disabled or impaired body does not necessarily have to imply a hopeless quality of life. It's a different life, perhaps, but not necessarily a bad one.

"In the philosophical literature," Goering says, "people push back and forth between objective measures of quality of life—which are often defined by nondisabled people, and employed problematically in policy—and subjective quality-of-life measures." Those subjective measures are influenced by the society we live in; they are mutable, if we want to put in the work. But for a single individual at a cusp of decision-making, an abstract conversation about policy may not feel particularly relevant. The question isn't whether we should live in a society in which disabled lives have value and are supported (yes, we should), but what world we live in right now, which needs are immediate in this moment, if and how they can be met.

And for some, a life with some form of disability is considered truly intolerable, whether or not there are mediating factors that might affect quality of life, because the impairment itself is the issue, a breaking point of suffering. Some cannot imagine moving through their lives with a given impairment, even if it's one that others view as manageable and survivable—frustrating at times, perhaps, but not intrinsically terrible. These feelings about end-of-life shouldn't be dismissed, and we shouldn't pretend all impairments are created equally, that all experiences of disability are equivalent, that everyone should feel the same way about their disability. All disabilities carry their own hardships, but some are extremely difficult, especially in our present culture; and while internalized disablism may interact with the way someone feels about an impairment, that's not the whole story. The cultural phenomenon of believing that disability is worse than death is pernicious and troubling, and it clearly influences the way people think about quality of life, but people shouldn't be forced to bear the burden of society's sins when they are making difficult decisions for themselves.

It would also be foolish to pretend that all forms of embodiment are negotiable; pain is a commonly cited end-of-life fear, illustrated by reviews of advance directives,[6] with people worrying both about uncontrollable pain in their last days[7] and pain associated with death itself. "It was painless" is a common reassurance when talking about a death. In 2005, *San Francisco Chronicle* journalist Alicia Rose Parlette took readers through the journey of her diagnosis with cancer, her subsequent treatment and struggles, and eventual death, and one thing that stuck with me was her description of Actiq, a pain medication provided in a lollipop-like format[8] to make it easier to take that she used to manage her acute, intractable pain: the kind of pain that people describe when they talk about wanting to die rather than endure continued suffering; the kind of pain that led her, ultimately, to focus on comfort care rather than continued aggressive medical interventions and more pain, as was her right.[9] The series resonated with me for its raw frankness, for her generosity in sharing her illness and eventual death with readers.

Sometimes that pain threshold is hard to predict or understand as an abstract, when it is not something that you are actually going through. If at times we catastrophize pain, sparking even more intense fears, we also live in a culture that minimizes and dismisses pain, especially chronic pain; we pressure people to accept it as part of life, in a world where poorly controlled pain is characterized as unavoidable. In that context, I can see why pain becomes a subject of intense fear.

We all fear the unknown, but talking with dying people themselves is a good start. Talking to people who interact with death and the dying can also be a helpful entry into answering questions about quality of life. Hospice nurses, death doulas, and palliative care physicians, for example, have extensive experience to draw upon and can offer advice and information rooted in that experience. They can also demystify some of the elements of dying and talk about what to expect: the sounds and sights and smells of death and dying. It can be less frightening to encounter a huge transition when you understand what's going to happen and how, whether that's a detailed discussion of how the body changes in the days and hours before death or a step-by-step discussion of the process of taking end-of-life medications. Understanding what your quality of life might look and feel like with various options lets you make a more informed choice.

I have never died and will get only one shot at it. I know this only as an observer—I can only guess at what my quality of life might be like as my senses slowly turn inward, my body more reflexive than responsive—so it behooves me to think about understanding and communicating my values.

How do you want to die? Do you want to die at home, perhaps surrounded by loved ones, in a space that is familiar, looking at the things and places you've known all your life, with your animals and routines of home and other familiar elements that enriched your life around you? Or do you think you will be more comfortable in a hospital, a standalone hospice? Are you interested in hospice and palliative care, which are gaining ground in the United States (so much so that private equity has swooped[10] in to take advantage of what it sees as a growing market)? This approach to care in death supports people through the dying process—with an aim to making it more comfortable, not necessarily to prolong life or stave off death—and does not leave you to your own devices without supportive care.

If you're not sure, sit down and pick through your fears and wants, think about which options might serve you better—and think about how you will feel if your best-case scenario doesn't work out. Have you talked with potential care providers and loved ones about what you want the dying process to look like?

Plans go awry, and plans are also hard to enact when people don't make them or don't think about how they will be enacted.

A 2017 Kaiser Family Foundation study found that about 70 percent of people want to die at home,[11] for example, but a 2019 analysis of mortality data[12] found that only about 31 percent of people actually get to do so.

While the idea of the birth plan has become widely popularized—and in some circles dismissed and even mocked, as things pertaining to birthing people often are—there's less acceptance of a death plan. Whether that plan is a few pieces of paper or a detailed binder, it's yours to write and circulate among the people who need to know. If you have specific concerns around medicalized elements of death and dying, make sure they are spelled out in an advance directive or similar document that's kept with your other medical information, and talk to the people named on that document about their responsibilities.

What do you want to happen with your body? Is that even important to you? Have you talked with the people around you about these wants and learned more about how they feel?

Perhaps you want to be buried in a traditional cemetery, or cremated. Maybe the idea of a green burial appeals to you, or you want to be composted. Or maybe, like me, you want to be burned on an open pyre or left out for the vultures to eat. Alas, there appears to be only one open pyre in the United States, at the Crestone End of Life Project in Colorado.[13] And the vultures won't eat my remains unless someone is willing to pull an Edward Abbey and violate the law,[14] sneaking my remains into the high desert or some other lonely place to fulfill my last wishes, which is a tall order. (Also, I do feel a certain degree of guilt at the idea that someone might stumble across my mortal remains while out on a nice nature hike.) With my preferred options out, I'm forced to think more conservatively: either alkaline hydrolysis (aka "aquamation") or dumping me in a hole in the ground with a shroud. Maybe, like me, you want to donate to organ and tissue banks, to medical research. Maybe you want to be shot out of a cannon, pressed into a diamond, mixed into substrates used to create artificial reefs.

How do those wishes interact with your faith, spiritual practices, potential lack thereof, and your surrounding community?

Do you want people to be able to mourn with your body? To sit vigil with you? For some, dressing and sitting with a body are an important part of the mourning process, while others don't find this important or may even find it uncomfortable and traumatic. If there are tensions between what you want and what the people around you might want, that could abridge your wishes in death. When the wishes of dying and griever conflict, negotiating those tensions before crisis, before death, creates the space for more time to reflect, more thoughtful conversations.

Do you want a witnessed cremation or burial, or would you prefer that those who knew you leave your body in the hands of professionals?

Some grieving traditions and methods of disposition are privileged over others, thanks to the role of white supremacy—a key consideration in conversations like these and in plans for carrying out people's wishes.

"Offerings left on the graves are also really a common part of our grief rituals, but most U.S. cemeteries have policies that items can't be placed on graves or they will be removed after twenty-four hours, to keep the cemetery looking clean. This aesthetic is prized: looking clean over grief," comments Sarah Chavez when describing the sanitation of mourning practices. This is something that may become a sticking point in conversations about what, exactly, we want to have happen to our bodies and at our gravesites, because what we want may conflict with societal or familial expectations, policies, and the law.

What kind of ritual do you want? How do you want to be remembered?

I ran into my therapist at a "celebration of life" a few months ago—the sort of thing that happens in a small town where, when somebody dies, the degrees of separation are never very distant. Both of us mourned the deceased in our session the following week, but we also expressed distaste for the sterility of the event: no body, some light refreshments, unmemorable music, a bit of milling around awkwardly before a few people said a few words and then things broke up. It could have been a meeting of the local Democratic club. I reflected that this was exactly what I wouldn't want, that I would rather have nothing than a bland event where everyone was afraid to use the *D*-word.

My father told me that he wanted me to throw a big party for him, with live music and good food, everyone having a good time as they came together to celebrate; what happened to his body, he said, wasn't terribly important to him, but going out with a bang was. He joked that he wanted me to hand out red envelopes with random amounts of money at the door, a little quirky tribute for people who decided to show up to mark his passing. (I happily accommodated.) It's something that speaks to his quixotic spirit, tinged with the fear so many of us have that we will pass into the vale unremembered, that no one will gather to mourn us.

"My family is from Mexico," says Sarah Chavez, "so there was always a lot of death talk in the house. My grandmother has always had her funeral planned, and she talks about it in almost every conversation: who's going to be there, what music she wants, what color car she wants the family to drive in. 'It's going to be a party and I have to miss it, I'm so mad.' It's very much talked about as any other subject would be." She notes this is an experience very different to that of many white families. The funeral is acknowledged as an inevitable life event, and a sad one, but also one that provides an opportunity for a little party planning from beyond the veil.

Ritual has social, emotional, and cultural importance. It is potent magic. This is a once-in-a-lifetime opportunity, featuring people who will never all be gathered together in this way again, linked by a shared loss that has affected all of them differently. Some of these people will never see each other again. We talk about memorable weddings but less often about banger funerals. I want my funeral to capture the distinct things about me, to celebrate the community I have built and contribute to. I want it to be funny and fun, because I am a deeply unserious person. I want people to remember it, to talk about it, to say, "That's the kind of funeral I'd love to have."

For some, it is also deep healing, whether that healing comes from ritual or conversation or an opportunity to collectively pause and mark a passing. In marginalized communities, these kinds of gatherings can be critical, not only for celebrating the dead but for contextualizing that death in a larger social sphere. The goal is not to be fixed or cured, to come out of a funeral feeling as though you have successfully completed something; the goal is to hold people close in a culture where grief and loss can be incredibly isolating and lonely.

Do you also want to take control of your parting words and mark on the world?

"At the tender age of ninety-six, in the Year of the Tiger 2070, Alice Wong died," wrote Alice Wong in her 2022 book, *Year of the Tiger.* "She took her time with both her work and the pleasures of life, as someone who did not find success until her late forties. Known for throwing excellent parties, savoring a good latte and a pastry, being a benevolent Bossy Boss to close friends and comrades, and messing around at all hours of the night."

As a writer and a ferocious advocate and a general all-round badass, Alice wanted to make sure her obituary was done right, especially because she was acutely aware that the way people talk about disabled people in death can be very dehumanizing. (I can also testify that an Alice Wong party was always a good time, filled with fantastic food and a well-curated group of people.)

Alice left us instead on November 14, 2025, the year of the Wood Snake. Ever the organized planner, though, she directed our friend Sandy to post her pre-written obituary, writing: "Hi everyone, it looks like I ran out of time. I have so many dreams that I wanted to fulfill and plans to create new stories for you. There are a few in progress that might come to fruition in a few years if things work out. I did not ever imagine I would live to this age and end up a writer, editor, activist, and more. As a kid riddled with insecurity and internalized ableism, I could not see a path forward. It was thanks to friendships and some great teachers who believed in me that I was able to fight my way out of miserable situations into a place where I finally felt comfortable in my skin. We need more stories about us and our culture. You all, we all, deserve the everything and more in such a hostile, ableist environment. Our wisdom is incisive and unflinching. I'm honored to be your ancestor and believe disabled oracles like us will light the way to the future. Don't let the bastards grind you down. I love you all."

If newspapers have prewritten obituaries that smolder on a file for years or decades, why shouldn't you get the jump on them and craft your own obituary, a chance to have the final word, something that I find immensely appealing? Obituaries written by or in collaboration with the dying have a special, beautiful spark that captures their personality in a way that I deeply love. They are an opportunity to speak from beyond, reminding people of our humanity, that we are more than names, dates, "survived by."

Legacies can take so many different forms. I especially love a memorial that speaks to the personality of the deceased in a way that invites engagement from beyond the grave, which is why I called archivist Rosie Grant, who runs a delightful project called the Ghostly Archive. The project started when she interned at Congressional Cemetery in Washington, D.C.—a place where she tells me she'd also like to be buried—and grew a life of its own from there.

Grant travels the country finding gravestones with recipes and then making them, sometimes with varying degrees of success on the first try. Her followers are quick to provide her with tips, tricks, and critiques. She tells me that most of them involve sweets, and many of the decedents are women, including Naomi Odessa Miller-Dawson, the Brooklyn woman with a spritz cookie recipe that started it all. Grant has collected fascinating stories about the people behind those headstones along the way, a rich slice of oral history that ensures these people live on along with the context of their lives.

I have to ask, and she has an answer ready to hand: "For my own headstone recipe, I have a clam linguine that I really like. It's pretty simple; it would fit on a headstone."

And then, of course, there are some other crude planning logistics that may be exceedingly boring but are also critically important because, as they say, you can't take it with you. This goes deeper than a will with basic legal information about what you want to happen. (And if you don't have a will, definitely write one!) There are more logistics and practicalities surrounding death that will be a lot easier to handle if someone thought ahead and tried to make the path a little smoother.

I have an "If I'm dead, look here" folder.

It contains all the information I think a person winding down the remains of my life might need: a complete list of bank accounts, credit cards, utilities, things that autobill and when, account numbers, and contact information for key people laid out across a two-page document. Where to find my car title and birth certificate, my safe deposit box keys, my advance directive and will—the legal things surrounding a life that can feel overwhelming to track down in a moment of grief. Contact information for Ash's and Tricycle's vet, and all their medical records. Listed beneficiaries on my accounts so people wrapping up my life can access money for things such as handling my body and paying bills immediately without waiting for probate. It's a surprising amount of bureaucracy for a single person who tries to live a low-impact life.

A person could, if they wanted—and someone is going to have to do it—sit down with it for half an hour and cancel all my credit cards, close my utility accounts, direct my (limited) assets to the appropriate places. At the same time that there is something kind of depressing about that, quietly breaking down a life and packing it away, I also hope that whoever has to do that appreciates that I took some time to make it as easy as possible for them. They don't have to fear zombie autopayments, wonder how to contact my agent, or go sleuthing to locate and reach out to the people who were important in my life. They don't have to wonder if I have savings or a life insurance policy squirreled away somewhere that might end up as unclaimed property. (According to the state of California, the state receives millions of dollars in cash, bonds, stocks, securities, insurance policies, and other assets each year that belong to people who haven't claimed them and might not even know they exist.)

Numerous companies sell an assortment of kits that are designed to facilitate the process of coming up with a detailed breakdown of the crude logistics of life, and some people seem to find them useful, though I am an inveterate cheapskate and refuse to pay for something that I feel I can assemble myself, especially in an era of capitalism when we have so much pressure to consume endless things, even in death. I also find myself haunted by and distrustful of a service I keep seeing in social media ads implying that compiling all this information is, of course, the responsibility of "the wife" in a traditional heterosexual, monogamous marriage. It's presented as a fun activity akin to scrapbooking, with a model who looks like a Mormon mommy blogger enthusiastically and painstakingly applying stickers to a series of gentrifier gray file folders. While I appreciate the uncanny accuracy of algorithms and their (usually correct) assumption that I want to see any and all death content, in this particular case, they're missing the mark.

Whatever floats your boat, I guess: The point is to get it done. Get it done now. You never know when someone might need it, and it might take a few hours with reminders to update it periodically, but it will save someone a lot of stress on the other end, one among a number of legacies that you can leave behind. Watching friends wrap up the estates of family members who did absolutely no preparation was a sharp lesson in not wanting to subject another human being to that. That might just be in my nature, but it should be in everyone's.

"The best gift you can give your family is to give them the confidence that they know how to make decisions on your behalf," says Lisa Pahl, a licensed clinical social worker who views her Death Deck game, a series of cards offering lively and provocative prompts for conversations about death, as one among a number of tools people can use to open up conversations about this topic and all the decisions that need to happen in and around death. The cards are rooted in her real-world experience, raising a number of practicalities without getting too heavy. It's always a hit at parties, but that might just be at my house.

"It's really stressful, and then in grief, people are second-guessing themselves all the time. Did I do the right thing? There's no do-overs, and people live with that, they wonder. It's really hard. If we can help people by having some conversations, at least starting the conversation, they can keep going back to it. It can help increase that confidence, so that time can be a little less chaotic."

In a death-avoidant culture, these conversations can be tense, and sometimes that means having them in bits and pieces, nibbling at them, finding a way into an uncomfortable topic through humor or indirect means, such as commenting on someone else's funeral or talking about the end-of-life choices someone else is making. The existential terror that we connect with death encourages us to deny the inevitable, but while some of us can evade taxes, we cannot avoid the thing that's waiting at the end of the hall for all of us.

I watch Ash and Tricycle zoom around the house, Ash sometimes getting fed up and launching himself onto a surface too high for Tricycle to reach, and I do find a kind of comfort in knowing that I've thought about the ends of their lives, what I want to happen and how, the choices I would make. It's freeing, in a sense, to know that when the inevitable comes, I can focus on spending time with them. I want the people around me to have that too, at the end. Who wouldn't?

Chapter 9

Little Grey // Euthanasia

Like many animal-loving children, I spent a brief period of my childhood longing to be a veterinarian, envisioning myself as a kindly doctor surrounded by happy kittens and horses taking their first steps, heavily influenced by the work of James Herriot, a veterinary influencer if ever there was one. Consequently, I spent several weeks each summer in high school working in my aunt's veterinary clinic, in the sweltering heat of Napa summers, when just walking back into the kennels brought on a wave of sweat; some days were so warm that I wanted to cry upon getting out of her car in the parking lot of the clinic.

One afternoon, a couple brought in a young gray cat in obvious distress after she had been hit by a car. X-rays revealed a break in her leg that Dr. Rock told them was fully treatable. She could recover to lead an active life, but the costs of surgery to repair the fracture and subsequent recovery could be quite high. Or, he told them, they could amputate, a less expensive option that she would quickly adapt to, but they shook their heads. All of this conversation and decision-making took place, as it often does in emergency veterinary settings, with Little Grey herself in the back of the clinic receiving basic supportive care while her family were counseled.

While she made herself at home in a kennel, comfortable on pain medication and purring and chirping for the staff, her guardians told us they wanted to euthanize—and they wouldn't surrender her to us to care for either, which is a not-uncommon situation in veterinary clinics when people cannot afford care for their animals; this is one reason every veterinary clinic and animal shelter seems to have a minimum of one very bedraggled cat skulking in the back office.

No one on the staff wanted to do it, though, and hours went by before we reluctantly drew up a sedative and Euthasol, only for her guardians to call at the eleventh hour: They'd changed their minds and wanted to opt for an amputation. Little Grey would live to run and jump another day.

It is a common understanding among those who love animals that we are likely to be the ones who make the decision about when and how their lives end. As a generation of people traumatized by *Old Yeller* can attest, we have been killing companion animals, ostensibly to alleviate suffering or mitigate danger, for a very long time. In 1963, the American Veterinary Medical Association formally convened a Panel on Euthanasia[1] to develop ethics and best practices, which are routinely updated to reflect current clinical practice and research. For decades, we have treated euthanasia for animals as a form of a final gift, arguing that it reduces fear and pain and allows animals a death with dignity, rather than a potentially traumatic, upsetting natural death; after witnessing Ember's horrific and violent death, I know firsthand that a natural death in animals does not always look like peacefully going to sleep and never waking again. In fact, as many vet med friends remark, a peaceful death is actually quite rare. As someone who cares deeply for my animals, this is one of the most difficult, and sacred, decisions I can make.

While we still shrink away from euthanasia conversations, often having them in a panic and too late, the notion of "putting her down" as the natural end point of an animal's life is deeply ingrained in American society. It was never in doubt that Little Grey's life would almost certainly end with euthanasia, it was simply a question of when.

The widespread acceptance of euthanasia for animals has also been implicated in another conversation: one about when, where, and how humans make end-of-life choices, with some proponents noting that we are allowed to ease the passing of beloved pets but do not provide the same to humans. If we value a "good death" for animals, surely we should want one for ourselves too? And unlike animals, we have the autonomy and understanding to make that very considered and active choice for ourselves when confronted with a terminal diagnosis, right?

Whether referred to simply as euthanasia or physician-assisted suicide (PAS), the right to die, medical aid in dying (MAID), death with dignity, or some other euphemism, the question of dying on our own terms is an incredibly fraught one, potentiated in growing years as a number of governments around the world expand access to it. Conversations on the topic can feel frustrating, as this is not simply a discussion about the absolute right to bodily autonomy but also one about how we value quality of life, who determines which lives are worth living, and the sociocultural and economic pressures that lead to forced decision-making among humans just as they do among animals.

If the discussion about end-of-life for animals can become conflicted and messy, it is much worse for humans. While life itself is a form of terminal diagnosis, as every birth must eventually end in a death, and we all dream of a gentle end—simply falling asleep and never waking, perhaps nodding off at a family picnic to the sound of birdsong and children playing—most of us will face some degree of medicalized death. Sometimes that experience will be brief, sometimes it will be prolonged, and sometimes it will be very, very painful. It will often involve some degree of impairment, as people with terminal illnesses experience a decline, and that decline often includes a cognitive element as well. Like animals, we can be handed terminal diagnoses that may be accompanied by intense agony and suffering, even with the most advanced medical care, with late-stage cancers a common and familiar example in conversations about euthanasia.

In the case of terminal diagnoses likely to cause significant pain and suffering, conversations are complicated by the fact that we have made astounding progress in medicine, expanding the kinds of treatment options available but also intensifying pressures around care and the imperative to try everything, sometimes even in the face of evidence that this isn't the best choice for the individual. With serious diagnoses come a conversation about the treatment options and prognosis that can be accompanied by a subtle undertone: Of course you want to try everything, to prolong life until the last possible moment, to buy precious minutes, hours, days with loved ones. It may be possible to buy more time, but at what cost—not just financially, but physically and emotionally?

To decide to decline some forms of care, for whatever reason, would be to "give up."

Fortunately, we are starting to see a shift in these conversations, with a glimmer of hope that people might be supported and empowered in their decisions about what they want at the end of their lives. Hospice and palliative care, which offer varying degrees of intervention, depending on the patient's wishes, are respected as forms of treatment and genuine care, not simply a last-ditch effort or a final shrug. The decision to stop aggressive treatment and pursue supportive or comfort care has become less stigmatized. The reality that sometimes treatment itself inflicts and prolongs suffering is more openly discussed. Euthanasia is one among many options that might be available to a patient at the end of their life, and with greater acceptance, it's more likely to be considered in some regions as an end-of-life option after other measures have been exhausted or no longer serve the patient. It can even be an early part of discussions about treatment planning and expectations to allow people to start thinking about their personal preferences and tolerance for treatment at the start, making it part of informed decision-making from the beginning, whether or not the patient decides to ultimately follow through.

Groups such as Death with Dignity and Compassion & Choices are actively engaged in both public education and legal advocacy work to move the needle (so to speak) on this conversation about how humans spend their final days. Death with Dignity states that their work "respects and honors an individual's choices, including how they choose to define a dignified death." Compassion & Choices concentrates on issues surrounding not just euthanasia but end-of-life comfort and respect, such as hospice and palliative care, voluntarily stopping eating and drinking (VSED), and palliative sedation, advocating for people with widely varied views on what they want from end-of-life care. The stories these organizations and the media highlight in this conversation are striking and sometimes heartbreaking, profiling people who suffered protracted, painful deaths while longing to die on their own terms, stripped of autonomy as humans and patients at the end of their lives in an experience that was traumatic for both them and their loved ones. Rather than passing peacefully in circumstances they could control, in the place where they felt most comfortable, they were subjected to the worst indignities and interventions of the medical system.

Advocacy organizations like these have access to a wealth of resources, national communications strategies, and other tools to keep their cause highly visible and shape the public face of what euthanasia looks like.

Notably, that face is usually white and elderly—reinforcing the attitude that age itself is an illness in need of correction—or dying of terminal cancer. The decision to foreground these cases is not unproblematic, suggesting that euthanasia is about a very specific number of people experiencing intractable pain and suffering.

In California, Brittany Maynard became the poster child of the state's euthanasia movement when she died at age twenty-nine in November 2014,[2] highlighting cancer patients' fight for the right to die on their own terms. Maynard, a California resident, became a ferocious advocate after facing a terminal diagnosis in California and ultimately moving to Oregon to access euthanasia, saying "the freedom is in the choice." Her life and death had a legacy not just in California—where euthanasia was legalized in 2015 with the End of Life Option Act[3]—but across the country, where as of 2025, according to Death with Dignity,[4] eleven states permit euthanasia, with another eighteen considering legislation pertaining to the topic. In California, patients must have less than six months to live, the capacity to understand their choice and self-administer the medication, and assent from consulting and attending physicians, with similar guidelines in other U.S. states; the standards are designed to act as safeguards to ensure that people aren't compelled into choosing death and are able to decide with a clear understanding of their options, with, advocates say, particular care for vulnerable populations.

But the faces of who opts for euthanasia or who is encouraged to do so don't always look like the ones on billboards, and here the line begins to blur between terminal illness and disability. Worldwide, euthanasia is becoming available for a growing list of conditions, including some that are not necessarily terminal, such as dementia and eating disorders. The Netherlands allows for it in people with severe mental illness, for example—called "psychiatric euthanasia"—along with Belgium, Canada, Luxembourg, Spain, and Switzerland.[5] In 2018, the topic made international headlines in the case of Aurelia Brouwers, a twenty-nine-year-old Dutch woman who successfully requested euthanasia for severe, treatment-resistant mental illness.[6] Given that suicidal ideation can be a powerful component of severe mental health conditions, it was incredibly hard to assess, and interpret, her request for death; in the United States, we invest heavily in suicide prevention, even starting a national psychiatric emergency hotline in 2024, and suicide is considered a bad outcome, a social failing. Did society fail Brouwers? Was her life one of intolerable pain and suffering that could not be ameliorated? Should severe mental illness be treated on par with an immediately terminal condition, such as organ failure or brain death?

As someone with a severe mental illness, these are not purely intellectual questions, and they shape the way society thinks about people like me, regardless of my own feelings about my mental health and quality of life.

While the concept of a death with dignity may feel like it should be an intuitive, absolute, basic right, the truth is much more complicated. What, after all, is the point of a death with dignity when the patient is not afforded the equally important life with dignity first? The community sitting at the nexus of this debate is one that is often marginalized and silenced: disabled people, for whom the outcome of the medical aid in dying debate has very real, immediate, and far-reaching consequences that determine not just when we die, but how we live. Is the existence of impairment considered reason enough to seek or recommend euthanasia?

Disability-focused critiques of euthanasia tend to make members of the public extremely unwilling to engage, because they touch upon the intrinsic value of disabled lives and society's role in this framework. They also highlight the incredible diversity of the disability community, because there is no grand unified theory or opinion about this topic and there never will be. Some disabled people fully support euthanasia, full stop, others are just as ardently opposed, and many more find themselves in a world of mixed emotions in the middle, just as two people can have radically different feelings about the same disability. It would be foolhardy and unwise to suggest that there is a neat solution to this question, although people are fond of cherry-picking opinions that affirm their own views on disability.

The work of disabled-led groups such as Not Dead Yet, which has led robust opposition to euthanasia since 1996, must be understood in a larger context that is not simply "Should people be allowed to die if they are in intractable physical or psychological suffering?" but rather "Who defines suffering and determines what should be considered intolerable?" and "Should disabled people be allowed to live?"

This is a conversation that makes some people deeply uncomfortable, cutting to the core of disablism—prejudice against disabled people that may manifest in policy, social attitudes, and personal beliefs—and our own complicity, including disabled people ourselves who may have internalized disablism that influences the way we think about ourselves and others. Disabled people and disability rights organizations are trying to participate in the regulatory processes surrounding euthanasia, with testimonies, briefs, direct actions in the halls of Congress, and more in an existential fight for their lives. Yet sometimes it feels like screaming into a void because being independent agents and activists runs contrary to how society thinks about the experience of disability.

One reason for our exclusion from these conversations and the larger failure to recognize disability as a social, cultural, and political identity revolves around the way people understand disability. In 2024, the Centers for Disease Control and Prevention concluded that one in four Americans are disabled,[7] and yet we are both unseen and unheard. For many nondisabled people, their first introduction to disability, and the framing that sticks with them, is the medical or medicalized model, which sets them up to understand conversations about euthanasia as a medical issue alone: If someone is suffering and all lines of treatment have been exhausted, euthanasia is another treatment option to consider. The medical model primarily positions disability as a personal problem, often a tragic one. This devalues disabled bodies and lives, posing them as problems to be solved. It does not make space for disability as an identity, for an understanding of disability as a collective experience, as seen for example with little people, who are intergenerational members of proud and interconnected networks with their own lively culture and rich history.

Under this model, nondisabled people thinking about disability may conjure up any number of mental images, but most will be characterized by some degree of impairment that appears to actively infringe upon someone's ability to navigate the world, often in a way that simply cannot be mitigated—at least until a cure is found. They think of disability as a medical issue a person lives with and suffers from, not as an element of someone's identity, reflected in the "people with disabilities"—

put the person first, not the disability!—language preferred by many advocates of the medical model. A person with a severe spinal cord injury, for example, may not be able to walk, requiring the use of a wheelchair for mobility and possible support with activities such as toileting and dressing. This exact scenario is viewed as a catastrophic tragedy that disrupts lives forever. In fact, it's such a horrible prospect that public safety campaigns surrounding behaviors such as drunk driving may specifically introduce it as a potential outcome—"being confined to a wheelchair"—threatening that a single bad decision could result in a shattering consequence, as if death wasn't bad enough. "Being confined to a wheelchair" means an endless list of lost opportunities and suffering, reiterating the framework of the medical model.

This contrasts with the social model, which instead focuses on the cultural attitudes around the impairment and the decisions society makes to consciously disable people on the basis of their identity: Failing to provide a ramp for a wheelchair user is a form of disablement, for example, as is failing to create and maintain a robust care infrastructure so that wheelchair users who need personal attendants can access them and pay them fairly for their labor. Failing to invest in research and development to support people where they are and improve their lives while also exploring cures for impairments for people who want them: This is also a conscious choice to disable people. Under this model, social attitudes and policy decisions introduce hardship to the lives of people with impairments who could be accommodated and fully integrated into society with better supports. These impairments may be a core part of someone's identity and will always introduce differences in the way they interact with the world, including, sometimes, suffering and distress that are innate to the impairment, in which case a cure may absolutely be the most desirable outcome. There should be room under this model for all relationships to disability.

Disability is not an inherent tragedy under this model. I do not, for example, view a cure for autism as something that society should be seeking. Instead, we should be building a world where the full expression of neurodiversity is welcome, and where autistics receive the level of support they need. Similarly, I view mental health conditions as part of human diversity. We need to make room for individuals to have their own opinions about their mental illnesses and how they opt to manage them, from members of the Mad Pride movement to those who want to be cured. The social model also does not mean that all disabilities are inherently good, or even neutral.

I'd like to see a cure for complex regional pain syndrome, an agonizing and debilitating condition that most people would rather not experience. In the meantime, though, I want better access to a diverse array of good pain management options; schools and workplaces that accommodate people who may need work from home, time off, or other options to manage living with their condition; and an end to the societal stigma that burdens people living with, or in, pain.

Society can also choose to engage in acts of mass disablement, whether these involve tolerating military pollution that leads to cancer clusters or passing mask bans that directly contribute to the spread of infectious disease, where the disability is both preventable and a symptom of deeper social inequities.

Sometimes disability is a symptom of a tragedy we should all scream about, something that should not exist but does because of cultural choices.

These are not just dull theoretical conversations about which model of disability is the right one to use, or how society in general should think about disabled people—though I would argue these conversations need not be dull and can in fact be quite interesting and provocative for those who are willing to take their time with them. Conversations about disability inclusion have a real impact on issues that affect the lives of disabled people, such as health care policy, frameworks of caregiving, and civil rights laws pertaining to discrimination, and they also have a knockdown effect on nondisabled people, particularly those who acquire disabilities, which can happen to anyone, at any time.

Pernicious societal disablism has ensured that many of these conversations go poorly. Investing in disabled people through reforms to health care, for example, is sometimes viewed as too costly, while disabled people struggle to access the basic services and supports they need to thrive. This ties directly into the conversation about euthanasia, because society has chosen to make it harder to live in a disabled body, thus putting a thumb on the scale of this conversation.

Perhaps after all this, the reasons some disabled people are so concerned about euthanasia seem obvious, but to understand why this issue is a third rail for the disability community, it's necessary to roll back the clock—to start not at death, but birth.

"He insists he doesn't want to kill me," wrote disability activist Harriet McBryde Johnson[8] in 2003 of infamous ethicist

Peter Singer, revered in some circles for his work on animal liberation and known in others for aggressively advocating for the deaths of disabled children and adults. "He simply thinks it would have been better, all things considered, to have given my parents the option of killing the baby I once was, and to let other parents kill similar babies as they come along and thereby avoid the suffering that comes with lives like mine and satisfy the reasonable preferences of parents for a different kind of child. It has nothing to do with me. I should not feel threatened."

The systematic devaluation of disabled people is rooted in the idea that life as a disabled person is "less-than," that impairments by their very nature mean disabled people are not fully capable of engaging with or appreciating society. Johnson lived in a society where Peter Singer was not the only person who questioned why she was alive, and we're all still living in it. For some, the idea of having a disabled baby, no matter the disability or the cause, is repugnant and upsetting, a notion embedded in the way we talk about pregnancy right down to new baby announcements touting "all ten fingers and toes." This does not distinguish between the fetus disabled by prenatal exposure to chemicals, the child born into a generationally D/deaf family, a random genetic fluke, or a baby born with a manageable chronic condition—positioning all as things to be prevented, things detrimental to the life of the child and burdensome on their parents. From birth, we are worth less, and when we acquire impairments as we move through life, this too is unacceptable, even though, arguably, disability is also a natural expression of human diversity and part of being alive.

Implying that disability is an inherent tragedy leads to the idea of "better dead than disabled," from birth forward. For some disabled people, the debate over euthanasia feels more like a personal attack, a belief that our lives are not worth living, a fundamental lack of understanding about the diversity of disabled people and their lives. It also propagates a larger worldview that disabled lives are not worth preserving, something that struck me acutely several years ago. I was working through an advance directive worksheet prior to a surgery, which included a series of questions relating to resuscitation and life support. One asked me if I wanted to be revived if I might be "a burden" on those around me.

The question was not whether I would be willing to keep living if I emerged from a surgery with paralysis, a brain injury, or another form of lasting impairment; rather, the question was about my impact on the people around me, a common situation for disabled people, who often find themselves objectified and talked over. My quality of life was not the core value under discussion; the paperwork was prompting me to think about how my existence might affect *other people's* quality of life, with no discussion of resources that might (and should) be available to help *me* live life on my own terms. In a society that prizes independence, interdependence—or, worse yet, dependence—is anathema.

This fight cannot be understood as one that is purely about how we die. It is also one about the systemic lack of services and supports that pushes people into decisions that aren't about their quality of life; rather, they're about the state's failure to prioritize good quality of life for disabled people, and about the isolation disabled people experience that cuts them off from both people and supports that allow them to lead full, active, participatory lives.

And this is where the conversation about euthanasia can take a turn toward the bleak. When advocates are using images of disability and namechecking diagnoses in campaigns encouraging states to legalize euthanasia, it's difficult to not recoil, difficult to not feel something sour bubbling up in our throats at the reminder that people think disabled people are inherently not worthy of life, that we cannot possibly enjoy being alive and would be better served by death.

"Their arguments for why we need dignified death are all grounded in ableism," Joseph Stramondo told me when I called to talk about euthanasia; the disabled bioethicist is an associate professor of philosophy and humanities at San Diego State University. "In something like a terminal cancer diagnosis, they weren't talking about physical suffering and pain relief, they were talking about the ability to wipe your own butt. They were talking about this idea of independence, so to speak, so it's always been about disability, because at the end of the day, what disability is, is differences in functioning. People presume that if you function differently, you're going to be losing something. You're going to be losing some kind of independence or something of value."

Stramondo notes that many of these conversations revolve around treating disability as a lack, evidence of something that is missing, a loss. For some people, it is: Someone whose leg is amputated is literally missing something, and they may feel that loss in changes to their life associated with the amputation. But, Stramondo says, the same doesn't hold true for everyone who acquires a disability. And congenitally disabled people aren't missing something; they are living precisely as they were born. Their disability is an inherent part of their identity and who they are. For people who acquire disabilities later in life, those experiences of impairment can also become part of their identity. Sometimes a disability even manifests as an addition, a source of personal growth and a different perspective on the world, a point of pride.

When "disability equals loss, equals grief," he says, that colors the way we experience and talk about disability. This creates an inherent conflict over our lives that spills over into policies about the services and supports we require, setting up a perfect storm in which someone believes their life is not worth living because society has told them it is not worth living—and not because *they* are able to think in a more value-neutral way about their quality of life and *they* have arrived at this assessment independently. Their disability is a tragedy, and society will not invest in their health and well-being, leaving them in intolerable living conditions that, indeed, contribute to a life not worth living.

The language of the euthanasia movement, to some disabled people, smells suspiciously like eugenics, made infamous in the Holocaust when the Nazi-run Aktion T4 program murdered hundreds of thousands of disabled people. The United States, however, has a long tradition of eugenics as well, dating to nineteenth-century beliefs about human improvement—that removing disabled people from society was "for their own good" but also for the supposed benefit of society itself—and that eugenics legacy is alive and well, not just in the United States but worldwide. The question of when killing becomes caring arose in a controversial 2005 *New England Journal of Medicine* perspective introducing the Groningen Protocol,[9] with physicians laying out the case for euthanizing infants with "poor prospects" in the Netherlands; tellingly, this paper predated the expansion of access to euthanasia in the Netherlands, establishing a baseline that some disabled people found very troubling.

"The question under consideration now is whether deliberate life-ending procedures are also acceptable for newborns and infants, despite the fact that these patients cannot express their own will," wrote authors Eduard Verhagen and Pieter Sauer in a paper exploring twenty-two cases of newborn euthanasia and making the case for establishing a clear protocol for deciding when an infant's future is "grim."

This goes beyond the palliative care some parents choose to provide in cases when a baby faces a terminal diagnosis, crossing the line from focusing on comfort with minimal interventions and into the decision to consciously kill—a decision the authors argued was rooted in compassion for a baby sentenced to a brief, tormented life due to severe congenital disabilities that might result in living for just hours or days. It puts forward an urgent moral case: If we can agree that suffering people should be allowed to end their lives on their own terms rather than endure the traumas of terminal illness, why should we sentence infants, whom we are supposed to love and care for, even when love means letting go, to brief, miserable lives? If we make other decisions for children in the name of "their own good," why not this one too?

But when your community includes people who were themselves considered poor prospects at birth, it can be troubling to see this kind of advocacy, to wonder how far the envelope will be pushed. This is one reason nondisabled anti-euthanasia activists have found a foothold in some disability spaces, presenting themselves as allies. It can be easy to cultivate fears around euthanasia, threatening the prospect of doctors chasing down disabled patients they deem unworthy of life by drawing upon very real-world evidence that disabled people's lives are not valued. The same underlying logic, incidentally, also shows up in right-wing rhetoric around termination on the basis of a fetal diagnosis. These advocates equate termination for an issue incompatible with life or a risk to the pregnant person's health (a true medical crisis for a possibly very much wanted pregnancy) with *any* abortion to push disabled people into supporting restrictions on abortion care because they fear the weaponization of abortion as a eugenic tool. These same people fail to advocate for good quality of life for the disability community: They think you shouldn't kill us, but they also don't think you should help us.

Nondisabled people still seem surprised that disabled people can and want to make their own decisions, that even people with "lives not worth living" actually live highly realized, happy lives when given the opportunity to do so. Perhaps they move or think in ways radically different from those of nondisabled people: use a ventilator to breathe or rely on a communication board to interact with people. But these are not tragic fates to be mourned: They are simply living their lives.

"Nothing about us without us," the disability community's rallying cry, is reflected in assumptions about quality of life with conditions that some people argue should be eligible for euthanasia, such as dementia, where interlocutors assume that the subject of their discussion cannot participate by nature of their disability and it may again be necessary to step in to make choices on their behalf. Hailee M. Yoshizaki-Gibbons, a professor in biomedical humanities at Hiram College, has worked extensively with people with dementia, writing about the experience in a striking 2023 essay included in *Lateral*'s Crip Pandemic Life Issue, "Leaving Evidence,"[10] a piece referencing the work of disability justice activist Mia Mingus. I called her on a warm July day to talk about her work and her fight for a deeper understanding of and respect for people with dementia.

"We have this social narrative that people with dementia are already dead, in a sense," she told me. "It's this idea that you're grieving this loss of this person whose body is still alive but is otherwise dead," with popular culture referring to dementia with terms such as "the long goodbye." This sense of death while still alive has a pervasive grip on society that undoubtedly contributes to the sentiment of fearing dementia more than death, of hoping for a swift end if ever diagnosed. But it doesn't reflect the lives of people with dementia, says Yoshizaki-Gibbons, who wrote compellingly about "Sylvia," a woman with dementia she interacted with in the course of her academic research.

Quality of life, and life itself, for people with dementia are often foreshortened when they are warehoused in nursing homes and other places "people go to die," she says, keeping people in a state of limbo and social death. She rejects the notion that people with dementia do not experience happiness and are slipping away from the world. She explains that the aphasia associated with dementia is frustrating for the people who experience it, for example, just as it would be for anyone else. A person may search for the right word and what comes out seems like nonsense to an observer, but it actually carries its own meaning for those who care to listen. It would be a mistake to assume that people with dementia are incapable of communicating, that there is nothing there.

"How do we let go of that idea that they have to make sense to us for us to connect with them? How do we co-create meaning, still find meaning in their words?" People with dementia aren't the only people who have aphasia or communicate via means that nondisabled people may find confusing or hard to understand. Using a communication board or another mode of communication doesn't make someone lesser, but these perspectives are often erased in conversations about the quality and value of disabled peoples' lives. If you cannot speak with your voice box and lips, you must have nothing to say.

Yoshizaki-Gibbons noted that she doesn't oppose euthanasia, especially after watching her father suffer with terminal illness, but that she has grave concerns about its potential applications. "Even when we just start with 'we're only allowing for terminal cases,' it does open the door. And then there are people who are going to push on that door."

Disabled people already have a deep distrust of health care systems, the current mediators of access to and oversight over end-of-life medication. Their fears are extremely valid. It's not just the day-to-day frustrations of encounters with the system that highlight why disabled people have room for concern. During the height of the COVID-19 pandemic, for example, multiple states engaged in health care rationing that deprioritized the lives of developmentally disabled people—again, a practice that sounds and feels a great deal like eugenics, with the state (and the health care system as a state actor) making decisions about whether people should live or die on the basis of their disability status. A damning 2021 report from the National Council on Disability[11] highlighted the experience of being "triaged out" of COVID care, left unprotected in long-term care facilities and denied equal access to supports and services. The case of Sarah McSweeney, a forty-five-year-old multiply disabled woman who died after doctors pushed to make her a do-not-resuscitate patient[12]—against her expressed prior wishes—became a cause célèbre for disabled people fearing the consequences of health care rationing. For disabled people, the reduction of our lives to data points or the rationalization that "they were already sick" meant that we never truly got to know, or mark the passage of, so many disabled people in institutional settings.

This radically changes the stakes and nature of the conversation about euthanasia: If it is about the dignified termination of suffering, then what is suffering? How much suffering is societally caused, rather than absolute? If society chooses to collectively invest in services and supports and people are made aware of the options and tools available to them, would they still choose death? Can you provide counsel in these conversations in a way that is not patronizing, not an attempt to push patients into choosing or rejecting euthanasia, while still respecting the ultimate autonomy of the person?

Every disabled person feels differently about their life and what they need to live a life of dignity and worth. Those who are aware of Aktion T4 and other eugenics enterprises are also acutely aware of the burden of history they carry on already bowed backs, something we consider in our advocacy around these topics, whether we oppose euthanasia or believe that it is a natural extension of bodily autonomy, if one that should be handled with greater care.

We exist in a state of strange tension where our choices and attitudes are not entirely our own, even as we insist on our bodily autonomy and personal rights. Those who support euthanasia may struggle with this position given the history behind it. At the same time, it is extremely challenging to discuss concerns about euthanasia without inadvertently giving fodder to society's desire to exert control over our lives—and frustrating to feel devalued by people on both sides who impose their own beliefs about disability upon us and our bodies.

But there's another critical element to this conversation: Little Grey's reprieve highlighted a fraught debate in veterinary medicine over when euthanasia is the humane, best outcome, and when it's a forced choice because of economics and circumstances. This tension has only become more extreme thanks to the increasing price of veterinary care and the economic pressures on pet guardians that make it so hard to make choices informed purely by prognosis, when treatment may cost thousands of dollars, thus giving rise to the phenomenon of "economic euthanasia."[13] Pets are not the only ones facing this outcome.

Expansion of eligibility for euthanasia across a range of

conditions that don't necessarily represent immediate, terminal diagnoses isn't the only trend emerging globally: There's also a growing pressure that has less to do with the patient's medical situation and more to do with their social circumstances and their ability to afford to live, creating a framework for a kind of economic euthanasia in humans. Deciding upon euthanasia because you lack the resources to live sounds ominously like a forced choice, and one that policies and regulations should be designed to prevent; but that's not how it's playing out in the real world, where costs of living crises are a systemic and widespread problem, and deaths of despair are the results.

For Little Grey, death, not disability, would have been a tragedy, something I thought about decades later as I watched Dr. Clare perform Tricycle's amputation and watched him quickly adapt into a curious, mischievous, highly active agent of chaos on three legs. At an under-resourced shelter, Tricycle would have been quickly euthanized as the most humane option in a context where limited veterinary services are available, his body stored in a garbage bag in a freezer until it could be incinerated or buried in a mass grave with other unwanted animals. That quality-of-life consideration would have been based on limited available options for care as the kindest outcome. It is chilling to think that disabled people may be put in the same position, one in which dying truly is better than being disabled by society, and this is not a hypothetical.

"Sophia," a disabled woman in Canada, requested medical aid in dying specifically because she could not locate accessible housing,[14] while Christine Gauthier, a Canadian Paralympic athlete, told Canadian lawmakers that she was advised to consider euthanasia when she approached Veterans Affairs Canada for assistance with getting a wheelchair lift.[15] A 2023 Research Co. poll found that nearly one in three Canadians supported euthanasia for "poverty" or "homelessness," without a qualifying medical condition.[16] We'll never know how many disabled people chose death because they could see no way forward in life, because society failed them so systemically.

This does not sound like an unforced choice made by someone whose quality of life cannot be ameliorated with existing medical care. It sounds like being backed into a corner of fear of debt, homelessness, hopeless economic circumstances—all things disabled people are at increased risk of experiencing. Should we kill people because they cannot afford to remain alive?

Ultimately, any conversation about euthanasia should foreground the voices of the people most affected, even when those voices spark discomfort. That includes the people with terminal illnesses and other conditions pushing for access, but it also includes disabled people drawing upon lived and professional experience to raise concerns about who is eligible and what kinds of guardrails are in place to protect people from making decisions motivated by economics, by lack of social supports, by isolation, by disablism.

Disabled people must be a part of the conversation about how to regulate euthanasia, what the criteria for eligibility are, how people should be counseled about making this choice. And it's impossible to advocate for euthanasia in isolation; it must be considered within a larger social context that invites conversations about interventions that might affect someone's decision-making. If you are not fighting to keep disabled people in their community with services and supports at the same time you are fighting to protect their right to die on their own terms, you are skipping some critical steps. If your advocacy is for options, then more than one option should be available and supported.

When this topic arises in conversation, people often ask me for my stance, sometimes because they value my opinion, but also sometimes because they assume they know what it is and just want a disabled person to validate their own beliefs about disability and impairment. My answer is often unsatisfying to both camps: to disabled people who believe there is no ethical euthanasia, that any form is tantamount to murder and access to it only entrenches disablism, and also to people who may expect full-throated support rooted in my beliefs about bodily autonomy.

The answer, as it often is, is complicated: I do support the right to make your own decisions about your health care, your life, and your death, but those choices do not occur in a vacuum and they must be fully informed. When they are surrounded by significant societal pressures, both cultural and functional, I believe in our collective ethical obligation to tread carefully; to provide people with as much information as possible about their condition, their prospects, and their options; and to back up abstract discussions about options with meaningful societal supports and a culture where interdependence is valued. Advocacy for euthanasia must include advocacy to abolish disablist systems, ensuring equal access to society for disabled people, which includes expanding and protecting services and supports that help us lead full lives. If—upon full consideration and in a society that affirms your right to exist and backs that up with meaningful policies and social supports—you are suffering and still want to control the way you die, I'll make the pharmacy run for you, because denying people autonomy is at its core disablist.

I can't tell you whether your life is worth living, and neither can anyone else.

Quality of life is dependent on a myriad of factors, some of which are solvable if we have the will, and some of which are not. Solving these problems wouldn't just benefit the disability community: Everyone wins when sufficient affordable housing is available, they can easily access health care, and their basic needs are met. Everyone wins in a society that values not just surviving, but thriving, living lives full of meaning and companionship and community, of joy and solidarity and hope. Fighting disablism is one small element in building a better world; and in a world where all our lives have value and worth, decisions about euthanasia can come from a place of genuine desire to allow people to pass peacefully, without suffering, on their own terms, in conditions they choose, to address the distress of dying. That freedom of true choice is what we should all be working toward, one where the Little Greys of the world lead fulfilling lives and experience compassion in death, when it's time, and that time is determined by the prevention of true suffering, not society and circumstance.

Chapter 10

All My Dead Ghosts // Complicated

The cool thing about having pets is casually using a pic of them being joyful and full of life as your lock screen and then they die and you can never change it," I wrote on social media late one night six months after Ember died, after tapping my phone awake to the same beloved and long-dead face, incapable of opening my settings to change it, feeling like doing so would wipe the last part of her from the face of the Earth.

The photo is an old favorite, one polydactyl paw stretched out as she lounges on the couch, looking off into the distance, to somewhere I cannot follow. One of her favorite things to do was wait for me to take a nap on that very couch, pulling the blanket over myself so she could worm her way underneath, tucking her head into my armpit, both of us breathing slowly, softly, together.

At the time, I still felt undone by Ember's death, and seeing her on my phone was both a comfort and a torment. I still thought of her every day, remembering the plush feeling of her fur under my fingers, the way she liked for me to tickle her between her many toes, her amber gaze fixing me in space and time. I felt like a tree along a storm-tossed shore, branches shredding in the wind. Entire days went by in which I did nothing, thinking of her, simultaneously wanting to avoid and wallow in the places she had lived, disinterested in any kind of interaction with other human beings, resentful that Ash was alive and she wasn't, filled with guilt and anger and frustration seeking outlets. I tried to convince myself that this was a nightmare that I would wake from, that it would be the morning of June 6 and she would be waking me up by pawing at my shoulder like she always did, demanding a place under the covers, hissing at Ash if he got too close, expecting me to share my morning yogurt with her.

Years later, I still think of her every day, and not simply because she's still on my phone, in photographs around the house, in the rings on my fingers. There are some days when I wake up and have to remember all over again that she is dead; when I push my empty yogurt bowl across the table to let her clean it; when I shake out a blanket and expect to see her come running; when I have to set aside whatever plans I might have made to sit with her memory. I have come to dread the lengthening days of late spring and early summer, thinking of how the light lingered late in the later weeks of her life, each evening seeming full of possibility, a late spring of brilliant wildflowers and golden hour after golden hour followed by livid sunsets.

I felt her death perhaps more intensely than that of any cat I've ever had, despite our brief time together, and I suppose I have a lifetime to unpack why that was, just as I also have a lifetime to carry her ghost with me.

There are some who would argue that what I feel for Ember,

the intensity of that feeling, how long it has lasted, is actually a sickness, a pathology, evidence that something is going wrong inside me. They might draw upon the diagnosis of complicated grief, now termed "prolonged grief disorder" (PGD); this kind of "extended" grief is seen as such a serious issue that in 2021 it was added to the fifth edition of the Diagnostic and Statistical Manual of Mental Disorders (DSM-5), the bible of psychiatric diagnoses, a text in which myriad facets of the human experience and mind are picked apart and presented as diagnoses.

Prolonged grief disorder situates grief and loss as personal issues rather than collective ones, rooted in the here and now, not intergenerational or intercommunal experiences of loss; like the medical model writ large, it attempts to distill and isolate individual feelings and turn them into diagnoses that can be quantified, entered in a chart, submitted to an insurance company, or murmured to family members. The mental health system often commits acts of violence in the guise of naming and helping, and for some people, prolonged grief disorder is one of them.

The DSM attempts to define ineffable aspects of being human by generating diagnostic criteria, themselves based in very white, Western understandings of mental health, psychology, and psychosocial relations. A patient can be evaluated against these criteria through conversations with a care provider, but also the applications of survey instruments designed to put emotions on a scale. People who have interacted with the mental health care industry in the United States may be familiar with one such self-report, the Patient Health Questionnaire, usually administered prior to appointments with providers. The PHQ-9 asks patients to respond to prompts on topics such as appetite, sleep, and "feeling bad about yourself" with a rating of "not at all," "several days," "more than half the days," and "nearly every day"; the answers convert to a numeric score as to how much these feelings interact with the patient's ability to complete activities of daily living. Such scales capture a point in time, adding to a body of evidence over the course of treatment as providers can see how responses shift between appointments; but the questions can be surprisingly difficult to answer, especially when patients are aware that admissions of suicidal ideation or severe depression may result in forcible treatment or other severe, disruptive consequences.

"Nearly every day" I feel sadness.

The flaws in the DSM—and psychiatric assessment and diagnosis in general—are on full display in conversations about grief, highlighting deeper social tensions around mental health topics, in which the eagerness to avoid distress can sometimes itself turn pathological in a society obsessed with positivity. Prolonged grief disorder, as a concept, can seem like a direct reinforcement of performative positivity, indicating that someone has "failed to move on," hasn't found their silver lining in grief, has stepped outside of space and time in their mourning. And while some mourners genuinely experience this as dysfunction and do find value in naming it, for others, the very diagnosis can actually exacerbate the symptoms they are being evaluated for, sparking feelings of guilt, inadequacy, and a sense of being judged.

In theory there is no timeline for the mourning process, except in the context of prolonged grief disorder, where there very literally is. The diagnostic criteria for prolonged grief disorder involve intense expressions of grief, such as depression, suicidal ideation, numbness, difficulty relating to other people, disbelief or denial, longing for the deceased, and loneliness within six months of a loss for children or twelve months for adults.[1] (We shall set aside, for a moment, the implications of cultural attitudes about children versus adults.) The patient must display at least three of the identified symptoms over the course of a month or more, in a pattern of emotions and behavior that suggests something more than a passing wave or moment of grief. It is sometimes described as being "stuck in grief," with the physical and emotional feelings of acute grief never abating and never allowing the mourner to start the process of integrating the loss into the rest of their lives.

Advocates for this diagnosis point to the way the grief described could impede functioning as a human being and disrupt a person's life, suggesting that naming it helps people get the help they need if they are struggling—not just in the practical sense of providing a diagnostic code so health insurance will pay for it, but also in the sense of making people understand that they are not alone in their feelings, that others have been where they are. On the flip side, it also raises the specter of that grief as something *wrong* with the griever, as evidence that someone needs to get over it and move on, who requires repair. Is visiting Grandfather's grave year after year a form of prolonged grief? What if you visit that grave once a week? Once a day? With offerings of flowers or other things? What about feeling continually depressed about his death, expressing feelings of intense longing and loneliness? What if part of you still wonders if he's really dead? How do your culture, faith, family, and history affect the way you think about him? Some of those things would point to a diagnosis of prolonged grief disorder. Some of these same things might point to the experience of being alive and to shared cultural values and attitudes about death and loss.

At what point does thinking about and living with the dead turn into a sickness?

The diagnosis of prolonged grief disorder tries to thread a needle—when is grieving "too much," and who gets to decide that?—while drawing upon beliefs about loss and quality of life that are rooted in white American life. There's a positioning of grief as difficulty, rather than a growth period. Notably for a society that tends to be death-avoidant, fear of death can increase the risk of developing overwhelming emotions in the aftermath of a loss.[2] These findings suggest that the culture of mainstream America and its relationship to death may be directly contributing to increased distress in the aftermath of a loss, suggesting the need for a shift in the way we conceptualize loss and difficult conversations; we should have them early and often rather than in crisis, and we should welcome sorrows into our lives as well as joys.

A *New York Times* article asked, "How long should it take to grieve?"[3] at a moment in the midst of national mourning of hundreds of thousands of COVID-19 deaths, as though this was a question with a concrete and universally applicable answer. The topic of complicated grief actually arose frequently during the height of the COVID pandemic, in part thanks to the DSM-5 addition and in part due to society's struggle with the sea changes wrought by COVID-19. Numerous outlets explored the topic and spilled reams of ink on their discomfort with the feelings of loss surrounding not just the personal deaths of loved ones in circumstances that were often traumatic and hard to process, but the larger social losses represented by coming to terms with living in a society that would permit the rampant spread of infectious disease in the face of scientific evidence and human suffering. These are the kinds of things that tend to create ghosts.

The sequelae of those losses lingered long after mask mandates and social distancing—themselves contributors to COVID grief as society confronted the loss of a way of life—were lifted. Children and youth, for example, experienced changes because of instructional loss[4] as well as isolation from friends and loss of opportunities for socialization during key periods of development. Those diagnosed with long COVID were facing severe mental health effects with both personal and social causes, including changes in ability and functioning that forced fundamental shifts in their lives, along with a feeling of being left behind as society reopened.

Meanwhile, other people were grappling with what it meant to lose a loved one at a time when it might have been impossible to visit with them, to participate in funerary rituals, to find fellowship in a death; such feelings were especially acute for those with family or religious practices that require community involvement and participation in mourning, such as sitting shiva in Jewish communities. The fracturing of human connections when they were needed most was a source of harm for many who lived through the pandemic. This is an issue the psychiatric profession was quick to recognize, with a 2021 assessment of prolonged grief disorder[5] warning that "increased prevalence of mental health conditions, including prolonged grief, may be a 'second wave' of the pandemic."

No small surprise that feelings of grief lasted much longer than six months, a year, two years, across the world and certainly in the "country that could not mourn," as journalist Sarah Jaffe put it in a feature for *The New Republic*.[6] The inability to find community, to express and explore loss, left many feeling a grief denied, resenting the return to normalcy pushed societally and culturally; it was as though talking about those deaths might dredge up old wounds and history, hearkening back to a time we are all desperate to forget, one that already seems to be fading in memory.

Under these circumstances, opening up a conversation about complicated grief might seem useful: With so many people experiencing grief, it could be possible to find more empathy for each other, to apply the concept to our lives more broadly. But our fear of grief kept that conversation superficial and quickly suppressed it.

Not all clinicians and researchers find the notion of complicated grief useful. Clinical psychologist Maarten Eisma noted in 2023 that this diagnosis tends to be heavily rooted in research on Western countries.[7] He concluded that "evidence that PGD is characterized by qualitatively different experiences than normal grief is yet unconvincing," especially given that there's incredible inconsistency in the definition of "normal" grief and that there likely will never be a wholly agreed upon definition of what "normal" grief should look like. The implied universality behind the notion does not reflect human reality among communities, individuals, and cultures, let alone individual deaths. In an era of legitimate pushback against the concept of normality, it feels glaring to attempt to apply the concept to grief.

Among clinical professionals who feel the diagnosis could sometimes be helpful for making people feel less alone in a potentially isolating time, or for accessing insurance coverage for therapy and other mental health supports as one avenue to pursue while growing with grief, some have expressed concerns about how the diagnosis might be understood and interpreted by mourners and those around them. Armchair psychiatry is a favorite national pastime in the United States, and the temptation to pathologize every uncomfortable aspect of the human experience without considering the implications runs deep; any dip into social media brings up yet another amateur psychologist making solemn pronouncements. It can feel, at times, as though simply being alive and having feelings is a clinical problem in the eyes of a general public seduced by the idea of neat and tidy definitions for diagnoses that can in turn be used to marginalize people: You're not mad or sad, you're sick, and therefore you need treatment, not a voice and space to use it.

In addition, some counselors and other professionals fear that individuals diagnosed with prolonged grief disorder might feel like they are grieving incorrectly, failing to follow the expectations and instructions set out by the society around them. That could add distress to an already challenging time, with societal pressure to conform shaping their feelings around loss. The people around them, in turn, might feel validated in attitudes that a griever is taking too long, demanding too much energy, being too dramatic, using the diagnosis to push a mourner to "get over it" and pursue fixes to the problem of grief, rather than creating more space for themselves. This is an especially big concern with lopsided power dynamics, such as manager and direct report, teacher and student, parent and child.

Concerned parties in the mental health profession aren't alone; many of the death doulas and other death workers I spoke to in the course of researching this book independently raised the topic of prolonged or complicated grief and expressed their frustrations with the concept, which both sets a timeline for grief and implies that there's a clear ending or finish for it, as well as some sort of yardstick of "normality" that is broadly applicable across generations, class, culture, background, existence.

Rather than caring for the psyche or the griever in situ, there may be a tendency to focus on the emotions as symptoms and address them instead of the bigger picture, and the griever is also placed in the context of a medical model. This is a problem to be fixed, a task some around the griever may take to with relish: At last, an action they can take!

This can be a particular issue for people who come from social and cultural backgrounds that differ from the white, Western mainstream that tends to dominate conversations about what is expected and acceptable in grief, especially for those who view grief as communal. Why is it okay to block traffic with a motorcade but not a protest? If it takes a village to raise a child, it should also take a village to bury an elder—and in many beliefs, death is not the end of the journey for that elder. In grief, especially in isolation, encountering attitudes that your community's way of being and interacting with grief are pathological can be an incredible act of cruelty.

"This whole conversation is so interesting," says community care practitioner and death worker Stefanie Lyn Kaufman-Mthimkhulu, who roots their work around support for, service to, and liberation of mentally ill people and those who identify with madness. "There's a lot to be said about what is the cultural underpinning: How do you get a diagnosis? I think you can only have a diagnosis like that in a culture that has decided life is only while you're alive. We have people all over the world who have culturally rooted practices that embed grief into every single day of life. The rituals that we do uplift our ancestors, we might pour water or wine on the ground, we're lighting candles, we're taking steps that honor these things.... Outside of the so-called United States and European colonial cultures, nearly every single culturally rooted ethnic practice involves some level of acknowledging the spirit world, an ongoing relationship with spirits."

Kaufman-Mthimkhulu views grief, whether it's surrounding a death, intergenerational trauma, or other significant life event, as a portal, "an opening into a very necessary dimension." This is a framing of grief that departs dramatically from the mainstream, very clinical norm, positioning it instead as something woven throughout our lives, not an isolated event.

Many cultures directly acknowledge this with rituals and practices repeated at intervals long after a death, sometimes for years, to acknowledge the role of the loss in the lives of the mourners. Tomb-sweeping day in Chinese Buddhist cultures, for example, allows people to gather at the site of burial to tidy it up and remember the dead, much like the Día de los Muertos in Mexico—or, for that matter, in theory, Memorial Day in the United States.

Some grievers do have intense psychiatric symptoms that warrant intervention, whether it be counseling, pharmaceutical options, complementary medicine, or anything else, and some may not realize in the thick of their distress that help is available. As Kaufman-Mthimkhulu notes, though, sometimes these things are symptoms of other issues that mental health diagnoses may obscure or cloud. For example, someone who loses their housing and family connections after a death may be understandably distressed, but they may find it extremely difficult to access supports to address their precarious situation and feelings of isolation and loneliness. A diagnosis of prolonged grief disorder, in that case, might cover up the larger systemic problems that person is going through, again turning the lens firmly back to the personal rather than the structural.

Advocacy for access to any and all tools to provide support for people in mourning must consider that loss occurs in the larger context of someone's life, and it may not be the only factor contributing to emotional distress or crisis. In a culture where people are used to facing rejection or dismissal when they reach out for assistance with larger structural problems, however, they may seek out or accept mental health services as a stopgap against the myriad emotions and problems they are facing. But six sessions of cognitive behavioral therapy paid for by your insurance company are not going to solve the problem that you are about to be evicted or your deceased partner's family is trying to take your children away.

And the question here is not whether we should support grievers who are struggling (of course we should, in every way possible that serves them and their loved ones), but what the trajectory and goal of that support should look like: Is the goal to allow someone to grow and move within grief, or to get the grief to stop? If at the outset a diagnosis has determined that grief has lasted too long, that does not inspire confidence when it comes to a conversation about compassionate support for the mourner.

I cannot help but think about how treating lengthy periods of grief as a sickness tells us a great deal about our society, and how there are perhaps healthier ways to approach people who have been grieving for an extended period of time or who appear to be perseverating on a loss. Perhaps open acceptance of grief would make it less "complicated," as would moving away from the concept of a neat timeline of grief that people must follow in order to be doing it right. And perhaps living with your ghosts is not a sickness. This is a hard thing to accept in a culture that hates ambiguity, that wants a rubric and guidance and solutions to everything.

There is no such thing as "normal" grief, a prescribed trajectory seeking a clear resolution, although there is an evolving understanding of grief that's more holistic, such as the widely adopted dual process model.[8] This positions grief as nonlinear and suggests that it may oscillate between active engagement and avoidance; this seems a more authentic expression of the human spirit and one that is less grinding than "facing up" to a loss until one has "gotten through" it. The idea of grief as an experience with an endpoint is perhaps exemplified by Sigmund Freud's approach to grief work, which integrates a sense of cutting ties and moving forward after confronting loss. In "Mourning and Melancholia," Freud identified a healthy form of grief, mourning, taking place in the conscious mind as someone adjusts to a loss and reaches a state of acceptance. Melancholia, though, is an unconscious struggle with loss that takes on a more pathological aspect, a deeply internalized form of distress that is also prolonged. (The phrasing may seem familiar to students of prolonged grief disorder.) Freud identified melancholia as an indicator that someone is stuck, unable to fully identify and resolve the grief that they are feeling.

The dual process model discusses how people can shift through deep mourning to practicality to the desire to pursue distractions in a single day, which explains why people who are rebuilding themselves and finding a new life after a loss may experience times of deep sorrow as they return to the topic of a loss. The notion of an oscillating grief—a term that comes up frequently in literature around the topic—also mimics many patterns in nature. So many things, from the movement of the ocean to processes inside the body, follow constantly moving and shifting lines rather than proceeding in a series of predictable, clearly defined steps. The brain is a fascinating organ that we still don't fully understand, despite the rise of more accurate and high-resolution imaging and other tools, and grief involves not just cognition but the whole body.

The dual process model identifies two very distinct stressors in the process of mourning and integrating loss. The first is loss-oriented, focusing on the primary immediacy of the loss, whether it be a death or another significant life event that represents irrevocable or significant change. The second is restoration-oriented, specifically exploring the process of adjusting to someone's absence, such as having to learn to cook for yourself, parenting on your own, or finishing a project. This person has died: How do you mean to go on? *Can* you go on? The latter reflects a step in the process of adaptation as a mourner explores what their new world looks like and how they want to live in it, something far too intense to do all at once. The dual process model creates space for both mourning and breathing, and it does not judge varied expressions of grief. In the course of grief, the brain is mapping out new pathways of memory and cognition,[9] fundamentally changing and reshaping itself.

If society sets aside the idea of a "normal" grief, it introduces the idea that perhaps grief and the myriad expressions surrounding loss and mourning are not a pathology but, rather, natural events that everyone will go through, events in which everyone should be an active participant—even when it is sometimes brutal, challenging, frightening. If grief is not a solitary endeavor, that invites the possibility of accessing the support and affirmations of the whole community, rather than navigating grief alone or in a purely rigid clinical context, and it integrates a perspective that goes beyond the immediate loss and into larger cultural contexts that may surround it. This isn't just true in the sense of finding grief groups, therapy, and other structured modes of support; it's also about building connections and cultivating a deeper, kinder understanding of one another.

Treating grief this way also makes space for cultural expressions of loss. Entering the homes of Chinese Buddhist friends, for example, I often encounter a family altar with photographs, ancestral tablets, joss sticks burning, offerings of fruit and hell money, and other objects of importance to the deceased and their families. The altar is ever present, a part of household life; people may make prayers and offerings regularly. Is this evidence of prolonged grief, the refusal to let go and move on, a fixation on the deceased rather than an adjustment to the reality of a life without them? Or is it a practice deeply rooted in tradition, in which the contemplation of loss and the embrace of spirits and ancestors is integrated into daily life?

Buddhists are far from the only ones who build altars to the dead; it's a widespread practice across faith traditions and people all over the world, from the temporary *ofrendas* associated with the Day of the Dead to ceremonial events held in many cultures to invite conversation with the dead, sometimes even welcoming spirits into the bodies of willing hosts. In Pomuch, Mexico, people mark the days leading up to Día de los Muertos with an annual "cleaning of the bones,"[10] where they open caskets to care for deceased family and friends, providing them with new shrouds and embroidered fabrics, and invite everyone to view them; this is a practice echoed in many parts of the world where people routinely revisit and handle the physical remains of deceased loved ones. These practices are sometimes described as "primitive" or "primal," but many Christian churches also engage in such ceremonies every Sunday, when they welcome the body and blood of Christ to congregants, who engage in a ceremonial anthropophagy as part of the observation of their faith, in the belief that doing so cultivates a deeper relationship with god.

"Discussions around grief rituals, particularly the use of

household altars, often reveal cultural misunderstandings. People ask, 'What is this witchcraft you're doing, why do you have an altar?'" says Maria Brown-Spence of Hearts2Heal, a support organization for and by Black and Brown communities, of conversations with people about household altars and the comfort and sense of belonging they may provide for grievers.

"Household altars are a long-standing practice in many African diasporic, Indigenous, and Latin American traditions, serving as spaces for remembrance, spiritual connection, and ongoing relationships with the deceased. While some may perceive this as an inability to accept loss, within these traditions, altars provide comfort and reinforce a sense of belonging.

"For those unfamiliar with this practice, the reaction is often: 'That's creepy, what's going on?' But grief rituals are deeply cultural, and understanding them should be part of our broader social awareness. People process loss in different ways, and as long as it's not causing harm, those expressions should be respected."

The practice of routinely revisiting the bodies of the dead and caring for the bones, as seen in cultures that maintain mummies or other reliquary objects, is an important demonstration of spiritual connection and care—as it was in the Greece of my childhood, where families played active roles in exhumations. Some cultures also value keeping bodies in the home for periods of time that may seem extended to Western outsiders who usually focus on removal as quickly as possible; they may do this to allow family members more time to mourn, to give restless spirits an anchor while they are adjusting to their change in circumstances, or simply to enjoy the company of their loved ones a little longer.

Outsiders may see an expression of grief that is deeply connected to faith, community, and culture as a sign of perseveration on the loss; it is sometimes even met with revulsion. It is unclean, even dangerous; a dead body is like a human ticking time bomb, ready to explode with disease at any moment. (Human bodies are not, for the record, inherently dangerous except in the cases of some specific instances, such as prion diseases, or handling techniques, as seen for example in Ebola outbreaks, where some traditional funerary practices are unsafe due to the presence of the virus.)[11] At a moment when buzzwords and phrases such as "cultural competence" are appearing in more and more conversations about diversity, equity, and inclusion—in an attempt to build a world that is more accommodating and welcoming of difference—some people become very stuck on mourning rituals that differ from their own, marking them as alien, uncomfortable, perhaps even gross. Yet, even the biological reality of death is not clearly defined or universal, as seen in debates about what, exactly, constitutes death on a biochemical and cultural level. So why should mourning practices be uniform?

Researchers are starting to recognize this in conversations about complicated grief, as Columbia University psychiatrist Geoffrey Reed and colleagues observed in a 2022 paper[12] that more closely investigates prolonged grief disorder alongside other new diagnoses in the DSM and introduces important nuances to these conversations.

"The experience of grief is often culturally bound and linked to distinct religious mourning rituals," the researchers wrote, "and so there have been concerns that any attempt to categorize persistent grief as a disorder may ignore this variability." While ultimately expressing support of the diagnosis, arguing that when symptoms of acute grief persist they represent a "pathological grief reaction," they stressed that conversations about grief need to consider a "balance" that reflects the spectrum of grief reactions, which includes cultural practices.

Approaching grief in a way that centers community and shared existence also directly confronts the role of capitalism in how we grieve and how we talk about mourning and loss. If capitalism presents a bootstrapping model in which people are expected to navigate losses alone—one in which people should solve their problems on their own and, if necessary, look for a quick fix from a professional—prolonged grief disorder is an exemplifier of these attitudes. The only circumstances in which you can miss work are those in which you have a clearly documented reason, a medical diagnosis, followed just as quickly by plans to fix it.

Grief, for many, takes time, with the dual process theory in particular pointing to the fact that grief is cyclical, wrapping in and around itself; it can be tremendously variable from day to day and over time. Capitalism asks us to put mourning on an accelerated schedule, denying opportunities to be together and take our time; and as with all things under capitalism, loss is heavily affected by race, gender, and class, all of which affect our responses.

Many marginalized communities experience systemic and cultural influences in loss and subsequent mourning that can make their grief deeper, longer, and more intense; in addition to the loss, they must reckon with the possibility that a loss was unjust, perhaps preventable. These losses are deeply personal for their loved ones, but they can also be accompanied by anger, frustration, and collective grief—not just at the death but what it symbolizes; and these feelings may multiply if the fundamental injustice is not addressed. In these cases, politicized, disenfranchised grief may interact with the fundamental loss, making mourning even more challenging. To be told that your cries for justice are evidence of "prolonged grief" and disorder is a rejection of your suffering.

Questioning the notion of prolonged or complicated grief also requires chipping away at another fundamental underpinning of the white cultural experience that dominates the United States: our grotesque and unhealthy relationship with the idea of happiness, with finding safe spaces in which we never have to interact with anything unpleasant; in which conflict and discomfort are treated as harmful rather than facets of our lives; in which "self-care" has become a buzzword for active avoidance and permission to disengage. The cult of positivity that dominates so much thinking in the United States is pernicious and toxic, its claws sunk deep in expectations about death, loss, and recovery, because the end goal is often treated as one in which the mourner "recovers" by returning to their prior self and getting back to their normal, happy lives.

"In the United States, grief is commonly associated with pain, sadness, and distress, and framed as something inconvenient," says Sarah Chavez, speaking to a cultural distaste for directly engaging with, let alone witnessing, pain in ourselves and others. "It's a temporary state, it will pass, this will pass too, we can restore our lives to some default of normal, a default of happiness. There's often this resistance to change, but particularly when it's out of our control. We struggle to frame grief for what it is, something that's transformative, something that changes us in ways we can't predict. We resist accepting this and don't agree to that transformation. We're in a society all about self-help, progress, transformation, but only when we control it."

That controlling approach to the uncontrollable plays a role in every aspect of our lives, from the slew of self-help books promising that it is possible to think your way into wealth, happiness, and love to prominent therapeutic modalities such as cognitive behavioral therapy, in which it sometimes feels that patients are expected to think themselves well: Simply change your thinking! Losing control, as is often the case when we express grief authentically, in the United States is presented as a failure, an expression of surrender; pausing to feel one's feelings is dangerous and suggests that perhaps there are some things in life that cannot be tightly controlled and regulated.

If it cannot be controlled, perhaps it can be swept under the rug and dealt with later, if ever or at all. That expectation of control, of thinking yourself happy, also transfers into how people interact with the grief of others; terms like "uncontrollable" or "uncontainable" imply that the mourner's intensity of emotions should be brought in check; or, again, their grief is a sickness that must be addressed for their good as well as the comfort of those around them. It can be intimidating, sometimes even distressing, to be confronted with raw grief that cannot be subjected to power and control.

Grief, it turns out, is a lot of work and something that can take a lot of time. It is also highly unpredictable work: the unreliable repairman of feelings, if you will, who promises to show up in a four-hour window and then doesn't but appears unexpectedly three days later. Our response to things that are time-consuming is often to seek shortcuts, hacks, little tricks to get through them faster, but some things can't be put on 1.5 speed and should, in fact, be experienced on their own timelines.

Society wants the expression of grief to go away, to stop, articulating this through a desire to fix it. But if death is a mirror of birth, it's not something that truly ends; there is always more to learn and grow into. A loss provides an opportunity to reframe the way we understand the world. Prolonged grief disorder's attempt at imposing order may treat someone as a patient, as someone sick who is struggling with a failure to leave memory in the past, refusing to reassign a deceased loved one to a different part of the brain and understanding; but it should also be understood as a diagnosis that targets something that makes people deeply uncomfortable—and our reaction to discomfort is to make it go away by any means possible.

When I catch the scent of A's shampoo on a breeze, or hear Ember's distinctive clicking toenails in the hall, or taste phantom Cheerios with brown sugar that take me back to Leonard's table in Albion, these things don't haunt me. When I am struck by a wave of sorrow, or need to take a day off to allow my body and mind a chance to explore a sudden rush of feelings, it seems like a voice from beyond, a reminder that my dead are with me, not a pathology that needs to be identified and cut out. These nudges from the dead make me feel surrounded by community that persists beyond death, even when sometimes they force me to take an unexpected or sometimes prolonged pause, giving my full attention to my ancestors and teachers. I do not come from a familial, religious, or cultural tradition that engages in practices such as keeping an altar, but I find other ways to nod to the dead who accompany me as I move through life.

Some might say that this is evidence of maladaptive grief, of disruptions in functioning; that it is unhealthy to spend a day in deep contemplation about someone who died a decade ago or more, describing it as an unhealthy rumination or obsession, an inability to move on or out of loss. I am not thinking positively or limiting my mourning to a photo in the hallway and perhaps some occasional moderate reflection: "Cady really loved these cookies and it's nice to be reminded of her when I bake them." I may even at times treat the dead as alive—denial!—because they are, in a sense, for me. The truly great are never dead, as Canadian writer Robertson Davies wrote in *The Rebel Angels,* and people live as long as our memories do.

Ghost stories may be designed to spark fear, tapping into our cultural distaste for death and the assumption that death must be wrapped in negativity and unfinished business, but my ghosts are not malevolent and do not have a harmful intent. They just are, in the same way that I shrug a jacket on when it is cold. It is far from unusual to carry your dead with you, metaphorically and literally in some cases, to feel sometimes hit by an unexpected wave and overwhelmed by a loss that happened long ago, to commemorate the dead in varying ways, to hold them in our memory, sometimes very closely. That experience should not be treated as an illness.

I'm struck by the characters in one of the worlds depicted by Philip Pullman in *His Dark Materials* who literally live with the embodiment of their deaths, constant physical companions from birth to the end, shocked at the idea that there are people who don't see a tangible expression of their mortality. In a series of books for children, Pullman explores death and loss in ways that many adults can't even begin to fathom: accessible but still confrontational, a vision of a different world. It is perhaps not surprising that the books have had a significant influence on children's fantasy novels while they've also been a subject of challenges ever since they were published in the 1990s, criticized for themes around the questioning of faith and the pursuit of knowledge, even when that knowledge is uncomfortable. For so many in the West, especially the United States, living with discomfort, let alone a familiarity and comfort with death, is anathema, but some people diagnosed with prolonged grief disorder may be on to something: a world in which it is appropriate, sometimes even necessary, to feel the full spectrum of grief, no matter how long it takes.

Afterword: Memento Mori

I write this with a heavy silver ring on my hand, curls of metal suggestive of petals surrounding a small, faceted orange stone. At first glance, the setting is strange; it appears streaked and stained, rather than perfectly polished. Ember's hair and ashes sit under the gem. This is one of several reliquary objects I keep, from a tiny toe bone that escaped Leila's cremation to traditional urns to more memorial jewelry made by Angela Kirkpatrick, an Olympia, Washington–based jeweler. These are a throwback to the charnel house and the power of carrying even a small piece of the deceased—and an important part of my own grieving process in a house where "Cremated remains or cookie jar?" is not always an academic question.

Knowing that I have my dead around me makes me feel warm, comforted, held, surrounded by friends. Choosing to weave grief through my life, rather than attempt to limit or compartmentalize it, has enriched the life I live and share with others, making me a kinder, better person. I do not believe in an afterlife or anything beyond death, but simply an ending, the complex and miraculous workings of the body brought to a halt. This is an incentive to build the world I want to live in, and say the things that need to be said, now, to lead with compassion.

This is a thing that needs to be said more often, and more forcefully: Grief is a living, breathing thing, and, as such, it must be cared for. It would be cruelty to chain it up in the yard to huddle in the elements, untended, or to hit it for growling and snapping because it is afraid or doesn't understand what you are asking of it. And it is not only my grief that needs care; all our griefs deserve to come in from the cold. I cannot in good conscience leave anyone to suffer, even if all I am able to do is sit in stillness with them for a time, even if that very inability to vanish their pain distresses me.

I also believe that we keep our dead alive by carrying their memories, that speaking their names and thinking of them deepens their mark on the world, and on our lives.

To be forgotten is to die all over again.

If religious reliquaries were my introduction to the world of death, it seems fitting that my own secular jewelry has become an entry point for so many conversations about what it means to live, die, and mourn in America. In a sense, my reliquary objects are a permission slip for talking about death, whether I'm on an airplane somewhere over the dark reaches of the Atlantic or gesticulating at a dinner party. I love it when people compliment my jewelry and ask questions about it. Let me tell you about this amazing person or animal that I love so much I want to take them with me everywhere, our relationship enduring beyond death.

Some find these objects interesting, sentimental, or beautiful, shyly wondering if they can touch my rings or look inside an urn to see what cremated remains look like. Others find reliquaries off and repulsive, a source of discomfort; though they are reluctant to openly comment, the shift in their body language or the downturn in their voice says it for them as they quickly hurry to another topic of conversation, another person to talk to. Displays of mourning such as these, as low-key as they are, are troublesome, and their response is reflective of our overall resistance to remembering that death is part of the human condition and grief is all around us. Death should be neither seen nor heard, something confined to a space behind closed doors and dusted off your dress pants after the funeral. It's weird, perhaps even pathological, to literally cling to the dead in this way, to refuse to close the book on the matter and move on.

I feel a kind of sadness for these people. A physical closeness to death is not necessarily part of everyone's mourning process or memory making and need not be; everyone grieves differently. But the deep, existential fear that lies beneath the disgust or discomfort is palpable. Their response is acculturated, deeply woven into their lives from birth, and it is very difficult to deconstruct. I am not offended by their distaste, but more regretful that their lives have not created space for death and living with grief, let alone learning from it and finding value in fellowship with others. The true pathology lies in refusing to engage with grief, in hiding from it, in telling others how they should experience and express their feelings.

Hold your breath driving past the cemetery, lest the dead swirl down your throat.

Our collective fear of death, particularly in the white, Western culture my life is rooted in, rejects visible memorial and returning to the site of mourning, because if we acknowledge that death exists, we also have to face the feelings that surround death and loss, including the ugly ones. We have to admit that grief is a continuous, evolving thing, and not a personal, interior, hidden one either. To grieve publicly is to be openhearted, a trait that many people deem suspect. When we are surprised by our emotions, it feels embarrassing, rather than an opportunity to explore those feelings and make room for them in our lives.

If we suggest that death is a natural end point of life, though sometimes it strikes in unnatural, awful ways, we have to question why we pathologize the emotions that come with loss; simply existing in the world and experiencing the good and bad it has to offer is not a sickness that needs to be cured. Neither is reacting differently to death than our neighbors. This is not an examination, where peering at your partner's paper will provide some insight into how you can answer. This is, perhaps, one of the most frustrating and exciting things about being alive: We all have to figure this out for ourselves, but it's a lot easier to figure out in community, where we can buoy each other up, giving to those who need it and—perhaps more frightening—accepting what others have to offer us. To accept, also, that some pain must be lived through, to reject the pressure of toxic positivity and admit that, sometimes, life is simply terrible; and it's okay to feel that way, to say so.

Talking about grief and loss and the practicalities of death opens up so many wonderful opportunities. I want to live in a world where all our wishes are honored in death, where we know what those wishes are and are prepared to meet them because we have talked about them, where our surviving mourners are able to memorialize us in the ways that feel right to them, without shame or judgment, because these are the things that make us human. For thousands of years, we have been observing this passage, honoring our dead with funerary objects and flowers, rituals and stones on their grave markers, wearing mourning garb to remind each other that we are bereft. It is astonishing and delightful to see how our ancestors grappled with this, the ebb of our lives. For much of history, we lived much closer to our dead than we do today. There are bones beneath the stones of so many religious sites, and there was a time when every church had a graveyard and a baptismal font, when graves were decorated with winged death's-heads and other icons of death, not sterile expiration dates. Do not mistake this as a simple fascination with death itself, because it is about a larger engagement with how we feel about it as witnesses, participants, voyagers through the unknown.

When I wear my own dead, I feel the strength of bonds that persist in death, but I also feel more deeply connected to the living around me; the lessons all my dead have taught me linger in their bones on my desk, their ashes in my jewelry, their images in the hallway. Some of those lessons are very concrete, others more abstract, and still others yet to be learned and understood. Whether I am haunted by grief or missed opportunities or stricken by too few years together, their tangible presence helps me understand my relationship to them and move with grief, rather than trying to push against it, to get over it, to consign it to a distant past and prior self. I hope that in bringing you along on this journey, you have been able to allow yourself to feel the influence of your own losses on your life, and perhaps to have compassion for yourself—and others—as you face navigating a world without these people and places and parts of yourself that are so important and integral to who you are. As long as you speak their names, they are still with you.

Without a kinder, better, more affirming shared understanding that all of us carry the dead with us in our own way, that our status as grievers is never truly revoked and Tab4 will never be deleted, we will continue to fail ourselves and each other in our journeys through death, dying, grief, and mourning. There is a raw tenderness in grief, a sense of deep personal exposure that can be exhilarating and terrifying all at once, but it is also something that must be held gently by those around us, while we are at our most open and vulnerable, most easily damaged. Surrender is frightening, I know, but it yields an incredible world of interdependent opportunity.

Grief is not Bloody Mary, summoned by repeating her name in the mirror. Naming grief, talking about it, exploring its complexities is not going to draw it closer. Honoring that grief will not make it go away either. Having kindness and care for each other, seeing the many iterations of grief and the social pressures to perform grief in particular ways: These allow us to live with and alongside grief as a friend and teacher, and to resist social pressures, creating a world where we are able to experience loss on our own terms. Naming the fact that grief is about far more than literal death but life's passages more broadly—sometimes, even those that seem like they should be happy ones—also invites us to consider a world where we find value in expressing, and allowing ourselves to fully experience, our feelings, rather than letting them rot us from the inside out.

Grief is not merely a sense of sadness, a void in your spirit created by a loss. It can be sadness, yes: pain, fear, and suffering. It can also be joy and acceptance, hope and relief, anger and indifference. It is whatever we make it to be, not what anyone tells you it should be.

In our ferociously capitalist and individualistic society, interdependence and collaborative activities are frowned upon, sometimes even actively suppressed. But mourning should be a collective enterprise: not something to be carried out alone in the dark, but something we do together in the light. It is something to be openly worn, whether literally or figuratively, in all its heart and messiness, rage and perplexity. Expressions of mourning are not just a reminder of death's presence but of life and our relationships to one another; grief is a thing we reserve for things we have deep relationships with, whether they be rooted in love or hate or other things. Grief is about connections, and grief shared strengthens the web of care around us, builds community, makes all of us stronger.

Collective mourning and invitations to take a pause are all around us, for those willing to look. There must be space for all of us here, lest we become islands unto ourselves, unmoored in grief, unable to integrate it into our whole and complex lives. Continuing with your grief and asking others to join you is not a sign of weakness, but one of strength. Open wide.

Acknowledgments

There is a bittersweet feeling to unleashing a book upon the world, one that, in some ways, can be accompanied by a sense of loss; something once secret and hidden is now available for anyone to see, in immutable form, mistakes enshrined to ruminate over.

I am thankful to the many living and dead cats who have crossed my path, from those named in these pages to those belonging to friends and family to those who belonged to no one to whom I was able to provide kindness in their final breaths.

A number of people helped this book come to life.

My friends Emily Lloyd-Jones, Ace Tilton Ratcliff, and Tristan Matthews were frequent providers of moral support and suggestions (as well as shared meals and stitch-and-bitches), without whom this book would not exist.

My father, Joe Smith, raised me in a house filled with books and reading, provided innumerable conversations about grief and loss, and was very much looking forward to reading this book. He died before it was published, but his favorite quote from *King Lear* (Act IV, scene vii) lives on above my desk:

> You do me wrong to take me out o' th' grave.
> Thou are a soul in bliss. But I am bound
> Upon a wheel of fire, that mine own tears
> Do scald like molten lead.

The many editors I've worked with over the years, including Jessica Reed, Christopher Shay, Evette Dionne, Gina Mei, Kevin Nguyen, Lauren Kelley, Matthew Wheeland, and Megan Greenwell, provided invaluable feedback throughout my career that made me a much better writer, informed many things about the structure and framing of this text, and encouraged me to pursue my special interests, wherever they led. Thanks to colleagues, comrades, co-conspirators, and friends in the internet who offered critical fellowship and support, sometimes without realizing it: Sarah Jaffe, Colin Dickey, Cherie Priest, Kelly Dunlap, Sarah Rees Brennan, Kim Kelly, Elizabeth Harper, Cindy Pon, Andrea Horbinski, Kate Elliott, Erin Biba, Heather Corinna, Matthew Cortland, Sarah McCarry, Nicole Chung, Andi Zeisler, Anna Hamilton, Alice Wong, Sandy Ho, Andrea Grimes, Danielle Glick, Brett Banditelli, Mara Pellittieri, Louise Hung, Melissa Gira Grant, Jesse Hirsch, Kelley Lonesome, Figbar Lonesome, Felicia Gealey, Jordan Weiger, Tina Vasqéz, Jacob Hewko, Nora Reed, Nicole Froio, Charlie Jane Anders, Aaron Sofaer, Malice Walker, and the many readers who support my work (and even some of you who send me mean emails).

The Omidyar Network and Economic Hardship Reporting Project both provided financial support at critical moments and enabled much of the reporting work in the "Tab4" chapter; I appreciate the hard work and support of the staff at both organizations, including Alissa Quart, Alexis Krieg, and Deborah Jian Lee.

Exploring our relationship with grief would not have been possible without the many sources who talked to me, generously giving up hours of their time, including death practitioners, mental health professionals, researchers, animal welfare workers, fellow death nerds, grievers, and many others represented in these pages. I am particularly thankful to the Death Positive and doula communities for their support and kindness; being received with so much excitement and joy every time I reached out for an interview, more information, or clarifications was a testimony to the collaborative and loving ethos of the death community, and I hope I do them credit here.

I'm grateful to my agent, Hannah Bowman, who is remarkably patient with my increasingly unhinged emails; and to my editor, Angela Guzman, whose enthusiasm for this project was tremendously heartening at a difficult time. I'm appreciative of everyone on the HarperOne team, including Judith Curr, Cristina Nunez Blanco, Suzanne Quist, Bob Castillo, Yvonne Chan, Zoe Norvell, Maya Alpert, and to the staff at Liza Dawson Associates. Book production itself is a process that involves a whole host of people, from the copy editor looking at this sentence right now to the press operator who will ensure this page is correctly printed. I salute the efforts of these often hidden workers who put books into our hands. Much love also to the independent bookstore and bookselling community: While it has been many years since I clerked at a bookstore, once a bookseller, always a bookseller, and our shared passion for books (and getting them into the right hands) is a collective project. Please pet all your bookstore cats for me.

Notes

Prologue: Into the Charnel House

1. Maria Petrakis, "Greece Had Long Banned Cremation—Until the Country Ran Out of Room for Bodies," *Los Angeles Times,* December 29, 2019, https://www.latimes.com/world-nation/story/2019-12-29/greece-had-long-banned-cremation.

Chapter 1: Sofie // Childhood

1. John Calvin, *Commentary on Psalms, Volume 5,* trans. James Anderson (Wipf and Stock Publishers, 2024).
2. Jeffrey Watt, "Calvinism, Childhood, and Education: The Evidence from the Genevan Consistory," *Sixteenth Century Journal* 33, no. 2 (2002), https://www.doi.org/10.2307/4143916.
3. Jane Hu, "The Myth of the 25-Year-Old Brain," *Slate,* November 7, 2022, https://slate.com/technology/2022/11/brain-development-25-year-old-mature-myth.html.
4. Bryan Kolb et al., "Experience and the Developing Prefrontal Cortex," *Proceedings of the National Academy of Sciences* 109, no. 2 (2012), https://www.doi.org/10.1073/pnas.1121251109.
5. Zara Abrams, "What Neuroscience Tells Us About the Teenage Brain," *Monitor on Psychology* 53, no. 5 (2022): 66, https://www.apa.org/monitor/2022/07/feature-neuroscience-teen-brain.
6. Lisa Tozzi, "He Wrote the Onion's Famous Mass-Shooting Headline. It Still Haunts Him," *Rolling Stone,* May 25, 2022, https://www.rollingstone

.com/culture/culture-news/onion-mass-shootings-no-way-to-prevent-this-headline-1358539/.

7. Erin Ice, "Bringing Family Demography Back In: A Life Course Approach to the Gender Gap in Caregiving in the United States," *Social Forces* 101, no. 3 (2023), https://doi.org/10.1093/sf/soac041.
8. Elizabeth Briones and Robin Cohen, "National Health Interview Survey, January–June 2024," National Center for Health Statistics (2024), https://www.cdc.gov/nchs/data/nhis/earlyrelease/insur202412.pdf.

Chapter 2: Mr. Shadow // Anticipation

1. "Lymphoma," Cornell University College of Veterinary Medicine, updated 2021, https://www.vet.cornell.edu/departments/cornell-feline-health-center/health-information/feline-health-topics/lymphoma.
2. Amy MacKenzie and Michelle Lasota, "Bringing Life to Death: The Need for Honest, Compassionate, and Effective End-of-Life Conversations," *American Society of Clinical Oncology Educational Book* 40 (2020), https://doi.org/10.1200/EDBK_27976.
3. Meghan Mallya and Leonard Wang, "Death, Dying and Suffering: The Need for Medical Education Reform," *In-Training,* April 24, 2022, https://in-training.org/death-dying-and-suffering-the-need-for-medical-education-reform-24025.
4. Amy Paturel, "Let's Talk About Death," *AAMC,* January 14, 2019, https://www.aamc.org/news/let-s-talk-about-death.
5. Rachel Douglas, Emily Sharpe, and Molly Kraus, "Mental Health Questions on State Medical License Applications and Evaluation of Updates," *JAMA Network Open* 6, no. 9 (2023), http://www.doi.org/10.1001/jamanetworkopen.2023.33360.
6. Therese Rando, ed., *Loss and Anticipatory Grief* (Lexington Books, 1986).
7. Julie Johnson et al., "Outcomes for End-of-Life Patients with Anticipatory Grieving: Insights from Practice with Standardized Nursing Terminologies Within an Interoperable Internet-Based Electronic Health Record," *Journal of Hospice and Palliative Nursing* 19, no. 3 (2017), https://www.doi.org/10.1097/NJH.0000000000000333.
8. Sherman Lee and Robert Neimeyer, "Grief Impairment Scale: A Biopsychosocial Measure of Grief-Related Functional Impairment," *Death Studies* 47, no. 5 (2023): 519–530, https:/www./doi.org/10.1080/07481187.2022.2113605.
9. "Grief, Bereavement, and Coping with Loss (PDQ®)," National Cancer Institute, June 26, 2024, https://www.ncbi.nlm.nih.gov/books/NBK66052/.
10. Rachel Martin, "Why This Poet Sees Grief as Its Own Kind of Spiritual Practice," NPR News, July 23, 2023, https://www.npr.org/2023/07/23/1189435741/why-this-poet-sees-grief-as-its-own-kind-of-spiritual-practice.

11. Sandor Szabo et al., "The Legacy of Hans Selye and the Origins of Stress Research: A Retrospective 75 Years After His Landmark Brief 'Letter' to the Editor of Nature," *Nature* 15, no. 5 (2012), https://www.doi.org/10.3109/10253890.2012.710919.
12. Kylie Rogalla, "Anticipatory Grief, Proactive Coping, Social Support, and Growth: Exploring Positive Experiences of Preparing for Loss," *OMEGA: Journal of Death and Dying* 81, no. 1 (2018), https://www.doi.org/10.1177/0030222818761461.
13. Barbara Ehrenreich, "Welcome to Cancerland," *Harper's,* November 2001, https://harpers.org/archive/2001/11/welcome-to-cancerland/.
14. Kristen Martin, "A Good Death," *The Baffler,* January 31, 2023, https://thebaffler.com/latest/a-good-death-martin.
15. Kikaru Suzuki, *The Price of Death: The Funeral Industry in Contemporary Japan* (Stanford University Press, 2000).
16. Mette Nielsen et al., "Do We Need to Change Our Understanding of Anticipatory Grief in Caregivers? A Systematic Review of Caregiver Studies During End-of-Life Caregiving and Bereavement," *Clinical Psychology Review* 44 (2016): 75–93, https://www.doi.org/10.1016/j.cpr.2016.01.002.
17. Scott Brown et al., "Employee and Worksite Perspectives of the Family and Medical Leave Act," ABT Associates, July 2020, https://www.dol.gov/sites/dolgov/files/OASP/evaluation/pdf/WHD_FMLA2018SurveyResults_FinalReport_Aug2020.pdf.
18. "State Bereavement Leave Laws and Legislation in 2023," Evermore, April 2023, https://evermore.org/wp-content/uploads/2023/07/Evermore-State-Bereavement-Leave-Policy-Brief-1.pdf.
19. Kelly Jones and Farah Tasneem, "FMLA Eligibility of Underserved Communities," US Department of Labor, October 5, 2022.

Chapter 3: Mr. Bell // Sudden

1. Sherry Murphy et al., "Mortality in the United States, 2023," NHCS Data Brief No. 524 (2024), https://www.cdc.gov/nchs/products/databriefs/db521.htm.
2. Mary-Frances O'Connor, "Grief: A Brief History of Research on How Body, Mind, and Brain Adapt," *Psychosomatic Medicine* 81, no. 8 (2019): 731–738, https://www.doi.org/10.1097/PSY.0000000000000717.
3. Wendy Marina Walker, "Sudden Cardiac Death in Adults: Causes, Incidence and Interventions," *Nursing Standard* 24, no. 38 (2010): 50–56, https://www.doi.org/10.7748/ns2010.05.24.38.50.c7803.
4. Felix Elwert and Nicholas Christakis, "The Effect of Widowhood on Mortality by the Causes of Death of Both Spouses," *American Journal of Public Health* 98, no. 11 (2008): 2092–2098, https://www.doi.org/10.2105/AJPH.2007.114348.

5. William Feigalman, "Stigmatization and Suicide Bereavement," *Death Studies* 33, no. 7 (2009): 591–608, https://www.doi.org/10.1080/07481180902979973.
6. Naomi Ennis et al., "Measuring Grief in the Context of Traumatic Loss: A Systematic Review of Assessment Instruments," *Trauma, Violence and Abuse* 24, no. 4 (2022): 2346–2362, https://www.doi.org/10.1177/1524838022109 3694.
7. Katherine Shear, "Grief and Mourning Gone Awry: Pathway and Course of Complicated Grief," *Dialogues in Clinical Neuroscience* 14, no. 2 (2012): 119–128, https://www.doi.org/10.31887/DCNS.2012.14.2/mshear.
8. Katherine Keyes, "The Burden of Loss: Unexpected Death of a Loved One and Psychiatric Disorders Across the Life Course in a National Study," *American Journal of Psychiatry* 171, no. 8 (2014), https://www.doi.org/10.1176/appi.ajp.2014.13081132.
9. Kyndaron Reinier et al., "Race, Ethnicity, and the Risk of Sudden Death," *Trends in Cardiovascular Medicine* 29, no. 2 (2019): 120–126, https://www.doi.org/10.1016/j.tcm.2018.07.001.
10. Marina Zhavoronkova et al., "Occupational Segregation in America," Center for American Progress, March 29, 2022, https://www.americanprogress.org/article/occupational-segregation-in-america/.
11. Adam Serwer, "The Cruelty Is the Point," *The Atlantic,* October 2018, https://www.theatlantic.com/ideas/archive/2018/10/the-cruelty-is-the-point/572104/.
12. Meg Bernhard, "Grief Guides," *n+1,* June 21, 2024, https://www.nplusonemag.com/online-only/online-only/grief-guides/.
13. Kirk Siegler, "A California Town Wiped Off the Map by Wildfire Is Still Recovering 5 Years On," *All Things Considered,* NPR News, November 8, 2023, https://www.npr.org/2023/11/08/1209471739/a-california-town-wiped-off-the-map-by-wildfire-is-still-recovering-five-years-o.
14. Phil Helsel, "PG&E Pleads Guilty to 84 Counts of Manslaughter in Devastating Camp Fire," NBC News, June 17, 2020, https://www.nbcnews.com/news/us-news/pg-e-pleads-guilty-84-counts-manslaughter-devastating-camp-fire-n1231256.
15. Zoe Todd et al., "Ahead of Camp Fire Anniversary, New Details Emerge of Troubled Evacuation," PBS News, October 25, 2019, https://www.pbs.org/wgbh/frontline/article/camp-fire-anniversary-new-details-troubled-evacuation/.
16. Claire Goforth, "'Literally Walking Over a Dead Body': Amazon Employees Accuse Company of Mishandling Holiday Warehouse Death," *Daily Dot,* January 4, 2023, https://www.dailydot.com/debug/amazon-employee-death-colorado-warehouse-work-continued/.

17. Salvador Hernandez, "She Was Killed in a Carrot Field. With Her Body Nearby, Workers Say, They Were Told to Keep Picking," *Los Angeles Times,* November 2, 2023, https://www.latimes.com/california/story/2023-11-03/she-was-killed-in-a-carrot-field-with-her-body-nearby-workers-say-they-were-told-to-keep-picking.
18. Josh Cobb et al., "'No Justice, No Streets': 4 Years After Murder, George Floyd Square Stands in Protest," MPR News, May 24, 2024, https://www.mprnews.org/story/2024/05/25/no-justice-no-streets-4-years-after-murder-george-floyd-square-stands-in-protest.
19. Paul Vercammen and Steve Almasy, "Derek Chauvin Sentenced to 21 Years in Federal Prison for Depriving George Floyd of His Civil Rights," CNN, July 7, 2022, https://www.cnn.com/2022/07/07/us/derek-chauvin-federal-sentencing/index.html.
20. Yolande Clarke-Jackson, "The Revolutionary Power of Grieving in Public," *Yes!*, July 2, 2024, https://www.yesmagazine.org/health-happiness/2024/07/02/public-healing-grief.
21. Eleanor Beardsley, "Israel Holds Memorial at the Music Festival Site Where Hamas Killed 364 People," NPR News, November 28, 2023, https://www.npr.org/2023/11/28/1215697613/israel-holds-memorial-at-the-music-festival-site-where-hamas-killed-364-people.
22. United Nations Human Rights Council, "Legal Analysis of the Conduct of Israel in Gaza Pursuant to the Convention on the Prevention and Punishment of the Crime of Genocide," United Nations, September 16, 2025.
23. Lisa Goldman, "When the Music Stopped and the Grief Began," *New Lines,* July 2, 2024, https://newlinesmag.com/spotlight/when-the-music-stopped-and-the-grief-began/.
24. Elad Nehorai (@eladnehorai), "A Note to the American Jewish Community," Instagram, October 7, 2024, https://www.instagram.com/p/DAzCsn1TICj/.
25. "Bush: 'You Are Either with Us, or with the Terrorists,'" Voice of America, September 21, 2001, https://www.voanews.com/a/a-13-a-2001–09–21–14-bush-66411197/549664.html.
26. Gilbert Burnham et al., "Mortality After the 2003 Invasion of Iraq: A Cross-Sectional Cluster Sample Survey," *The Lancet* 368, no. 9545 (2006): 1421–1428, https://www.doi.org/10.1016/S0140-6736(06)69491-9; "Human and Budgetary Costs to Date of the US War in Afghanistan," Watson Institute for International and Public Affairs, Brown University, https://watson.brown.edu/costsofwar/figures/2021/human-and-budgetary-costs-date-us-war-afghanistan-2001–2022.
27. Susan Silk and Barry Goldman, "How Not to Say the Wrong Thing," *Los Angeles Times,* April 7, 2013, https://www.latimes.com/nation/la-oe-0407-silk-ring-theory-20130407-story.html.

Chapter 4: Leila // Guilt

1. Matt Wade, "'The Giving Layer of the Internet': A Critical History of GoFundMe's Reputation Management, Platform Governance, and Communication Strategies in Capturing Peer-to-Peer and Charitable Giving Markets," *Journal of Philanthropy and Marketing* 28, no. 28 (2023), https://www.doi.org/10.1002/nvsm.1777.
2. Megan Cerullo, "Their Twins' Medical Costs Total $750,000—Each. They and Thousands of Others Are Counting on GoFundMe," CBS News, January 28, 2019, https://www.cbsnews.com/news/crushed-by-medical-bills-many-americans-go-online-to-beg-for-help/.
3. "If I'm Out of Insulin, I'm Going to Die," Human Rights Watch, April 12, 2022, https://www.hrw.org/report/2022/04/12/if-im-out-insulin-im-going-die/united-states-lack-regulation-fuels-crisis.
4. Christopher Su and Scott Ramsey, "Medical Debt—An Iatrogenic Epidemic with Mortal Consequences," *JAMA Network Open* 7, no. 3 (2024), https://www.doi.org/10.1001/jamanetworkopen.2023.54707 .
5. Emily Harris, "Medical Debt in US Linked with Worse Health, More Deaths," *Journal of the American Medical Association* 331, no. 16 (2024): 1354–1355, https://www.doi.org/10.1001/jamanetworkopen.2023.54707.
6. Eric Elbogen et al., "Financial Strain and Suicide Attempts in a Nationally Representative Sample of US Adults," *American Journal of Epidemiology* 89, no. 11 (2021): 1266–1274, https://www.doi.org/10.1093/aje/kwaa146.
7. Per Ostmo, "Rural Hospital Closures: 2023 Update," *Rural Health Research Gateway,* June 2023, https://www.ruralhealthresearch.org/recaps/19.
8. Ruqaiijah Yearby et al., "Structural Racism in Historical and Modern US Health Care Policy," *Health Affairs* 41, no. 2 (2022), https://www.doi.org/10.1377/hlthaff.2021.01466.
9. Mark L. Hatzenbuehler et al., "Structural Stigma and LGBTQ+ Health: A Narrative Review of Quantitative Studies," *The Lancet* 9, no. 2 (2024), https://www.doi.org/10.1016/S2468-2667(23)00312-2.
10. S. E. Porter, "The Complicated—Yet Inspiring!—History of Spiritualism in America," *Lithub,* February 16, 2024, https://lithub.com/the-complicated-yet-inspiring-history-of-spiritualism-in-america/.
11. Sloane Crosley, "The Tail End," *The New Yorker,* August 12, 2024, https://www.newyorker.com/magazine/2024/08/12/the-tail-end.
12. Nicole LeBlanc et al., "Shame, Guilt, and Pride After Loss: Exploring the Relationship Between Moral Emotions and Psychopathology in Bereaved Adults," *Journal of Affective Disorders* 263 (2020): 405–412, https://www.doi.org/10.1016/j.jad.2019.11.164.

Chapter 5: Tab4 // Witness

1. Madeline Bilis, "When Bonnie Came Home," *Slate,* June 19, 2021, https://slate.com/human-interest/2021/06/dog-bite-training-behavioral-euthanasia.html.
2. Beth Miller, *The Most Painful Choice* (McFarland Publishing, 2023).
3. Marcy Hammerle et al., "2015 AAHA Canine and Feline Behavior Management Guidelines," *Journal of the American Animal Hospital Association* 51, no. 4 (July/Aug. 2015), https://www.aaha.org/globalassets/02-guidelines/behavior-management/2015_aaha_canine_and_feline_behavior_management_guidelines_final.pdf.
4. Charlie Reeve et al., "The Caring-Killing Paradox: Euthanasia-Related Strain Among Animal-Shelter Workers," *Journal of Applied Social Psychology* 5, no. 1 (2005): 119–143, https://www.doi.org/10.1111/j.1559–1816.2005.tb02096.x.
5. Rachel MacNair, *Perpetration-Induced Traumatic Stress: The Psychological Consequences of Killing* (Praeger Publishers/Greenwood Publishing Group, 2002).
6. Rachel MacNair, "Causing Trauma as a Form of Trauma," *Peace and Conflict: Journal of Peace Psychology* 21, no. 3 (2015): 313–321, https://www.doi.org/10.1037/pac0000116.
7. Benjamin Marton et al., "Exploring the Loss and Disenfranchised Grief of Animal Care Workers," *Death Studies* 44, no. 1 (2020): 31–41, https://www.doi.org/10.1080/07481187.2018.1519610.
8. Janet Hoy-Gerlach et al., "Social Workers in Animal Shelters: A Strategy Toward Reducing Occupational Stress Among Animal Shelter Workers," *Frontiers in Veterinary Science* 8 (2021), https://www.doi.org/10.3389/fvets.2021.734396.
9. Rochelle Stevenson and Celeste Morales, "Trauma in Animal Protection and Welfare Work: The Potential of Trauma-Informed Practice," *Animals* 12, no. 7 (2022): 852, https://www.doi.org/10.3390/ani12070852.
10. Allison Andrukonis and Alexandra Protopopova, "Occupational Health of Animal Shelter Employees by Live Release Rate, Shelter Type, and Euthanasia-Related Decision," *Anthrozoös* 33, no. 1 (2020), https://www.doi.org/10.1080/08927936.2020.1694316.
11. In the midst of people complaining about not being able to access veterinary care or that it's "too expensive," there is an absolute crisis. In 2023, the American Veterinary Medical Association noted a spike in patients delaying care due to cost concerns (Nolen, 2023), and a rise in "lapsing patients" who had established relationships with clinics but who weren't bringing their animals in, which is unsurprising when two in five pet guardians (Metz, 2023) can't cover an emergency medical expense. Those rising costs, argue the British Veterinary Association, which is encountering similar cost pressures as American vets, are the consequence of a constellation of factors, including the increased professionalism of the field, the wider scope of treatment practices, and long-lagging

adjustments of compensation that have finally come due. See R. Scott Nolen, "Facing Economic Uncertainty, Clients Delay Veterinary Visits," AVMA, November 28, 2023, https://www.avma.org/news/facing-economic-uncertainty-clients-delay-veterinary-visits; Jason Metz, "42% of Pet Owners Can't Cover a Surprise Vet Bill amid Inflation," *Forbes,* August 18, 2023, https://www.forbes.com/advisor/pet-insurance/pet-cost-inflation/.

12. "2024 Annual Analysis: Comparing 2024 to 2023 and 2019," Shelter Animals Count, March 13, 2025, https://www.shelteranimalscount.org/wp-content/uploads/YearEndReport_3.13_Website_FINAL.pdf.
13. "National Animal Welfare Statistics," Shelter Animals Count, https://www.shelteranimalscount.org/explore-the-data/data-dashboards/national-animal-welfare-statistics-dashboard.
14. s. e. smith, "No, People Aren't Giving Up Pandemic Pets Because They're Bored," *Washington Post,* May 17, 2021, https://www.washingtonpost.com/opinions/2021/05/17/pandemic-pets-shaming-animal-welfare/.
15. Caroline Anders, "As Evictions Rise, People May Have to Give Up Their Pets. Animal Shelters Are Calling for Help," *Washington Post,* August 15, 2021, https://www.washingtonpost.com/nation/2021/08/15/animal-shelters-evictions-surrenders/.
16. Vicki Kilmer, "Latest Data Analysis Reveals Most Common Reasons for Owner Surrender," Best Friends, accessed March 18, 2024, https://network.bestfriends.org/proven-strategies/program-spotlights/data-analysis-reveals-reasons-owner-surrender.
17. Leah Fieser, "Warehousing Isn't Working," Brother Wolf Animal Rescue, December 5, 2019, https://www.bwar.org/warehousing-isnt-working/.
18. "Expanded training in EBI have driven the gas chamber to the brink of extinction (only Missouri and Wyoming are now known to have active chambers for domestic animals)." See James Hettinger, "Online Humane Euthanasia Training," HumanePro, accessed March 15, 2024, https://humanepro.org/magazine/articles/online-humane-euthanasia-training.
19. "Bringing an End to Inhumane Euthanasia," Humane Society of the United States, accessed March 15, 2024, https://www.humanesociety.org/resources/bringing-end-inhumane-euthanasia.
20. "Comps & Benefits Survey Reveals State of the Animal Welfare Workforce," Association for Animal Welfare Advancement, March 30, 2022, https://theaawa.org/comps-benefits-survey-reveals-state-of-the-animal-welfare-workforce/.
21. "Animal Care and Service Workers," Occupational Handbook Outlook, Bureau of Labor Statistics, accessed March 18, 2024, https://www.bls.gov/ooh/personal-care-and-service/animal-care-and-service-workers.htm.
22. Tracy White et al., "Suicides and Deaths of Undetermined Intent Among Vet-

erinary Professionals from 2003 Through 2014," *Journal of the American Veterinary Medical Association* 255, no. 5 (2019), https://www.doi.org/10.2460/javma.255.5.595; Emilie Lucchesi, "Researchers Try to Understand High Suicide Rate Among Veterinarians," *Discover,* May 12, 2022, https://www.discovermagazine.com/mind/researchers-try-to-understand-high-suicide-rate-among-veterinarians.

23. Ellen Jefferson, "Are Animal Welfare Workers at Greater Risk of Suicide?," *Psychology Today,* November 20, 2023, https://www.psychologytoday.com/us/blog/helping-people-help-pets/202311/are-animal-welfare-workers-at-greater-risk-of-suicide.
24. Sarah Jaffe, *Work Won't Love You Back* (Bold Type Books, 2021), ch. 5.
25. Nathan Cheek and Elder Shafir, "The Thick Skin Bias in Judgments About People in Poverty," *Behavioral Public Policy* (2020), https://www.doi.org/10.1017/bpp.2020.33.
26. Lindsay Kalter, "Compassion Begins with the Cadavers," Association of American Medical Colleges, April 5, 2019, https://www.aamc.org/news/compassion-begins-cadavers.
27. Alexandra Claveria et al., "A Comparison of Student Perspectives on Body Donation Across Healthcare Professional Programs: From Prosection- to Dissection-Based Curricula," *Anatomical Sciences Education* 17, no. 2 (2024), https://www.doi.org/10.1002/ase.2383.

Chapter 6: Loki // Performance

1. Surviving a mass shooting is costly. Researcher Matthew Czaja and colleagues found in a 2022 study for *JAMA Network Open* that among 403 survivors of mass shootings from 2012 to 2019, the mean charges per patient at discharge were $65,000. This does not include ongoing physical and occupational therapy or mental health services. See Matthew Czaja et al., "Injury Characteristics, Outcomes, and Health Care Services Use Associated with Nonfatal Injuries Sustained in Mass Shootings in the US, 2012–2019," *JAMA Network Open* 5, no. 5 (2022), https://www.doi.org/10.1001/jamanetworkopen.2022.13737.
2. Elisabeth Kübler-Ross, *On Grief and Grieving: Finding the Meaning of Grief Through the Five Stages of Loss* (Scribner, 2014).
3. Kate Avis et al., "Stages of Grief Portrayed on the Internet: A Systematic Analysis and Critical Appraisal," *Frontiers in Psychology* 12 (2021), https://www.doi.org/10.3389/fpsyg.2021.772696.
4. Marianne Eloise, "How Grief Affects Autistic People Differently," *The Conversationalist,* January 19, 2024, https://conversationalist.org/2024/01/19/grief-autism-processing-death-buffy/.
5. The states are California, Illinois, and Oregon. See "Bereavement Leave," State

of California Civil Rights Department, accessed September 2, 2024, https://calcivilrights.ca.gov/wp-content/uploads/sites/32/2023/04/Bereavement-Leave_AB-1949_FAQ_ENG.pdf; "Family Bereavement Leave Act FAQs," Illinois.gov, accessed September 2, 2024, https://labor.illinois.gov/faqs/flbafaqs.html; "Oregon Family Leave Act," Oregon.gov, accessed September 2, 2024, https://www.oregon.gov/boli/workers/pages/oregon-family-leave.aspx.

6. Katharine Seelye, "Carrie Ann Lucas, Champion for Disabled Parents, Dies at 47," *New York Times,* February 27, 2019, https://www.nytimes.com/2019/02/27/obituaries/carrie-ann-lucas-dead.html.

Chapter 7: Ember // Disenfranchised

1. Diane Bezucha, "Burned Out and Understaffed, Veterinary Clinics Are Struggling to Catch Up After Pandemic Challenges," Wisconsin Public Radio, October 5, 2021, https://www.wpr.org/animals/burned-out-and-understaffed-veterinary-clinics-are-struggling-catch-after-pandemic-challenges.
2. "COVID-19 Dashboard," Center for Systems Science and Engineering (CSSE) at Johns Hopkins University (JHU), https://coronavirus.jhu.edu/map.html.
3. Meghan Daum, "Species of Grief," *Gen,* May 1, 2019, https://gen.medium.com/species-of-grief-b60e494b71c6.
4. Kenneth J. Doka, ed., *Disenfranchised Grief: Recognizing Hidden Sorrow* (Lexington Books, 1989).
5. Rachel Martin, "Though Not a Death Sentence, HIV/AIDS Still Holds a Powerful Stigma," NPR News, August 16, 2015, https://www.npr.org/2015/08/16/432435481/though-not-a-death-sentence-hiv-aids-still-holds-a-powerful-stigma; David Bennett et al., "Shame Among People Living with HIV: A Literature Review," *AIDS Care* 28, no. 1 (2016), https://doi.org/10.1080/09540121.2015.1066749.
6. Eliza Henry-Jones, "The Grief of Losing a Pet Is Traumatic and Universal. So Why Don't We Talk About It?," *The Guardian,* December 22, 2016, https://www.theguardian.com/lifeandstyle/2016/dec/22/the-grief-of-losing-a-pet-is-traumatic-and-universal-so-why-dont-we-talk-about-it.
7. Kavitha Cardoza and Clare Marie Schneider, "The Importance of Mourning Losses (Even When They Seem Small)," *NPR Life Kit,* June 14, 2021, https://www.npr.org/2021/06/02/1002446604/the-importance-of-mourning-losses-even-when-they-seem-small.
8. Tara Parker-Pope, "Disenfranchised Grief in a Year of Pandemic Losses," *New York Times,* March 15, 2021, https://www.nytimes.com/2021/03/15/well/mind/grief-pandemic-losses.html.
9. Nora Feely, "Grieving When You Can't Gather," *Catapult,* April 12, 2021, https://catapult.co/stories/nora_feely_grief_loss_pandemic_cancer_family_st_louis.

10. Lena Sun, "My Mom Died While I Was Covering Covid. It Changed My Views on Grief," *Washington Post,* March 9, 2023, https://www.washingtonpost.com/health/2023/03/09/covid-grief/.
11. Philippa Perry, "How Do I Handle the Death of My Secret Lover?," *The Guardian,* December 11, 2022, https://www.theguardian.com/lifeandstyle/2022/dec/11/how-do-i-handle-the-death-of-my-secret-lover-.
12. Carla Dugas and Valori Slane, "StatPearls: Miscarriage," National Center for Biotechnology Information, June 27, 2022, https://www.ncbi.nlm.nih.gov/books/NBK532992/.
13. Julia Pelly, "I Had a Miscarriage, and It Forced Me to Rethink Everything I Believed About Abortion," *Vox,* January 21, 2016, https://www.vox.com/2015/8/5/9095959/miscarriage-abortion-pro-choice.
14. T. S. Mendola, "Rivers of Babylon: The Story of a Third-Trimester Abortion," *The Rumpus,* January 30, 2018, https://therumpus.net/2022/07/05/rivers-of-babylon-the-story-of-a-third-trimester-abortion-2/.
15. The Dougy Center, "Death Rituals & Funeral Practices as Resistance: Dr. Kami Fletcher," *Grief Out Loud*, podcast, episode 156, July 14, 2020, https://www.dougy.org/news-media/podcasts/death-rituals-funeral-practices-as-resistance-dr-kami-fletcher.
16. Gabi Del Valle, "Surveillance Has a Body Count," *The Verge,* March 20, 2024, https://www.theverge.com/2024/3/20/24106098/cbp-migrant-deaths-border-surveillance.
17. James Verini, "How U.S. Policy Turned the Sonoran Desert into a Graveyard for Migrants," Pulitzer Center, August 18, 2020, https://pulitzercenter.org/stories/how-us-policy-turned-sonoran-desert-graveyard-migrants-0.
18. "Secretary Haaland Creates New Missing & Murdered Unit to Pursue Justice for Missing or Murdered American Indians and Alaska Natives," Department of the Interior, April 1, 2021, https://www.doi.gov/news/secretary-haaland-creates-new-missing-murdered-unit-pursue-justice-missing-or-murdered-american.
19. Hannah Gold, "Voices of Mourning," *The Baffler,* April 9, 2024, https://thebaffler.com/latest/voices-of-mourning-gold.
20. Judith Butler, "Judith Butler: Precariousness and Grievability," *Verso,* November 16, 2015, https://www.versobooks.com/blogs/news/2339-judith-butler-precariousness-and-grievability.

Chapter 8: Ash and Trycicle // Inevitability

1. Alice Wong, "Living with Muscular Dystrophy at 50 Makes Death My Shadow Partner," *Time,* March 27, 2024, https://time.com/6960765/alice-wong-muscular-dystrophy-essay/.

2. According to the National Funeral Directors Association's 2024 Cremation and Burial Report, the median cost of a funeral with viewing is $7,848. Meanwhile, Bankrate's 2024 Annual Emergency Savings Report found that 27 percent of adults in the United States have no emergency savings.
3. Ian Duncan et al., "Medicare Cost at End of Life," *American Journal of Hospice and Palliative Care* 36, no. 8 (2019), https://www.doi.org/10.1177/1049909119836204.
4. Karolos Arapakis, "How Should We Fund End-of-Life Care in the US?," *The Lancet Regional Health: Americas* 15 (2022), https://www.doi.org/10.1016/j.lana.2022.100359.
5. Rob Haskell, "Serena Williams on Motherhood, Marriage, and Making Her Comeback," *Vogue,* January 10, 2018, https://www.vogue.com/article/serena-williams-vogue-cover-interview-february-2018.
6. George Luck et al., "Fearing Pain at the End of Life: A Review of Advance Directives," *American Journal of Hospice and Palliative Care* 41, no. 7 (2024), https://www.doi.org/10.1177/10499091231190063.
7. Ankur Sinha et al., "End-of-Life Evaluation and Management of Pain," StatPearls, February 26, 2023, https://www.ncbi.nlm.nih.gov/books/NBK568753/.
8. Alicia Parlette, "The Dark and Seductive Side of Pain Management—Addiction—Becomes Yet Another Battle to Fight," *San Francisco Chronicle,* November 3, 2006, https://www.sfgate.com/entertainment/article/ALICIA-S-STORY-The-dark-and-seductive-side-of-2484711.php.
9. Meredith May, "Alicia Parlette Faces Final Stages of Journey," *San Francisco Chronicle,* April 16, 2010, https://www.sfgate.com/news/article/Alicia-Parlette-faces-final-stages-of-journey-3192305.php.
10. Markian Hawryluk, "Hospices Have Become Big Business for Private Equity Firms, Raising Concerns About End-of-Life Care," KFF News, July 29, 2022, https://kffhealthnews.org/news/article/hospices-private-equity-firms-end-of-life-care/.
11. Liz Hamel et al., "Views and Experiences with End-of-Life Medical Care in the U.S.," Kaiser Family Foundation, April 27, 2017, https://www.kff.org/report-section/views-and-experiences-with-end-of-life-medical-care-in-the-us-findings/.
12. Sarah Cross and Haider Warraich, "Changes in the Place of Death in the United States," *New England Journal of Medicine* 381, no. 24 (2019): 2369–2370, https://www.doi.org/10.1056/NEJMc1911892.
13. Ruth Graham, "'Being the Smoke': One Man's Choice to Be Cremated Under the Open Sky," *New York Times,* May 18, 2022, https://www.nytimes.com/2022/05/18/us/colorado-funeral-pyre.html.
14. Blaine Harden, "A Friend, Not a Role Model; Remembering Edward Abbey, Who Loved Words, Women, Beer and the Desert," *New York Times,*

April 29, 2002, https://www.nytimes.com/2002/04/29/books/friend-not-role-model-remembering-edward-abbey-who-loved-words-women-beer-desert.html.

Chapter 9: Little Grey // Euthanasia

1. "Humane Endings," American Veterinary Medical Association, accessed August 23, 2024, https://www.avma.org/resources-tools/animal-health-and-welfare/animal-welfare/humane-endings.
2. "Brittany Maynard, Advocate for Death with Dignity, Ends Her Life," ABC News, November 2, 2014, https://abcnews.go.com/Health/brittany-maynard-advocate-death-dignity-ends-life/story?id=26644431.
3. California Health and Safety Code, Division 1, Part 1.85, Section 443–443.22.
4. "In Your State," *Death with Dignity,* August 1, 2024, https://deathwithdignity.org/states/.
5. Caroline Favron-Godbout and Eric Racine, "Medical Assistance in Dying for People Living with Mental Disorders: A Qualitative Thematic Review," *BMC Medical Ethics* 24, no. 86 (2023), https://www.doi.org/10.1186/s12910-023-00971-4.
6. Linda Pressly, "The Troubled 29-Year-Old Helped to Die by Dutch Doctors," BBC News, August 8, 2018, https://www.bbc.com/news/stories-45117163.
7. "CDC Data Shows Over 70 Million U.S. Adults Reported Having a Disability," Centers for Disease Control and Prevention, July 16, 2024, https://www.cdc.gov/media/releases/2024/s0716-Adult-disability.html.
8. Harriet McBryde Johnson, "Unspeakable Conversations," *New York Times,* February 16, 2003, https://www.nytimes.com/2003/02/16/magazine/unspeakable-conversations.html.
9. Eduard Verhagen and Pieter Sauer, "The Groningen Protocol—Euthanasia in Severely Ill Newborns," *New England Journal of Medicine* 352, no. 10 (2005): 959–962, https://www.doi.org/10.1056/NEJMp058026.
10. Hailee M. Yoshizaki-Gibbons, "The Dedication: Leaving Evidence of Life, Death, Care, and Confinement During COVID-19," *Lateral* 12, no. 1 (2023), https://www.doi.org/10.25158/L12.1.10.
11. "The Impact of COVID-19 on People with Disabilities," National Council on Disability, 2021, https://www.ncd.gov/assets/uploads/reports/2021/ncd-2021-progress-report-covid-19.pdf.
12. Joseph Shapiro, "As Hospitals Fear Being Overwhelmed by COVID-19, Do the Disabled Get the Same Access?," NPR News, December 14, 2020, https://www.npr.org/2020/12/14/945056176/as-hospitals-fear-being-overwhelmed-by-covid-19-do-the-disabled-get-the-same-acc.
13. Barry Kipperman, "Economic Euthanasia: A Disease in Need of Prevention,"

Humane Society Veterinary Medical Alliance, August 10, 2010, https://www.hsvma.org/economic_euthanasia_disease_in_need_of_prevention.

14. Avis Favaro, "Woman with Chemical Sensitivities Chose Medically-Assisted Death After Failed Bid to Get Better Housing," CTV News, April 13, 2022, https://www.ctvnews.ca/health/woman-with-chemical-sensitivities-chose-medically-assisted-death-after-failed-bid-to-get-better-housing-1.5860579.
15. Bevan Hurley, "Paralympian Claims Canada Offered to Euthanise Her When She Asked for a Stairlift," *The Independent,* December 4, 2022, https://www.independent.co.uk/news/world/americas/christine-gauthier-paralympian-euthanasia-canada-b2238319.html.
16. Mario Canseco, "Most Canadians Back Status Quo on Medical Assistance in Dying," Research Co., May 5, 2023, https://researchco.ca/2023/05/05/maid-canada-2023/.

Chapter 10: All My Dead Ghosts // Complicated

1. "APA Offers Tips for Understanding Prolonged Grief Disorder," American Psychiatric Association, September 23, 2021, https://www.psychiatry.org/News-room/News-Releases/apa-offers-tips-for-understanding-prolonged-grief.
2. Goda Gegieckaite and Evaldas Kazlauskas, "Fear of Death and Death Acceptance Among Bereaved Adults: Associations with Prolonged Grief," *OMEGA: Journal of Death and Dying* 84, no. 3 (2020): 884–898, https://www.doi.org/10.1177/0030222820921045.
3. Ellen Barry, "How Long Should It Take to Grieve? Psychiatry Has Come Up with an Answer," *New York Times,* March 18, 2022, https://www.nytimes.com/2022/03/18/health/prolonged-grief-disorder.html.
4. Erin Fahle, "School District and Community Factors Associated with Learning Loss During the COVID-19 Pandemic," Education Recovery Scorecard, May 2023, https://cepr.harvard.edu/sites/hwpi.harvard.edu/files/cepr/files/explaining_covid_losses_5.23.pdf.
5. Kristin Szuhany, "Prolonged Grief Disorder: Course, Diagnosis, Assessment, and Treatment," *American Journal of Psychiatry* 19, no. 2 (2021), https://www.doi.org/10.1176/appi.focus.20200052.
6. Sarah Jaffe, "The Country That Could Not Mourn," *The New Republic,* September 23, 2022, https://newrepublic.com/article/167838/country-not-mourn-after-life-covid-pandemic-grief-book-review.
7. Maarten Eisma, "Prolonged Grief Disorder in ICD-11 and DSM-5-TR: Challenges and Controversies," *Australia and New Zealand Journal of Psychiatry* 57, no. 7 (2023): 944–951, https://www.doi.org/10.1177/00048674231154206.
8. Margaret Stoebe and Henk Schut, "The Dual Process Model of Coping with

Bereavement: Rationale and Description," *Death Studies* 23, no. 3 (1999), https://www.doi.org/10.1080/074811899201046.

9. Katherine Shear, "Grief and Mourning Gone Awry: Pathway and Course of Complicated Grief," *Dialogues in Clinical Neuroscience* 14, no. 2 (2012), https://www.doi.org/10.31887/DCNS.2012.14.2/mshear.
10. Paul Koudounaris (@hexenkult), "Cleaning of the Bones," Instagram, November 2, 2024, https://www.instagram.com/p/DB35KI_xJAF/.
11. Carrie F. Nielsen et al., "Improving Burial Practices and Cemetery Management During an Ebola Virus Disease Epidemic—Sierra Leone, 2014," Centers for Disease Control and Prevention, *Morbidity and Mortality Weekly Report* 64, no. 1 (2014): 20–27, https://www.cdc.gov/mmwr/preview/mmwrhtml/mm6401a6.htm.
12. Geoffrey Reed et al., "Emerging Experience with Selected New Categories in the ICD-11: Complex PTSD, Prolonged Grief Disorder, Gaming Disorder, and Compulsive Sexual Behaviour Disorder," *World Psychiatry* 21, no. 2 (2022): 189–213, https://www.doi.org/10.1002/wps.20960.

About the Author

s.e. smith is a journalist, essayist, author, and critic who explores contemporary culture and topics around labor, disability, technology, feminism, death and dying, and animal welfare. smith's cultural criticism and reported features have appeared in publications such as *The Washington Post*, *Time*, *The Guardian*, *Rolling Stone*, *The Verge*, *Esquire*, and *The Nation*, and were recognized with a National Magazine Award in 2020 in Columns and Commentary for the "An Unquiet Mind" column in *Catapult Magazine*. smith's work also appears in numerous anthologies, most recently *Disability Intimacy* and *Body Language*. smith is a cofounder and worker-owner of The Flytrap, a feminist journalism collective. Accompanied by cats Ash and Tricycle, smith lives amongst the redwoods of Northern California.